FILM PROPAGANDA

FILM PROPAGANDA

SOVIET RUSSIA AND NAZI GERMANY

RICHARD TAYLOR

CROOM HELM LONDON

BARNES & NOBLE BOOKS NEW YORK 035260

(a division of Harper & Row Publishers, Inc.)

© 1979 Richard Taylor
Croom Helm Ltd, 2-10 St John's Road, London SW11

British Library Cataloguing in Publication Data

Taylor, Richard, b. 1946
    Film propaganda.
    1. Propaganda, German – History. 2. Moving-pictures
    in propaganda – History   3. World War, 1939-1945
    – Propaganda   4. Moving-pictures – Germany –
    History   5. Propaganda, Russian – History
    6. Moving-pictures – Russia – History
    I. Title
    301.15'4   DD253
    ISBN 0-85664-099-9

Published in the USA 1979 by
Harper & Row Publishers, Inc.
Barnes & Noble Import Division
ISBN 0-06-496778-6

Printed in Great Britain by
Biddles Ltd, Guildford, Surrey

CONTENTS

CONTENTS

ACKNOWLEDGEMENTS

The subject of this book reflects a fusion of several of my interests. Ever since leaving school I have hovered uneasily between an interest in things German and an interest in things Russian, and to this day the dilemma remains unresolved. I owe an incalculable debt to Alan Hornsey, who taught me German at school and who first stimulated in me that seed of doubt, that critical intelligence that must lie at the heart of all true education. My interest in Germany was encouraged and developed by Trevor Jones and that in Russia by Nikolay Andreyev, both of the University of Cambridge: to them too I owe a great deal. My doctoral thesis on the Soviet cinema was completed under Leonard Schapiro at the London School of Economics and I should like to express my profound gratitude to him for his generous supervision and patronage.

I should also like to thank the friends and colleagues who have, directly or indirectly, commented on sections of this book: George Boyce, Eleonore Breuning, Neil Harding, Peter Nicholson and Ifor Rowlands. I am grateful to Alan Bodger for his assistance with translations from the Russian, and to Bruce and Marliese Waller, for similar help with German. My thanks also go to David Welch and Jeffrey Richards for our various discussions of a shared enthusiasm and for their generosity in making research materials available, and to David Croom, for his exemplary patience in waiting for the end result. I am grateful to Roger Davies of Swansea and to the staff of the British Film Institute for their assistance with the illustrations and to Transit-Film for permission to reproduce stills from their films. I should also like to acknowledge the help that I have received from the staff of the following institutions: British Library, British Library of Political and Economic Science, Imperial War Museum, British Film Institute (London); Staatliches Filmarchiv der DDR (Berlin, GDR); Lenin State Library, Institute for the History of the Arts (Moscow); University College of Swansea Library. The University College of Swansea has also been generous with research funds.

Finally, I should like to thank my friends, Alan and Vanessa Bodger, George and Kathleen Boyce, Hugh and Kirstine Dunthorne, Neil and Deanna Harding, Sandra Hawkins, and Ifor and Lynda Rowlands, and their respective children, for putting me back together again on the all too frequent occasions when I have threatened to fall apart, and above all I should like to thank my mother and my late grandmother for all their selfless support. The strengths in this book are theirs, the weaknesses are mine. It is to the memory of my grandmother, and her healthy scepticism, that I lovingly dedicate this book.

Richard Taylor

Swansea
July 1978

NOTES

Transliteration from Russian into English always creates problems and I have therefore used two slightly different systems. In the text and index I have used a system that I hope renders the Russian into a form that can more easily be understood by the non-Russian speaker. In the notes and bibliography I have used a system that accurately reproduces the Russian for anyone wishing to consult my sources. I have translated all film titles into English: in the case of the Soviet cinema there is an accepted English version for most films, but in the case of Nazi Germany there is not. The original version of every title is therefore given in the index after its translation. The italics in the quotations appear in the original.

The sources for the quotations that introduce each part of the book are as follows:

Part 1: V. Shklovskii, *Eizenshtein* (Moscow, 1973), p. 246.

Part 2: Lenin, quoted in: K. Tsetkin, *Vospominaniya o Lenine* (Moscow, 1966), pp. 9-10.
D. Vertov, 'Eshchë o Mayakovskom', first published in full: S. Drobashenko (ed.), *Dziga Vertov. Stat'i. Dnevniki. Zamysli* (Moscow, 1966), p. 187.

Part 3: Goebbels' speech of 28 March 1933, quoted in: G. Albrecht, *Nationalsozialistische Filmpolitik* (Stuttgart, 1969), p. 441.
Hans Steinhoff, director of *Hitler Youth Quex, The Old and the Young King, Uncle Kruger* and *Rembrandt*, in *Völkischer Beobachter*, 5 March 1941.

Hamlet: O God, I could be bounded in a nut-shell, and count myself a King of infinite space; were it not that I have bad dreams.

Guildenstern: Which dreams indeed are ambition: for the very substance of the ambitious is merely the shadow of a dream.

Hamlet: A dream itself is but a shadow.

Rosencrantz: Truly, and I hold ambition of so airy and light a quality that it is but a shadow's shadow.

Hamlet: Then are our beggars bodies, and our monarchs and out-stretched heroes the beggars' shadows.

Hamlet, Act Two, Scene Two.

PART ONE: INTRODUCTION

The past does not die. We must contemplate it and know how to recognise the future in it.

Viktor Shklovsky

1 PREFACE

Question: Have you become a liberal? Are you somewhat
   afraid of ideologies?
Answer: A little . . . even a lot.

From the Marcel Ophuls film *The Sorrow and the Pity*[1]

The significance of propaganda in the politics of the twentieth century
continues to be underestimated, and the importance of the cinema in
that propaganda is similarly undervalued. This is partly because propaganda has become a dirty word: it describes a phenomenon to be
found in 'totalitarian régimes' but not, so we like to think, in 'liberal
democracies'. It is also because historians and political scientists on the
one hand, and film aesthetes and semiologists on the other, continue,
at least in Britain, to place the cinema on one side in its own ghetto.
While the importance of radio and especially television in the formation
of popular political and moral attitudes is beginning to be generally
recognised, the treatment of the cinema as a subject for serious academic research is still regarded by many as somewhat eccentric. I hope
that this book will at least point the way to an appreciation of the
significance of both propaganda and the cinema for the politics of the
twentieth century.

The choice of Soviet Russia and Nazi Germany as case studies will,
I trust, seem obvious to most readers. Some, however, will find that
choice controversial, perhaps even provocative. I have chosen them as
examples not because I necessarily equate communism with National
Socialism (I don't), nor because I think that Stalin was cast in the same
mould as Hitler (I do), but because Soviet Russia and Nazi Germany
are the two best known and best documented examples of highly politicised societies that the world has ever seen. To say this is not to give
approval to the concept of a totalitarian model, one that can be
applied to both extremes of the political spectrum. The ideology that
underpins the Soviet system differs very obviously, and fundamentally,
from the *Weltanschauung* that inspired the Third Reich. The one
claimed to be based on a scientific analysis of the economic class conflict in human history, while the other relied on a faith in innate racial
superiority. It would be dishonest of me not to admit that I find the
ideals of the October Revolution largely congenial, whereas I feel the

15

beliefs of the National Socialist movement to be completely abhorrent. However, these ideals, which have the same broad appeal to humanity as the ideals of the French Revolution or the fundamental tenets of Christianity, have never been put into practice. Nor perhaps are they ever likely to be. That is our loss, and it is a loss whose consequences we must face up to. One of those consequences must be the admission that, in terms of its intervention in the individual lives of its citizens and its direction of them, the Soviet political system has impinged at least as much as did the Nazi régime: that is what I mean by a highly politicised society. Nor can it be claimed that this is a Stalinist deviation from orthodox Marxism, for the intolerance and the Jacobinism that have been manifested in the name of Marxism-Leninism have their direct origins in the doctrine of Marxist infallibility, the arrogant claim that the Marxist analysis is not merely correct, but uniquely correct, because it is the only one based upon scientific criteria, and the equally patronising assertion that anyone who disagrees is suffering from an ailment called false consciousness. It was these same theoretical assumptions that led to the enormous sacrifices imposed upon the Soviet people in the 1930s and to the argument that these sacrifices were historically necessary if the Soviet Union and its economic, social and political order were to survive. One cannot and should not deny that the sacrifices of the Soviet people both during the purges of the 1930s and during the Second World War played a decisive part in the defeat of Nazism and thus, ironically, in the preservation of pluralist democracies in Western Europe. Nor can we deny that those sacrifices are now bringing their reward and giving the population of the Soviet Union the highest material standard of living in their entire history. But the point that really concerns us here is not the rationale for the purges or the camps: it is the fact that, in demanding great sacrifices, the political system has intervened directly and constantly in the lives of individuals and has politicised vast areas of life that elsewhere have little or no apparent political significance. It is here that propaganda plays an important part in placing individual events and actions in a broader political framework, and the films that are discussed in this book have, in their turn, played an important part in that propaganda.

In selecting individual films for discussion and analysis I have borne two considerations in mind: first and foremost, that the film itself should be available for hire, and second that it should exemplify an important aspect of the propaganda of Soviet Russia or Nazi Germany. Of course these two considerations sometimes conflict: I have, for instance, not been able to include an anti-Soviet Nazi film (such as

GPU or *Frisians in Peril*) simply because they are not available outside the archives. To write about a film that the reader could not see for himself seemed pointless. On the other hand, I have included *Triumph of the Will*, although it has already been written about, because it was too important to be left out. But I have left *Battleship Potemkin* out precisely because it has been much written about, and concentrated on *October* and *Alexander Nevsky* – and I make no apologies for including two Eisenstein films. On the Soviet side I have chosen a fictional story from the history of the pre-revolutionary workers' movement (*Mother*), a re-creation of the Revolution itself (*October*), a documentary account of the progress of the Soviet Union since the Revolution (*Three Songs of Lenin*) and an anti-German film (*Alexander Nevsky*). On the German side I have selected *Triumph of the Will*, which really stands on its own as a portrait of the movement, a re-creation of German history (*Kolberg*), an anti-British film (*Uncle Kruger*) and an anti-Semitic one (*The Wandering Jew*). For reasons of space it has not been possible to include more films for detailed comment. Clearly this means that there are significant gaps in my treatment of propaganda through the feature film, and I have not dealt with the newsreels, which both Lenin and Goebbels considered important,[2] at all. These are the subjects for other books. This book is not intended to be either comprehensive or definitive. Instead it aims to point the way for further discussion of the many issues involved and to provide some of the material necessary for that discussion. It is only through such discussion that the issues can be clarified and the cinema raised to its proper place in the political history of our time.

The cinemas of Soviet Russia and Nazi Germany are worth studying for their intrinsic interest alone. Their films are given added interest by their importance as works of art and by the fact that they have helped to shape the histories of their respective countries and to carry the image of those countries abroad. The success of *Battleship Potemkin* in Berlin, and its banning in Britain, are ample evidence of that. But these films have another significance for us. Soviet Russia and Nazi Germany are by no means the only countries in which propaganda has been used for official political purposes, nor are they the only countries in which the cinema has been utilised to this end. They merely provide what I have described as the best known and best documented examples, the clearest instances of the deliberate and consistent manipulation of public opinion through the film. For this reason they also provide a yardstick against which the subtler manipulations of public opinion in more pluralistic political systems can be judged and analysed. Then at last we shall know in what ways 'Of all the arts, for us the cinema is the most important'.

Notes

1. From an interview with Christian de la Mazère, a former member of the Waffen S.S. The script of the film is available in English: M. Ophuls, *The Sorrow and the Pity* (London, 1975) and this quotation comes from p. 153.

2. Lunacharsky recalls Lenin's remark that 'The production of new films imbued with Communist ideas and reflecting Soviet reality should start with the newsreel.' This is taken to imply that Lenin thought that the newsreel was the most important medium for the transmission of propaganda through film. See: G. Boltyanskii, *Lenin i kino* (Moscow, 1925), pp. 16-19. However Lunacharsky later maintained that Lenin considered that the fictional film was 'no less – on the contrary, even more – important' for the transmission of propaganda. See: A. Lunacharskii, *Kino na Zapade i u nas* (Moscow, 1928), p. 64. For Goebbels' views, see: G. Albrecht, *Nationalsozialistische Filmpolitik* (Stuttgart, 1969), pp. 94-5.

2 PROPAGANDA AND FILM

> Millions of people who have never visited a cultural establish-
> ment have been won over to art by the film. Breaking out of
> the restricted conditions of their daily working lives they have
> lived to see that life can be immeasurably greater and more
> profound!
>
> Emil Jannings, 1942[1]

The term 'propaganda' has for various reasons been devalued in its
usage. In particular, it has come to have pejorative connotations, so that
the word itself is often used for 'propaganda' purposes.[2] 'Propaganda'
becomes what the enemy engages in, while one's own 'propaganda'
parades under the disguise of 'information' or 'publicity'. It therefore
ceases to be a useful concept. But if 'propaganda' is to be a useful concept, if it is to be distinguished from 'information' and 'publicity', it
must first of all be divested of these associations. It must provide a
value-free definition of a recognisably distinct activity.

What are the characteristic features that distinguish 'propaganda'
from other cognate activities? There is a veritable plethora of defini-
tions available to the student of the subject, and they cover a remarkable and sometimes incompatible range of attributes. Some observations are distinguished by their brevity, if not their clarity. Driencourt's
repeated and somewhat melodramatic assertion that 'everything is
propaganda'[3] is not very helpful as a definition. On the other hand,
those who have tried to encapsulate in a single sentence, loaded with
qualifications, all the distinctive and distinguishing features of 'propaganda' have been equally unsuccessful in a different way.[4] It seems
therefore that writers on the subject must steer a difficult course
between the Scylla of a definition that is concise but far too general
and the Charybdis of one that is so complex and highly qualified that
it has only descriptive rather than definitive value.[5]

'Propaganda' is concerned with the transmission of ideas and/or
values from one person, or group of persons, to another. Where 'propagation' is the action, there 'propaganda' is the activity. It would therefore seem sensible, rather than searching on a more abstract plane for a
more satisfactory definition, to begin with the particular and examine
more closely the various stages in the process of transmission.

19

Where better to begin than with the propagandist himself? How
important to the definition of 'propaganda' is the purpose of the propagandist, or his sense of purpose? Doob regards this question of purpose
as irrelevant to the definition of 'propaganda'; for him the decisive factor is the use of suggestion:

> If individuals are controlled through the use of suggestion . . . then
> the process may be called propaganda, regardless of whether or not
> the propagandist intends to exercise the control. On the other hand,
> if individuals are affected in such a way that the same result would
> be obtained with or without the aid of suggestion, then this process
> may be called education, regardless of the intention of the educator.[6]

The very word 'suggestion' however implies a degree of deliberation
that Doob does not necessarily allow for. It would be a very peculiar
propagandist indeed who suggested something that he had not intended
to suggest. A similar objection may be made to Mackenzie's definition,
where the use of the word 'attempt' also implies a degree of deliberation: 'Propaganda is an attempt, either unconsciously or as part of a
systematic campaign by an individual or group holding certain beliefs or
desired ends, to influence others to adopt identical attitudes.'[7] An
attempt of this nature must be both conscious and deliberate: there
must be a purpose. Without purpose 'propaganda' can have no aim and
no direction, and without direction it can have no distinctive political
function separating it from other social and political activities. But this
does not mean that the purpose, or indeed the effect, of the propagandist's activity can always be measured with any degree of scientific
accuracy. These are areas for reasoned deduction and historical judgement, using all the sources, albeit defective, that are available to us. The
absence of conclusive proof of purpose is not of course synonymous
with the absence of purpose itself, although the problems of proof and
even deduction will naturally tend to increase with historical distance.
But these problems are not confined to the study of 'propaganda': they
are the problems that confront every historian.

   If then we insist upon the importance of purpose in discussions of
the nature of 'propaganda', we must dismiss the possibility that 'propaganda' can be either unintentional or accidental. If we can establish
purpose, then we have also established a link, albeit tenuous, between
the propagandist and his 'audience': there is a connection between the
activity of the propagandist and his intended result, to exert influence
on their opinions, which also connects him with them regardless of

whether his intentions are achieved or his activity successful. That connection is also an essential feature of 'propaganda', a prerequisite for the transmission of ideas and values that I have already mentioned. If we cannot establish such a connection, then we cannot describe the activity as 'propaganda'. The activity may have 'propaganda potential' but that potential may remain unrealised. This does not however mean that the activity will have no effect on opinion, for opinions are influenced by all kinds of factors, deliberate or otherwise. For example, an elector may find that his actual resolve to vote is more profoundly affected by the weather on polling day than by election manifestos or campaign broadcasts. He may stay at home because it is raining. On the other hand, he may vote for the government if the sun is shining, for the opposition if the weather is overcast. But until such time as that weather can be controlled by man in order to influence the voter's decision, we cannot attribute his decision to the effects of 'propaganda'.

If we accept that purpose is of prime importance in the definition of 'propaganda' then it is worth asking *whose* purpose is important and, by extension, *who* the propagandist *really* is — the technician or his political master? Is the propagandist the originator of the idea or the man who puts the idea into practical effect? The difficulty is well illustrated by the series of broadsheets issued for the British Army during the First World War. Each one contained a short piece of poetry or prose of an apparently patriotic or otherwise inspiring nature, and this was printed on a sheet of paper small enough to be folded into a letter to a soldier at the front or carried in bulk and dropped from the air over the trenches. The whole exercise was arranged by Lord Northcliffe, later Director of Propaganda in Enemy Countries, through *The Times*.[8] Some of the pieces used were obviously written either specifically for the purpose or at least contemporaneously. In these cases there is no reason to suspect any divergence of view or purpose between the poet (who is here both artist and technician) and the person who ordered, organised or financed the production and distribution of the broadsheet. In this instance there is therefore little point in pursuing the distinction between the technician and his political master. But among the other authors that the broadsheets quoted were Bacon, Wordsworth, Sheridan, Dickens, Shelley and Shakespeare. Even the Bible was cited. For obvious reasons of chronology none of these authors can have had the opportunity to develop an attitude towards the First World War or to play an active 'propagandist' role in it. None the less their work was deemed to have some relevance to the war and was used *by someone else* for a purpose specifically connected with it.

We have here two possible 'propagandists'. The authors may be seen as 'propagandists' only in the sense that any artist who commits his ideas to paper, to canvas, to the screen or whatever, may be regarded as intending those ideas to be transmitted to a wider audience. They are the purveyors of broad, perhaps even universal, statements on the human condition. The organiser, the political master, who uses their broader statements for narrower purposes, is acting as the 'propagandist' for a more specific purpose in the context of 1914-18. While Shakespeare may well have had a 'propagandist' purpose in writing his historical plays in the context of Elizabethan England, it is Northcliffe who is the 'propagandist' in the context of the First World War: Northcliffe is activating the 'propaganda potential' that Shakespeare's works for various reasons still have. Similar observations may be made about Olivier's film of *Henry V*, made towards the end of the Second World War. There is here then 'propaganda' on two levels, the specific harnessing the general, drawing upon moments from a cultural tradition to evoke particular associations and responses, in the same way that the significant symbol such as the swastika, the hammer and sickle or the cross evokes them. It is inevitable that the 'propagandist' should do this even in his elementary use of words. Words are our basic means of communication and in the course of their usage they acquire associations that the 'propagandist' can and must draw upon as part of his armoury. This does not mean that 'propaganda' is a passive phenomenon: it cannot create opinion out of a void, but it can build upon what is already there. Aldous Huxley is surely correct when he writes:

> Political and religious propaganda is effective, it would seem, only upon those who are already partly or entirely convinced of its truth . . . The course of history is undulatory, because (among other things) self-conscious men and women easily grow tired of a mode of thought and feeling which has lasted for more than a certain time. Propaganda gives force and direction to the successive movements of popular feeling and desire; but it does not do much to create those movements. The propagandist is a man who canalizes an already existing stream. In a land where there is no water he digs in vain.[9]

The 'propagandist' uses all the weapons that are available to him at a given time and in a given context. In the case of the broadsheets he is using the weapons left to him by 'propagandists' of a different order, a different age: he is activating 'propaganda potential'.

If the 'propagandist's' purpose is important, is it fundamental to the nature of 'propaganda' that this purpose should be concealed? It is implicit in the writings of several authors that the origins of 'propaganda' should be concealed, but Lumley, in particular, is quite specific: 'Propaganda is promotion which is veiled in one way or another as to (1) its origin or sources, (2) the interests involved, (3) the methods employed, (4) the content spread, and (5) the results accruing to the victims – any one, any two, any three, any four, or all five.'[10] His view is supported by Albig[11] who maintains further that advertising cannot be classified as 'propaganda' because its sources are revealed.[12] If the purpose is effectively concealed from contemporaries, it might well be that it will also be concealed from the historian, so that in many cases this problem will not arise. This does not, however, permit us to escape from the problem entirely. It is undoubtedly true that there are many situations in which 'propaganda' is *more effective* if its origins are concealed. It was Goebbels who remarked that 'Propaganda becomes ineffective the moment we are aware of it.'[13] Hence the concealment of origin becomes an important part of enemy leaflets dropped in wartime, of 'Fifth Column' infiltration and disruptive activities, and of 'black propaganda' such as the radio stations set up by both sides in the Second World War.[14] If the origins of such activities were to be revealed, they would doubtless be much less effective, in some cases perhaps completely ineffective, but such a revelation would not mean that they ceased to qualify as 'propaganda'. As Lasswell observes, 'One propaganda group may flourish in secret and another may invite publicity.'[15] If, on the other hand, we were to accept the Lumley/Albig prerequisite, then almost all Nazi and Soviet domestic 'propaganda' would have to be called something else. Only international 'propaganda' of certain types, like the 'black' radio stations, would qualify as such. Clearly this limitation would be unacceptable.

Another problem we must face if we are to accept the value of purpose in the definition of 'propaganda' is that of the possible conflict between its purpose and its effect. It is notoriously difficult to measure the effects of 'propaganda' with any degree of scientific accuracy. It is indeed difficult enough to measure public opinion with any consistent degree of accuracy on relatively clear-cut issues, and a shift in opinion and the reasons for it are shrouded in numerous imponderables. For the sake of the argument we must therefore assume an effect, just as we may have to assume a desired effect (i.e. purpose) with all the necessary reservations. The televised confrontations between Nixon and Kennedy during the 1960 presidential election campaign provide an interesting example. It has been argued that Nixon's heavy beard

growth, his 'five o'clock shadow', made him look untrustworthy, so
that his opponents, by asking the telling question, 'Would *you* buy a
used car from this man?', were able to undermine effectively much of
the image that his campaign managers were trying to project. This error
may have been due to gross incompetence or to mere lack of experience,
but we may safely assume that it was an error and that the effects of
Nixon's television appearances ran counter to their intended effects. Do
we therefore agree with Ellul that 'Ineffective propaganda is no propaganda'?[16] If we do feel that success is an essential feature of 'propaganda' then we must decide at what point in the historical process that
success is to be measured. Do we say that Bolshevik 'propaganda'
before October 1917 was not 'propaganda' because at the time it had
failed? Or do we say that, as the movement's activities were crowned
with success by the October Revolution, the word 'propaganda' can be
applied with benefit of hindsight? Similarly, is Nazi 'propaganda' *not*
'propaganda' at all, either purely or partly because the Third Reich is
no longer with us? Clearly, if we explore all these possibilities fully we
shall open up a veritable Pandora's Box. We shall find ourselves up a
blind alley as well. Surely we can and must confine ourselves to the
rather obvious observation that ineffective 'propaganda' is quite simply
ineffective, that its purpose remains unfulfilled. This leaves both the
purpose intact and the attempt. Only the result is missing, but it is
usually not possible to measure that anyway. Such a solution also
leaves intact the concept of 'propaganda' as a means of transmission
from the 'propagandist' to his audience, for the link, though not in
fact achieved, remains in the purpose.

The success or failure of 'propaganda' is not then relevant to its
definition. The technique of the 'propagandist' and the content of his
material may well be. Many writers have defined the essential element
of 'propaganda' as the manipulation of either significant symbols or the
emotions,[17] that is, the use of methods that are in some way subversive
of man's powers of reason. Is this necessarily so? Can there be rational
'propaganda', or does emotion necessarily reign supreme? If we can
have rational 'propaganda', how do we distinguish it from information
or education? Perhaps the balance between reason and the emotions in
'propaganda' reflects the balance in man himself. As Pope wrote:

The ruling passion, be it what it will
The ruling passion conquers reason still.[18]

If man's reason is ultimately ruled by his passions then it is likely that

'propaganda' will echo this and use it, just as it uses the associations
connected with words and symbols. The distinction between 'propaganda' on the one hand and publicity or information on the other is an
extremely fine one, unless we accept the somewhat crude rule of
thumb that 'propaganda' does play upon the emotions, whereas information or publicity appeals to man's reason. But such a crude rule will
not work in practice for the majority of case studies to which it is
applied. Let us look, for instance, at the warning that appears on the
side of every cigarette packet sold in the United Kingdom: 'H.M.
Govt. Health Dept.'s Warning: Cigarettes can seriously damage your
health'. In a sense, this is a bald statement of medically proven facts
about the dangers of cigarette smoking: it is therefore information
rather than 'propaganda'. But one could also argue that the 'statement'
is presented in an emotionally subversive manner. It is a summary of the
dangers, a significant symbol rather than a detailed exposition. It is a
vague threat bolstered by the reference to authority, the whole being
designed to stimulate fear and persuade people not to smoke cigarettes.
This vague fear is further aroused by the notice on all cigarette advertisements that is itself more vague: 'Every packet carries a Government health
warning'. The statement therefore has a purpose connected with the
transmission of the idea that smoking is harmful, so that smokers will
be frightened into abandoning their cigarettes. It is therefore 'propaganda' and we are back where we started. Clearly the distinction is of
little value if it can be interpreted in these two opposing ways.

Writing of the distinction between education and 'propaganda',
Brown remarks that 'education' teaches people *how* to think, while
'propaganda' teaches them *what* to think.[19] This is a distinction that
might usefully be adapted to distinguish between information and
'propaganda'. Information offers people opportunities, while 'propaganda' tells them how to use those opportunities. This distinction is
admittedly also crude, but it does have the merit of placing the focus
of attention back on purpose rather than technique or content. It also
serves to underline the *narrowing* tendency of 'propaganda' in contrast
to the *broadening* perspective of information or education. This does
not mean however that all interested or value-loaded transmission of
ideas must necessarily be classified as 'propaganda'. It is, after all, almost
inevitable that any system of education will transmit the values of the
society of which it is an integral part. But education is concerned with
opening minds, 'propaganda' with closing them. Therein lies the vital
difference, for education will ultimately lead its audience to question
the values upon which it is itself based, whereas 'propaganda' aims only

to make its audience accept those values, and sometimes to act upon the acceptance as well.

This is in direct contrast to the view expressed by Lasswell that 'The spread of controversial attitudes is propaganda, the spread of accepted attitudes and skills is education.'[20] One of the guiding principles for the successful 'propagandist' is surely to make the attitudes that he wishes to spread appear as uncontroversial as possible. The whiff of controversy would invite the possibility of debate and open these same attitudes to contradiction: hence the importance to the 'propagandist' of historical continuity. The 'propagandist' deals not in the drugs of stimulation but in those of sedation: it is through anaesthesia that he hopes to achieve a reaction. None the less, the 'propagandist' may still use controversy as a weapon in his arsenal, to manufacture a simulated debate on an issue for which he then provides a ready-made solution. Both the Nazis and the Bolsheviks used this technique to provoke a 'demand' for the solution that they intended to impose anyway, in order to bestow a spurious legitimacy upon their activities. The most notorious recent example of this technique concerns the events surrounding the Soviet-led occupation of Czechoslovakia in August 1968, and the subsequent arrangement of a request from workers' representatives for such intervention.[21] The 'propagandist' then may use controversy, though he will not wish the views that he is transmitting to be themselves controversial, or so to appear. Again, like success or failure, controversy does not form an essential part of the definition of the term 'propaganda'. It illustrates in this case one of the techniques that may be used. Similarly, 'propaganda' does not necessarily have to be composed of lies. Indeed, the most effective 'propaganda' is the truth, for in the long run the use of the truth will enable the 'propagandist' to gain the trust of his audience, and in the Second World War this was ultimately recognised by both sides.

There is one further point about 'propaganda' that we must examine before attempting to offer a definition, and that concerns the public nature of 'propaganda' as an activity. Does 'propaganda' always have to be in some sense a *public* activity, or is it sometimes applicable to *private* activity as well? If it does have to be public, how are we to delimit the parameters of 'public activity'? Is an academic lecture, for example, an instance of 'propaganda'? Would our judgement alter if it were published or broadcast, or produced as a wall-poster? Here we must remember the changing nature of the political public and therefore of the audience for the 'propagandist'. The introduction of compulsory education (or 'education'?) and universal suffrage has broadened

the political public to include almost every member of society. Thus
has mass man emerged and, to cope with him, the mass media have
arrived. Whereas the 'propagandist' of the Middle Ages was often aiming
to influence an élite, the 'propagandist' of the twentieth century aims
to influence the mass. This may affect the methods and the media employed, but it does not alter the essence of the activity. Some writers
have claimed that 'propaganda' is only 'propaganda' if it uses the mass
media of communication: if it does not, then it is something else.

Qualter, in his rather long though otherwise generally excellent definition, limits 'propaganda' in this way to matters transmitted by the
'instruments of communication':

> Propaganda is thus defined as the deliberate attempt by some
> individual or group to form, control, or alter the attitudes of other
> groups by the use of the instruments of communication, with the
> intention that in any given situation the reaction of those so in-
> fluenced will be that desired by the propagandist.[22]

But unless we are prepared to stretch the meaning of 'instruments of
communication' to hitherto unaccepted limits, Qualter's definition is
too narrow to be applied with conviction to what has been termed the
'propaganda of the deed'. This would seriously restrict the use of the
word 'propaganda' to its detriment. It would also exclude many of the
media of 'propaganda', such as architecture, coinage and postage
stamps, without providing an adequate alternative refuge for them. It
would exclude the practice of commemorating people and events
through naming places after them, and it would exclude the use of
significant symbols, from the 'deed' of the Hitler salute to the image
on a flag or badge. These are things that people identify with and relate
to, but they are hardly 'instruments of communication' in the conven-
tionally accepted sense of the term. This semantic argument does conceal a more important and fundamental point: 'propaganda' *is* an essentially public activity. It is directed at exerting an effect on public opinion or, more correctly, on the public opinions of individuals. The
private opinions of individuals are no concern of the 'propagandist',
except in so far as they impinge upon public matters as defined by the
'propagandist' himself. In societies that are highly politicised the
distinction between the public and the private world is of course difficult to maintain. In this context it will presumably be part of the task
of the 'propagandist' to reduce the frontiers of the private world as
much as possible, but in a liberal, pluralist or democratic system the

distinction still retains its meaning. It is not a question of whether the opinion is publicly or privately expressed, but of whether it impinges upon a matter deemed to be of public interest. It is at the point at which, for whatever reason, the private opinion acquires public meaning that the 'propagandist' becomes interested. He is concerned with the public opinions, and the public activities based upon them, of individuals and with the public significance of those opinions and those activities. The dividing line is of course a thin one, but it is also a clear one. It means that a particular activity can have public significance in one context but not in another. In Britain, for example, the attitude of the individual towards reproduction and contraception is generally considered to be a matter for that individual's conscience, whereas in India, Italy or the Irish Republic this is a public issue. Where there is a public issue upon which people can in this sense have a public opinion, there an attempt will be made to influence that opinion through the means that we can call 'propaganda'.

What then is 'propaganda'? Propaganda is the attempt to influence the public opinions of an audience through the transmission of ideas and values. The use of the word 'attempt' implies both that the purpose of the activity *is* important and that the result is *not*. Propaganda can fail, and be seen to have failed. The verb 'influence' is employed in preference to 'control' because the latter is too total in its implications, and to 'persuade' or 'change' because propaganda has a wider meaning. Propaganda can encompass both the confirmation of existing inclinations and the 'conversion' to ones that were hitherto not apparent; propaganda both confirms and 'converts' (but subject to the reservations expressed by Huxley and already cited). Propaganda aims to influence the 'public opinions of an audience': it is concerned to influence opinions and attitudes towards matters of public interest, as already elaborated, matters that may be of such interest in one context but not in another. Hence we must include the word 'audience': propaganda is aimed at a particular audience and manipulates that audience for its own purposes. Finally, propaganda exerts its influence through the 'transmission of ideas and values': it is thus distinguished from more overt pressures, such as financial reward, or the threat or use of violence. But these ideas and values may be transmitted either directly, as in a political speech, or indirectly by association, through the use of significant symbols such as the flag or emblem. These distinctions are clarified by Fraser:

The central element in propagandist inducements, as opposed to compulsion on the one side and payment, or bribery, on the other, is that they depend on 'communication' rather than concrete penalties or rewards. To affect a donkey's behaviour by whipping is not propaganda, nor is plying it with carrots. But if its owner shouts at it in a threatening manner, or tries to coax it with winning words or noises then the word begins to become appropriate.[23]

This 'communication', as I have already made clear, does not however have to be exercised through the mass media, or the conventional 'instruments of communication', for communication is a much wider process.

This then is what I mean by propaganda. But where does the film fit in? The significance of the cinema as a potential propaganda weapon has been widely recognised. Lenin remarked that 'of all the arts, for us the cinema is the most important'.[24] Stalin described it as 'the greatest means of mass agitation'[25] and Trotsky called it 'the best instrument for propaganda'.[26] Goebbels echoed these sentiments when he called the cinema 'one of the most modern and far-reaching media that there is for influencing the masses'.[27] Why was the cinema seen in these terms?

When people talk about the mass media, they are really talking about the media that are aimed at the mass of the population. From these mass media — the press, radio, television, the cinema — it may fairly be argued that the cinema has been, and indeed still is, the only truly mass medium. There are several reasons for this argument, some of which apply mainly to the silent cinema but which have none the less left their mark upon subsequent developments. Above all the cinema is a visual medium, and the silent cinema a purely visual medium. Its appeal is therefore universal, unlimited by considerations of language, literacy or culture. Only the blind cannot see and understand what is happening on the screen. The appeal of the sound cinema is of course more limited in this sense. The language of the sound track obviously narrows down the audience, although this effect can be modified by dubbing or subtitling. But the sound film, because it is technically capable of conveying more complex and more subtle information, will be limited, in its effective appeal, to audiences that can achieve the requisite level of comprehension. In other words, a simple silent film could be understood by almost anybody, but a less straightforward sound film requires an audience that is at least experienced, if not 'trained', in understanding its language, both visual and spoken, and its conventions. But even the sound film makes a primarily visual impact. If we recall the films that

we have seen, there will be certain spoken phrases that we find memorable: 'Here's looking at you, kid' from *Casablanca* is an obvious
example. For the most part, however, we recollect a film from its visual
phrases: the Odessa Steps sequence in *Potemkin*, the ritual slaughter in
The Wandering Jew, or the smashing of the bottle of Vichy water at
the end of *Casablanca* itself. Because of this visual appeal, the cinema
acts (*pace* Eisenstein's concept of intellectual montage) on the emotions
of an audience rather than its intellect. For the same reason the cinema
is more accessible to its audience — less demanding, easier to compre-
hend than the written or the spoken word. It appeals to us at a more
primitive, more subconscious level.

The cinema is also the only medium of mass communication that
appeals to an audience that is at the same time a mass. The press, radio
and television, while communicating crowd events, convey their message
to the individual and, in the case of radio and television especially,
almost always to the individual in his own home. The cinema appeals to
him as a member of a crowd. In this context it contains elements of
theatre: the member of a cinema audience, like a spectator in a theatre,
is uniquely susceptible not only to his own emotions, but to those of
the mass around him, and to the interaction between his own emotions
and those of the mass. When his enthusiasm is aroused. he is like a
member of a football crowd, or a spectator/participant at a mass rally.
He is like putty in the propagandist's hands.

In its early stages the cinema had other strengths that have since
been taken over by radio and television. The press, even after the
Northcliffe revolution, had appealed only to a section of the population. The cinema, on the other hand, attracted its audience from all
classes and social groupings. It therefore had a capacity for binding a
nation together, or for strengthening a national political movement,
that was unique at that time. In its early days too the cinema had the
advantage of being widely admired as a technological marvel and
novelty: this was an advantage that the Bolsheviks eventually put to
good use. The cinema, because of its mechanical basis, was also the first
medium that was reproducible for a mass audience. The audience for a
film was limited only by the number of copies that could be made
available and by the number of cinemas that were equipped to show it.
In practice of course these considerations proved to be severe handi-
caps, but *in theory* the entire population of the world could have been
watching the same film at the same time. Now of course we can all
watch television and see man walking on the moon, but in the 1920s
this was seen as an amazing breakthrough. The cinema was the first

universal mass medium and its potential appeared to be unbounded. There was one other aspect of the cinema's mechanical reproducibility that appealed to the propagandist. The cost of producing and distributing a film, as compared for instance with a poster or a printed leaflet, was enormous and required a vast capital outlay. But this also meant that the number of points at which films could be made was severely limited, and thus easier to control. The cinema was therefore a *reliable* propaganda medium: a film, unlike a theatre group, could be despatched from the centre to the periphery and the content of the performance could be determined and guaranteed in advance.

All these considerations combined to make the cinema the ideal propaganda weapon for the second quarter of the twentieth century. In the two most highly politicised societies of that time, Soviet Russia and Nazi Germany, that weapon was used on a large scale. It is the purpose of this study to examine in context how the cinema was used as a propaganda weapon in those countries — how the industry was organised, how the message was conveyed — and to see what lessons we can draw. It was, after all, Lenin himself who told us that we should 'Study, study, study'.

Notes

1. E. Jannings, 'Über den Film. Aus einer Rundfunk-Rede zu seinem Film *Ohm Krüger'*, *Nationalsozialistische Monatshefte*, June 1942, 342-3.
2. This pejorative connotation is by no means a twentieth-century development. The *OED* gives an earlier such usage in: W.T. Brande, *A Dictionary of Science, Literature and Art* (London, 1842): 'Derived from this celebrated society (i.e. the Sacred Congregation for the Propagation of the Faith), the name *propaganda* is applied in modern political language as a term of reproach to secret associations for the spread of opinions and principles which are viewed by most governments with horror and aversion.'
3. J. Driencourt, *La propagande. Nouvelle force politique* (Paris, 1950), p. 18.
4. e.g. H.D. Lasswell, 'The person: subject and object of propaganda', *Annals of the American Academy of Political and Social Science*, vol. 179, p. 189.
5. I take here the distinctions made in the *Shorter Oxford English Dictionary* between the verb 'define' ('To set forth the essential nature of', p. 471) and 'describe' ('To give a detailed or graphic account of', p. 489).
6. L.W. Doob, *Propaganda. Its Psychology and Technique* (New York, 1935), p. 80.
7. A.J. Mackenzie, *Propaganda Boom* (London, 1938), p. 35.
8. Introduction by G. Dawson in: *A Book of Broadsheets* (London, 1928), p. xi.
9. A. Huxley, 'Notes on propaganda', *Harper's Monthly Magazine*, vol. 174, December 1936, 34, 39.
10. F.E. Lumley, *The Propaganda Menace* (London, 1933), p. 44.
11. W. Albig, *Public Opinion* (New York, 1939), p. 287.
12. Ibid., p. 305.
13. Speech of 5 March 1937, quoted in: W. von Bredow and R. Zurek (eds), *Film und Gesellschaft in Deutschland. Dokumente und Materialien* (Hamburg, 1975), p. 33, note 41.

14. The Germans established the New British Broadcasting Corporation, The Workers' Challenge Station (in an attempt to exacerbate class divisions in Britain) and Radio Free Caledonia and Radio Free Wales (aimed at encouraging Scottish and Welsh nationalism respectively); C. Roetter, *Psychological Warfare* (London. 1974), p. 17. The British established Soldatensender West; J.A.C. Brown, *Techniques of Persuasion: From Propaganda to Brainwashing* (Harmondsworth, 1963), p. 99; R.H.S. Crossman, 'Psychological warfare', *Journal of the Royal United Services Institution*, vol. 97, no. 587 (1952), 321-2.

15. H.D. Lasswell, 'The theory of political propaganda', *American Political Science Review*, vol. 21, August 1927, 629.

16. J. Ellul, *Propaganda. The Formation of Men's Attitudes* (New York, 1973), p. x.

17. e.g. B. Russell, 'Free thought and official propaganda' (1922 Conway Memorial Lecture), in: *Let the People Think. A Selection of Essays* (London, 1941), p. 35; Lasswell, 'The theory of political propaganda', 627; and: The person . . .', p. 189; and also *Encyclopedia of the Social Sciences*, s.v.; Albig, p. 309; F.C. Bartlett, *Political Propaganda* (Cambridge, 1940), p. 65; B.L. Smith in *International Encyclopedia of the Social Sciences*, s.v.

18. A. Pope, *Moral Essays*, Ep. iii. 'To Lord Bathurst', ll. 153-4. Cf. D. Hume, *Treatise of Human Nature, II*, iii, 3.

19. Brown, *Techniques of Persuasion*, p. 21.

20. Lasswell, 'The person', p. 189.

21. R. Littell (ed.), *The Czech Black Book* (London, 1969), p. viii.

22. T.H. Qualter, *Propaganda and Psychological Warfare* (New York, 1962), p. 27.

23. L. Fraser, *Propaganda* (London, 1957), p. 3.

24. G. Boltyanskii, *Lenin i kino* (Moscow, 1925), pp. 16-17.

25. *Trinadtsatyi s"ezd R.K.P. (b). 23-31 maya 1924 goda. Stenograficheskii otchët* (Moscow, 1924), p. 132.

26. L. Trotsky, *Problems of Life* (London, 1924), p. 38.

27. 9 February 1934; quoted in E. Leiser, *Deutschland, erwache! Propaganda im Film des Dritten Reiches* (Reinbek bei Hamburg, 1968), pp. 40-1.

PART TWO: SOVIET RUSSIA

In a society based on private property the artist produces goods for the market; he needs buyers. Our revolution has freed artists from the yoke of these highly prosaic conditions. It has transformed the Soviet state into their protector and their customer. Every artist, anyone who considers himself as such, has the right to create freely, according to his ideal, independent of anything else.

But you must understand that we are Communists. We should not stand by with our arms folded and let chaos develop in all directions. We should guide this process and mould its results fully and systematically. We are still far, very far, from doing this.

Lenin, 1920

If an artist is so hungry for creative work that he can no longer sustain the torture of waiting, the torture of standing idle, and if then, averting his gaze, he agrees to make a film in obviously hopeless circumstances – he is making a mistake . . .

I myself am extremely hungry for work . . . If I depended only on pen and paper, I should write day and night, write and write and write. But I have to write with a movie camera. I write not on paper but on film. My work is dependent on a whole series of organisational and technical factors.

I must win my rights in my place of work. And if I cannot get anything from this administration or that governing body, I shall still not surrender. Surely we all remember what Mayakovsky said in a similar situation: 'Governing bodies come and go, art remains'.

Dziga Vertov, 1934

3 RUSSIA: THE HISTORICAL BACKGROUND

> I consider that the cinema is an empty, totally useless, and
> even harmful form of entertainment. Only an abnormal person
> could place this farcical business on a par with art. It is com-
> plete rubbish and no importance whatsoever should be
> attached to such stupidities.
>
> Nicholas II, 1913[1]

The October Revolution of 1917 took place in the year in which the
Russian cinema quite literally came of age. The first public demonstration of the Lumière brothers' new cinematograph in Russia was given
on 4 May 1896 at the Aquarium variety theatre in St Petersburg,
between the second and third acts of an operetta called, quite fortuitously,
Alfred Pasha in Paris.[2] From these very humble beginnings the cinema
was to experience, in Russia as elsewhere, a mushrooming growth in
popularity. But despite, or in some cases perhaps because of, this
popularity, it was not until after the First World War that the cinema
achieved 'respectability', both as an art form and as a medium for the
transmission of ideas and propaganda.

The new invention was so successful in St Petersburg and in Moscow,
where it was demonstrated shortly afterwards, that it became a major
attraction at the Nizhny Novgorod Fair in the summer of 1896. Here
it was seen by visitors from all over Russia including the writer, Maxim
Gorky, who saw the Lumière brothers' film *The Arrival of the Train in
the Station*. In his local newspaper column, Gorky vividly describes the
impressions that his visit to the 'kingdom of the shadows' left on him:

> If only you knew how strange it is to be there. There are no sounds,
> no colours. There everything — the earth, the trees, the people, the
> water, the air — is tinted in the single tone of grey: in a grey sky
> there are grey rays of sunlight; in grey faces grey eyes, and the leaves
> of the trees are grey like ashes. This is not life but the shadow of
> life and this is not movement but the soundless shadow of move-
> ment . . .
> A railway train appears on the screen. It darts like an arrow
> straight towards you — look out! It seems as if it is about to rush
> into the darkness in which you are sitting and reduce you to a

mangled sack of skin, full of crumpled flesh and shattered bones,
and reduce this hall and this building, so packed with wine, women,
music and vice, and transform it into fragments and into dust.[3]

The initial impact of the film was thus profound, and this impact continued to be felt amongst the Russian peasantry well into the 1920s,
before the moving picture ceased to be a novelty and became accepted
as an everyday method of communication and entertainment. In the
early years, however, the novelty value of the cinema combined with
its background as a fairground attraction to stifle its emergence as a
serious social and political force.

The structure, if it may so be called, of the nascent Russian film
industry was extremely fluid in its first decade. Film showings were
arranged at first by wandering exhibitors who had been to Paris to
purchase their projection equipment and supply of short films and
travelled from place to place showing their films until the audience
in a particular town had been exhausted. They were restricted by a
variety of considerations, ranging from the Lumière patent monopoly
to the absence of electricity outside the very largest centres of population. None the less they survived and prospered until such time as the
audience potential in Russia had been built up to the point where the
establishment of permanent cinemas was deemed to be a viable
commercial proposition. The first such cinemas were opened in Moscow
in 1903.[4] The new cinemas were given names like 'Illusion', 'Marvel',
'Mirage', 'Fantasia' and 'World of Wonders' and the generic term
developed from 'theatres of living photograph' or 'electrotheatres' to
the more popular 'illusions'. These names of course reflected the preoccupations of both the cinema and the cinema audience of the time.
Still in its infancy, the film could attract large numbers merely because
of its technical ingenuity and its novelty value. Most films still followed
the Lumière pattern as reflected in films like *The Arrival of the Train in
the Station* and *The Sprayer Sprayed*: they were short, simple, and used
the cinema's potential to amuse and surprise. In other words, these
films may be characterised as entertainment pure and simple.

The opening of permanent cinema theatres generated a further
expansion. As the audience for the cinema increased, so too did the
demand for longer and more elaborate films. The two major French film-
producing firms, Pathé and Gaumont, opened their own offices in
Moscow and swamped the growing Russian market with their films. The
first film to be shot in Russia had been of Nicholas II's coronation in
May 1896 and this footage had been shown in the West. Newsreel or

actuality film was boosted by both the Russo-Japanese War of 1904-5 and the 1905 Revolution. For the first time people were curious to *see* what was happening. This phenomenon marks an important stage in the cinema's growth towards respectability: people were beginning to tire of mere novelty and to demand something more. But the Russian government was certainly not going to give them what they wanted in 1905: it confiscated all film taken of the 1905 events so that one French company felt obliged to fabricate 'Russian' newsreels in Paris for its French audiences in order to avoid Russian censorship and satisfy French curiosity at the same time.[5] In 1907 the first film studio was set up in Russia by Drankov. In 1908 Pathé, wary of the prospect of competition and appreciating the attraction of films on Russian themes for Russian audiences, released *Don Cossacks*, which proved to be a phenomenal success. The press advertisement proclaimed: 'Up till now the Russian public, sitting in Russian theatres, paying Russian money, has not seen subjects from Russian life.'[6] Drankov replied with the first all-Russian production, *Stenka Razin*. Despite his successes, based mainly on the exploitation of sensation, as late as 1910-11 Pathé still controlled 75 per cent of the market.

The sensationalism, of which Drankov was but one exponent, tended to give the cinema a bad name. Writing in 1910 Kornei Chukovsky denounced the cinema as 'that collective creation of those very Kaffirs and Hottentots who live "below" '.[7] Three years later, Mayakovsky was writing:

Can the cinema be an independent art form? Obviously not . . . Only an artist can extract the images of art from real life and the cinema can only act as a successful or unsuccessful multiplier of his images . . . The cinema and art are phenomena of a different order . . . Art produces refined images, whilst the cinema, like the printer's press for a book, reproduces them and distributes them to the remotest and most distant parts of the world.[8]

These strictures were only ominous in the longer term; in the short term, the cinema faced more dangerous enemies. Mayakovsky himself also predicted that the cinema might ultimately replace the theatre[9] but it was the theatre owners and their lobby who forced the government to take steps to curb the growth of the new medium. In 1908-9 the government introduced restrictions on the number and location of cinemas and on cinema opening hours, and eventually banned the musical accompaniment of films altogether.[10] Contemporary commenta-

tors made the same kind of accusations against the cinema as have subsequently been levelled against television, and with equally little justification: the cinema, it was said, harmed the eyesight[11] and acted as 'the
breeding ground of fire, blindness and moral perversion'.[12] The restrictions caused a significant drop in box-office takings but they also
caused an outcry and had soon to be lifted. The cinema had by now
attracted a mass audience, one that outstripped the audience for
theatres, concerts, circuses and music halls combined. A contemporary
observed:

> If you walk in the evenings along the streets of the capital, of the
> large provincial towns, local towns, large settlements and villages, on
> every street you will see the same phenomenon with the solitary,
> flickering kerosene lights: an entrance illuminated by lamps, and by
> the entrance a crowd waiting in a queue – the cinema.
>   If you look in the auditorium the composition of the audience
> will amaze you. Everyone is there – students and gendarmes, writers
> and prostitutes, officers and cadets, all kinds of intellectuals,
> bearded and with pince-nez, and workers, shop assistants, tradesmen,
> society ladies, fashionable women, officials – in a word, everyone.[13]

It seemed that the cinema had become respectable.

At about this time the first steps to introduce the cinema into Russia
for educational purposes were being taken. In 1911 the Russian firm of
Khanzhonkov set up an Educational Section which produced its first
film entitled *Drunkenness and its Consequences*. In 1912 Pathé per-
fected a new projector which had its own dynamo and could therefore
be used in the countryside where there was no electricity supply. But
until the outbreak of the First World War, the government never took
the cinema seriously, the Tsar regarding it as an amusing toy. The war
was to change this state of affairs dramatically.

By the outbreak of war the cinema was already the most popular
form of public entertainment amongst the urban masses of the population. But 90 per cent of the films shown in Russia were still imported,
and the largest importer was Pathé. Soon, however, the British and
French governments decreed that film stock was to be classified as a
strategic commodity and could therefore not be exported. Obviously,
film could not be imported from the other major supplier, Germany,
because Russia was now at war with her. The war thus forced the
Russian film industry to stand on its own two feet. The foreign film
producers went out of business and Russian domestic production

boomed. rising from 129 films, mostly short, in 1913 to 499, mostly feature-length films, in 1916.[14] As a contemporary film journal remarked:

> From the beginning of the War the borders were closed and Russia left without foreign films. At first Russian cinematographers went to pieces.
> — The end! No films; the cinemas will have to close.
> But this only lasted for a very short time. And then we began to use our own means.
> And what happened?
> Such a short time has passed, yet look where the Russian cinema has got to now.
> Look at a Russian film and you will wonder: where did they attain such perfection? Where did they acquire such taste, such feeling, technique and artistry?
> And the explanation is quite simple: they did not acquire them from anywhere — they were already there.[15]

Russian film production was constrained only by the shortage of materials: in the cinema, as in many other fields of industry, Russia had relied too heavily on imports from its European neighbours.

The First World War also brought with it the first attempt by the Russian authorities to use the cinema for propaganda purposes. In March 1914 the Skobelev Committee, originally established as a charitable institution to assist veterans of the Russo-Japanese War, set up a Military Film Section.[16] On the outbreak of war it was given the exclusive right to film at the front[17] but the press complained about the quality and the sparsity of its films and the monopoly had eventually to be revoked. The government had lost its opportunity to harness the cinema for patriotic purposes. Commercial producers, however, were not slow to take advantage of the war. There was a rush of films with titles like *The Holy War* (allegedly a First World War newsreel, but in fact a collection of pre-war film with new and falsified subtitles),[18] *Down with the German Yoke!*,*The Antichrist, Glory to Us! Death to our Enemies!* and *For the Honour, Glory and Fortune of Slavdom*. Because the shortage of materials favoured the larger producers, who could afford to pay higher prices, smaller producers turned to the sensational and the pornographic. In the first year of the war a leading right-wing deputy to the Duma, Purishkevich, was outraged to discover that he had been lampooned in a film. He demanded the introduction of censorship and the establishment of a government film monopoly, and proposed:

> ... the prevention of the spread of cinemas into the villages without film censorship through the establishment of a legally based special mixed commission with representatives of the Ministries of People's Education, Internal Affairs, War, the Navy and the Holy Synod ... and the introduction of a government monopoly of cinemas.[19]

In the following year these ideas were further developed in a closely argued pamphlet entitled 'The Cinema as Government Regalia', written and published by V.M. Dementyev. Using a mixture of quasi-military arguments Dementyev proposed the establishment of a government cinema monopoly, along the lines of the spirit and salt monopolies, which could be used as a weapon for propaganda and education among the masses. He envisaged that the cinema should be run as a military operation, the personnel being given different ranks and the cinemas themselves being renamed 'royal pavilions'.[20] If this were not done, Dementyev argued, the government would lose the initiative and the present situation would continue: 'In the capital everything is being done to make the foreigner feel at home and the Russian feel that he is an alien.'[21]

In 1916 the Minister of the Interior, Protopopov, suggested that a government commission should be set up to investigate the feasibility of a government film monopoly 'in order to utilise it for educational and moral ends'.[22] The Minister of Finance rejected this proposal and Protopopov established his own commission which reported later in the same year. In the light of its findings the newspaper *Russkoe slovo* commented:

> In the plan, which has been transmitted through the relevant government organs into the highest spheres, it is pointed out that the cinema, if it were established on a broader basis, could be used by the government to instil healthy political and social opinions among the populace. It could lessen the sharpened conflict between classes and bring patriotic and monarchist ideas to the people. Government cinemas should be aimed largely at the lower classes of the nation.[23]

The events of 1917 swept this particular proposal into oblivion and it was left to the Bolsheviks to realise the plans that were being suggested to the Tsarist government.

By 1917 the Russian cinema was on its feet. In the towns and cities the cinema attracted a larger audience than all other forms of entertainment put together. Although still frowned upon in many theatrical circles, the cinema was beginning to achieve a certain respectability, at least amongst the more progressive of the intelligentsia. Meyerhold had filmed *The Portrait of Dorian Grey* and Mayakovsky had modified his earlier attitude. By 1917 many more people would have agreed with the sentiments expressed in 1913 by Leonid Andreyev:

The miraculous Kinemo! . . . If the highest and most sacred aim of art is to create contact between people and their separate souls, then an enormous unimaginable socio-psychological role is destined to be played by this artistic Apache of the present! . . . Having no language, being equally comprehensible to the savages of St Petersburg and those of Calcutta, it truly becomes the genius of international contact, brings nearer the ends of the earth and the spheres of the soul, and gathers into a single stream the whole of quivering humanity.[24]

But despite its enormous potential, the cinema remained unharnessed by the Provisional Government. The Skobelev Committee was reorganised on several occasions and in June 1917 it began production of a government propaganda newsreel called *Free Russia*. Censorship was abolished in May, but this measure was probably aimed as much at relieving the government of an unnecessary administrative burden as at signifying any positive policy of cultural enlightenment. The abolition of censorship did not give rise to a flood of revolutionary propaganda, mainly because the means of production and distribution lay firmly in the hands of commercial interests. Instead the new freedoms were abused to produce salacious films about the fallen imperial family and their court: titles such as *Dark Forces – Gregory Rasputin and His Associates, In the Tenacious Clutches of the Double-headed Eagle,* and *The Trading House of Romanov, Sukhomlinov, Myasoyedov, Protopopov and Co.* abounded. Fearful of government intervention, the Union of Patriotic Cinematography, which represented the interests of the entrepreneurs, resolved in March 1917:

In view of the immense power of the screen, for which such a wide field of activity as a truly democratic theatre amongst the popular masses has been opened, we consider that the people, having opened the doors to knowledge and enlightenment for themselves, should see in the screen the cultural force that will convey these things to

all four corners of our great fatherland. In addition, it is with great
regret that the conference declares that people for whom the cinema
is exclusively a source of profit and who have no scruples about their
methods, are striving to use the liberation of artistic expression for
the demonstration of pornographic themes relating to the old order,
the very titles of which are obscene, and are cynically connecting
them with the sacred cause of the Russian Revolution.[25]

To distinguish itself from such elements, the union further resolved to
pool what little film of the actual events of the February Revolution
had been shot and present it to the government for charitable causes.
The film, *The Great Days of the Russian Revolution from 28 February
to 4 March*, was handed over on 17 March and eventually raised a sum
of 40,000 roubles.[26]

The only tangible effect of the February Revolution upon the
Russian cinema was, however, a negative one. For the first time, but
not the last, the government took steps to reduce the consumption of
electricity. Electricity supplies for film production alone were initially
cut by 60 per cent,[27] the opening hours of cinemas were drastically
curtailed and a large number were forced to close altogether. The
Moscow City Soviet, which was concerned with the day-to-day imple-
mentation of the government's policy, protested loudly, pointing out
that the electricity consumption of individuals in separate households
was considerably higher than that of a mass of people gathered together
in the darkness to watch a film. This was an argument that was to be
heard again and again when the disruption of the Revolution, the Civil
War and the post-revolutionary period forced the Provisional Government and then the Soviet authorities to impose similar restrictions on
electricity consumption and on the cinema. In late October the government announced that cinemas would only be allowed to open for three
days a week. The November issue of the film journal *Proektor* denounced the new restrictions in its editorial but they had already been
overtaken by events; as *Proektor* observed:

> The preceding lines had already been set up in type when events
> took place in Moscow that will radically alter the pattern of our
> lives. The City Duma, which was supposed to ratify the . . . decision,
> has ceased to exist. The attitude of the new authorities towards the
> cinema is not known.[28]

The events referred to were, of course, those of the October Revolution which would in the long run radically alter the pattern of the Russian cinema, but the exact shape of the new pattern was to emerge only slowly in the coming months and years.

Notes

1. A note scribbled in the margin of a police report by Nicholas II in 1913; I.S. Zil'bershtein, 'Nikolai II o kino'. *Sovetskii ekran*, 12 April 1927, 10.

2. N.A. Lebedev *Ocherk istorii kino SSSR: Nemoe kino (1918-1934)* (Moscow, 1965), p. 3.

3. Pacatus (pseudonym of Maxim Gorky), 'Beglye zametki', *Nizhegorodskii listok*, 4 July 1896.

4. B.S. Likhachëv, *Kino v Rossii (1896-1926)*. *Materialy k istorii russkogo kino*. *Chast' I: 1896-1913* (Leningrad, 1927), p. 25.

5. G. Sadoul. 'Progressivnye techeniya vo frantsuzskom kino (1900-1958)', *Voprosy kinoiskusstva*, 1 (1957), pp. 360-1.

6. *Cine-Phono*, 1907-8, No. 7.

7. K. Chukovskii, *Nat Pinkerton i sovremennaya literatura* (Moscow, 1910), p. 26.

8. V.V. Mayakovskii, 'Otnoshenie segodnyashnego teatra i kinematografa k iskusstvu'. *Kine-Zhurnal*, 1913, no. 17.

9. V.V. Mayakovskii, 'Teatr, kinematograf, futurizm', *Kine-Zhurnal*, 1913, no. 14.

10. Likhachëv, *Kino v Rossii*, p. 26, note 1, and p. 34.

11. Quoted in ibid., p. 27.

12. Quoted in: A.A. Khanzhonkov, *Pervye gody russkoi kinematografii* (Moscow, 1937), p. 26.

13. A. Serafimovich, 'Mashinnoe nadvigaetsya', *Cine-Phono*, 1911-12, no. 8.

14. S.S. Ginzburg, *Kinematografiya dorevolyutsionnoi Rossii* (Moscow, 1963), p. 157.

15. *Cine-Phono*, 1914, no. 4/5.

16. Khanzhonkov, *Pervye gody russkoi kinematografii*, p. 80.

17. Ginsburg, *Kinematografiya*, p. 181.

18. Ibid., pp. 178-9.

19. Quoted in: Khanzhonkov, *Pervye gody russkoi kinematografii*, p. 76.

20. V.M. Dement'ev, *Kinematograf kak pravitel'stvennaya regaliya* (Petrograd, 1915), p. 47.

21. Ibid., p. 14.

22. Ginzburg, *Kinematografiya*, p. 172.

23. *Russkoe slovo*, 5 October 1916.

24. L. Andreev, *Polnoe sobranie sochinenii*, vol. 8 (St Petersburg, 1913), pp. 305-6.

25. *Vestnik kinematografii*, 1917, no. 124.

26. V. Rosolovskaya, *Russkaya kinematografiya v 1917 godu. Materialy k istorii* (Moscow, 1937), p. 47.

27. *Proektor*, 1917, no. 15/16.

28. *Proektor*, 1917, no. 17/18.

4 RUSSIA: THE NEEDS OF REVOLUTION

Of all the arts, for us the cinema is the most important.

Lenin, 1922[1]

The role of propaganda in the revolutionary struggle was a common-place of Russian socialist thought. Forced to work underground or in exile, the Russian Social Democratic and Labour Party had seen it as its principal task to arouse in the workers a consciousness of their separate identity as a class. From this it would be but a small step to convert that sense of identity into a feeling of common interest and thus of class solidarity. This transformation was to be achieved, where possible, by a combination of agitation, propaganda and organisation. In the period before 1905 especially it was difficult for the Party to organise the workers into a coherent movement and it was therefore forced to rely on methods of persuasion – pamphlets and speeches which utilised particular events (such as strikes or lock-outs) or specific issues (such as the length of the working day) – to unite passive and isolated individual workers into a coherent, active and militant mass, fighting the autocratic system to establish and protect their rights as a class. In this struggle, as in the struggles that were to occur after the Revolution, the Party saw itself as the vanguard of the working mass. Russian Marxists of this time distinguished between two forms of political persuasion – agitation and propaganda. This distinction was made originally, and most clearly, by Plekhanov, the 'father of Russian Marxism', when he wrote in 1892 that, 'A propagandist presents *many* ideas to one or a few persons; an agitator presents *only one or a few* ideas, but he presents them to a *whole* mass of people.'[2] Ten years later Lenin developed the distinction in *What is to be Done?*:

> . . . the propagandist, dealing with, say, the question of unemployment, must explain the capitalistic nature of crises, the cause of their inevitability in modern society, the necessity for the transformation of this society into a socialist society, etc. In a word, he must present 'many ideas', so many, indeed, that they will be widely understood as an integral whole only by a (comparatively) few persons. The agitator, however, speaking on the same subject, will take as an illustration a fact that is most glaring and widely known

to his audience, say, the death of an unemployed worker's family from starvation, the growth of impoverishment, etc., and, utilising this fact, known to all, will direct his efforts to presenting *a single idea* to the 'masses', e.g. the senselessness of the contradiction between the increase of wealth and the increase of poverty; he will strive *to rouse* discontent and indignation among the masses against this crying injustice, leaving a more complete explanation of this contradiction to the propagandist.[3]

At the turn of the century, with the Party operating in secret and underground, the distinction meant in practice that, in Lenin's words, 'the propagandist operates chiefly by means of the *printed* word; the agitator by means of the *spoken* word'.[4] Propaganda was, then, more of a long-term activity, a preparation of the background. Agitation, on the other hand, was more immediate and more specifically directed. This distinction is maintained in the Soviet Union to the present day, but in practice it is a difficult distinction to maintain. Plekhanov himself defined agitation and propaganda in terms of one another:

> In general it is not easy to draw the line between agitation and what is usually called propaganda. Agitation is also propaganda, but propaganda taking place in particular circumstances, i.e. in circumstances that compel even those people who would not normally have paid any attention to them to listen to the words of the propagandist. Propaganda is agitation conducted in the normal everyday course of the life of a particular country. Agitation is propaganda, occasioned by events that are not entirely ordinary and evoking a certain upsurge in the general mood . . . Propaganda, in the proper sense of the word, would lose all historical meaning if it were not accompanied by agitation.[5]

The distinction between agitation and propaganda is not normally made in English and I do not intend to make it in this book. The reader should however be aware of its existence in the Russian language and in Soviet theory. In practice the distinction is difficult to maintain, and not particularly useful when it can be maintained. It was clearly agitation rather than propaganda, to use their own terminology, that the Bolsheviks required in the aftermath of the October Revolution and in the early years of Soviet power. The *agitki* (short agitational films) of the Civil War were clearly agitational rather than propagandistic but, as the 1920s wore on and the Soviet cinema began to be organised on a more permanent basis, the distinction becomes less clear. The elements of agitation and propaganda in a film such as *Battleship Potemkin* are inextricably intertwined. I feel that to discuss each film in terms of whether it may be regarded as agitation or propaganda would be a worse than fruitless exercise, for it would actually obscure the real value of the film. I shall therefore use the word propaganda to apply to both agitation and propaganda in the Russian sense.

The principal unifying force in Marxist propaganda before the Revolution had been the press, first *Iskra* and then *Pravda*; the masthead of *Iskra* (The Spark) had proudly proclaimed: 'From this spark there shall arise a flame' and that precisely described its function in arousing the mass to revolutionary class consciousness. After the Revolution the masses had to be further aroused and actively involved in the struggle to create a new order. What *Iskra* and *Pravda* had been to the underground Party, the cinema would be to the Soviet government: a rallying point and a weapon in the struggle for unification. Hence, for Lenin, the cinema was to be 'the most important of all the arts'. The October Revolution had given the Bolsheviks control only of the commanding heights of the political and administrative machinery of the state: it had not given them effective power in large areas of the country. They had in their hands the structure of government, or what remained of it: they had to win the hearts and minds of the population. The media that had served them well before the Revolution were inadequate for the task that now lay before them: the Bolsheviks needed a medium that would appeal to the broad masses of the population who were overwhelmingly illiterate, and who spoke over a hundred different languages and came from many different cultures. They therefore needed a medium that was primarily and fundamentally visual in its appeal, thus overcoming problems of language, culture and literacy. They needed a medium that was dynamic and modern. The essence of the cinema was the *moving* picture: as a contemporary wrote, 'The soul of the cinema is the movement of life.'[6] The association of the cinema with the machine underlined its role as the art form of the twentieth century, its novelty, especially in the outlying areas of the Soviet countryside, and its symbolic function as an agent of progress. The cinema was universal in its appeal: the 'great silent', as it was called, could be viewed simultaneously in Petrograd and Vladivostok, Murmansk and Baku, and its message could be understood in all these places, unimpeded by barriers of language or culture:

The curse of the theatre – THE UNREPEATABILITY OF THE

SPECTACLE – does not frighten the cinema, which reproduces its spectacles for the whole world . . . Hence the colossal profitability of the cinema, which gives it the chance for the most powerful development and a tremendous advantage over the theatre – ECONOMY OF ARTISTIC RESOURCES WITH AN INFINITE AUDITORIUM. In order to give millions of people the chance to enjoy a beautiful spectacle involving world artists the cinema has only to play once . . . And the great Asta Nielsen or Jackie Coogan excites and shakes simultaneously both Berlin and Singapore.[7]

Its universality also meant that the cinema could be controlled more easily than, say, the theatre by the authorities at the centre. The making of a film required a great deal of complex and expensive equipment to which access was limited. Whereas a play on tour could be changed at the whim of the actors involved, the film remained largely as it had originally been made: in this sense the cinema was a more reliable medium for the spread of propaganda from the centre to the regions. In the early 1920s the theatre was often compared unfavourably with the cinema:

The theatre's day is done and there is only one thing left for it to do – die . . . The theatre is for *a few epicures*, it is not for the people. The cinema belongs to everyone The cinema does not talk, leaving us the opportunity to complete the spectacle, at the same time *training* our self-creativity. The theatre gives us long, boring, alien words which are 99% banal and empty. Which of them do we need now? Of course there can only be one answer.[8]

Before the Bolsheviks could use the cinema for propaganda purposes, they had to gain control of it, or what remained of it, in as far as that was possible. Just as the normal administrative structure of the state had been disrupted by war and revolution, so the production and distribution system of the existing cinema network had crumbled under the combined strain of political and economic pressures. It was therefore virtually impossible for the government to realise its policy through conventional channels. The situation was complicated by the behaviour of many of those active in the film industry. Fearing national-isation or sequestration, several of the leading pre-revolutionary film makers had fled, first to areas held by the White forces such as the Crimea, and then abroad. In many cases they took with them their leading directors, actors or cameramen, thus impoverishing the nascent

Soviet cinema even further.[9] In addition a number of those left
behind took steps to ensure that their property did not fall into the
hands of the new government: cases were reported of cinema owners
burying their entire stock of film in the hope that the Bolsheviks were
but a passing nightmare.[10] In these circumstances both Lunacharsky, the
People's Commissar for Enlightenment, and Lenin favoured a policy of
gradual nationalisation. If the cinema were ever to be used effectively
it would have to be brought under state control, but if this were done
too quickly, it could provoke destructive opposition. Even slight moves
in this direction were denounced as the 'sword of Damocles' hanging
over the cinema.[11] None the less the cinema industry, production,
distribution and exhibition, were subjected to a process·of gradually
increasing central and municipal control throughout the Civil War
period until on 27 August 1919 Lenin signed the decree that finally
nationalised all cinema enterprises, [12] although even this decree took
more than six months to put into effect.

From the beginning the cinema had been placed under the ultimate
control of Lunacharsky's ministry, the People's Commissariat for
Enlightenment, known in Russian as Narkompros for short. The newly
nationalised industry was organised under the All-Russian Photographic
and Cinematographic Section of Narkompros, VFKO.[13] But this only
meant that the state controlled the bare bones of the cinema industry:
much of the flesh and blood – the cinemas themselves, the films, the
trained personnel – was in no fit state to be used as a propaganda
weapon. Writing a few years later, Huntley Carter has described a visit to
a Moscow cinema:

> I visited the 'Mirror' kino in Tverskoi, another of Moscow's fashion-
> able thoroughfares. As the name implies, the 'Mirror' was once a
> hall of mirrors. When I saw it, it was the remains of mirrors, many
> of which got bent when the Reds and the antis were slaughtering
> each other. The decorated ceiling had been newly decorated by shot
> and shell, and had a special ventilation system introduced by the
> method of dropping eggs from aeroplanes. The windows were
> patched with odds and ends of timber, and the seats were in splints
> and looking unusually frowzy. Most of them were just plain wooden
> benches. Two dim lights made their appearance during the intervals
> which were pretty frequent. An ancient screen, suffering from
> jaundice, and a worn-out projector, buried in an emergency structure
> and half hidden by a dirty curtain as though ashamed of itself,
> completed the fitments.

The film was a genuine antique of pre-war Russian manufacture. It was in rags, and the reel was so broken that the 'curtain fell' every few minutes.[14]

There were virtually no new feature films being made at this time and none were as yet being imported; cinemas therefore had to fall back on old, worn films which most people had already seen. In addition they had to cope with increasing power cuts which were supposed to save precious energy. In other words the conventional cinema network could not cope with the propaganda needs of the new government. They therefore looked elsewhere for an emergency solution to an emergency situation.

A vast country with a widely scattered population and a rapidly changing Civil War front required above all a mobile, flexible and reliable medium of communication between the centre and the regions, at least until those regions had become sufficiently stable to permit the establishment of more permanent and conventional organisations. The Soviet government developed for its propaganda activities a network of stationary *agitpunkty* (from the Russian for an agitational point or centre), situated in strategic places like railway junctions or large settlements; combined with this were an increasing number of travelling agitational trains and a steamer. The trains were to act as the standard-bearers of revolutionary agitation, moving wherever they were most urgently required, while the *agitpunkty* were to concentrate on propaganda saturation of the population in a given place.[15] The trains were equipped with living quarters for the crew, a library and bookshop, printing press, radio and cinema equipment. It was the cinema that helped to make the visits of the trains memorable, for most peasants had never before seen a moving picture. The Bolsheviks were able to take advantage of this in two ways: first, they associated themselves in the popular mind with technology, mechanisation and progress, and second, they could use the new medium to bring pictures of the new leadership to the population at large. In these circumstances Lenin might appear as a god-like figure and indeed in 1918, following the attempt on his life, Lenin was shown in a widely distributed newsreel walking in the Kremlin with Bonch-Bruevich. This particular sequence was filmed and used quite specifically to scotch rumours that Lenin was dead.[16] The film section of the agitational trains had a two-fold function: first, the demonstration in the provinces, and especially in areas recently evacuated by the White forces, of agitational films produced at the centre (the Lenin newsreel sequence would have fallen into this category) and second, the supply of newsreel and documentary footage from the provinces back to the centre, where it was to be edited by Lev Kuleshov, Dziga Vertov, Esfir Shub and others who were to play a leading role in the subsequent development of the Soviet cinema. The needs of the moment gave rise to two new types of film: the so-called agitational film poster and the *agitka* (agitational film) proper. The former was quite simply what it claimed to be, a filmed version of a poster theme, and in essence it was the cinematic equivalent of a Mayakovsky poster poem. The *agitka* proper was also short and explicit conveying a simple message on a single subject with directness and economy. This type of film had a decisive influence on the stylistic development of the Soviet film: the essence of economy and dynamism in the visual presentation of material was developed in the principles of editing or, as Eisenstein was later to call it, 'dynamic montage'. The *agitka* had to convey its message entirely by simple, visual means. It had to attract and hold the attention of a varied audience and leave them with an impression of dynamism and strength. These principles were embodied in different ways in the theoretical teachings of Kuleshov and his workshop, in the documentaries and manifestos of Dziga Vertov's Cine-Eye group and in the films of Shub, Eisenstein and Pudovkin.

The conventional cinema remained locked in a vicious circle and the Civil War made the situation even worse. Cut off from new supplies of film stock and equipment from abroad the cinema industry ground to a halt. In his workshop, deprived of basic facilities, Kuleshov was forced to put his students through the motions of making 'films without film', in other words they acted out the films thay they would have made had the equipment been available. Generally the picture was bleak: as the existing supply of films was exhausted, as electricity supplies were constantly interrupted, and as the economic crisis worsened, so the number of cinemas still in operation fell. This further reduced the income which might have been used to stimulate production. As late as 1923 the journal *Kino* observed:

> We shall not deceive ourselves with faint hopes. The path of regener-
> ation for a shattered industry is difficult. Not only are there no
> serious resources in the cinema, but the workers and producers are
> dispersed, disorganised and, to a significant extent, technically
> backward and unqualified.[17]

The continued existence of a tax on cinema seats, levied by the

central government, made it more difficult for cinemas to attain
commercial viability but at the same time, made the struggle to attain it
all the more desperate. Hence, where possible, cinemas showed foreign
'hits' (*boeviki*). In June 1923 the back page of the Party newspaper
Pravda carried a most un-Soviet advertisement for the American film
Sodom and Gomorrah: 'A poem of human passions in two parts and
fourteen reels. In the principal role the famous artiste Lucy Dorney. In
the richness of its settings and in its techniques the picture surpasses
everything seen hitherto on the screen.'[18] In the early 1920s these
films were almost entirely those which had been produced and imported
before the Revolution. Some attempt was made to counter their effect
by accompanying their showing with a lecture from a Party worker, but
this method proved counterproductive.[19] After 1924, when imports
had been resumed, the Soviet market came increasingly to be dominated
by Hollywood films. Mary Pickford, Charlie Chaplin and Buster Keaton
were familiar figures in the pages of Soviet film journals. It was not
until 1927 that the box-office income from Soviet films exceeded that
from imported films[20] and many of these Soviet films could scarcely be
described as revolutionary in their ideological content. In September
1927 the Soviet film authorities released a film entitled *The Kiss from
Mary Pickford*, a comedy about a star-struck film studio worker which
utilised some newsreel footage of Mary Pickford and Douglas Fairbanks
on a visit to the Soviet Union to bring them into the plot. The original
idea for this film came from none other than the People's Commissar
for Enlightenment, Anatoli Lunacharsky himself.

The Party leadership showed itself to be aware of the considerable
deficiencies in the organisation of the Soviet cinema. Also writing in
1923, Trotsky lamented:

> The fact that we have so far, i.e. in nearly six years, not taken
> possession of the cinema shows how slow and uneducated we are, not
> to say, frankly, stupid. This weapon, which cries out to be used, is
> the best instrument for propaganda . . . a propaganda which is
> accessible to everyone, cuts into the memory and may be made a
> possible source of revenue.[21]

Trotsky felt that, whereas religion had been the opiate of the people
in feudal society, and vodka had played a similar role in the capitalist
stage of Russia's development, the cinema would serve as the great eye-
opener for the masses, the liberating educational weapon of a socialist
society. In January 1922 Lenin had issued a directive to Lunacharsky's

deputy, Litkens, outlining areas of development on which the Soviet cinema should concentrate. Although Lenin distinguished between feature and documentary or newsreel films, there is no evidence in this document for what has become known as the 'Leninist proportion', namely, that 75 per cent of Soviet films should fall into the first category, and the remaining 25 per cent into the latter:

Narkompros must organise the supervision of all institutions and systematise these matters. All firms exhibited in the R.S.F.S.R. should be registered and catalogued by number in Narkompros. For every film programme a definite proportion should be determined:

(a) entertainment films, especially for publicity purposes and their receipts (without, of course, any obscene or counter-revolutionary content),

(b) under the heading 'From the Life of the Peoples of the World', films of a particularly propagandist content, such as the colonial policy of the British in India, the work of the League of Nations, the starving in Berlin, etc., etc.[22]

In other words Lenin was urging that only a certain proportion of films should have a definite propaganda content: the rest should provide the entertainment that would attract audiences in the first place and also provide the revenue that would assist in the reconstruction of the Soviet film industry. Lenin also demonstrated his awareness of the particular strengths of the cinema as a propaganda weapon when he wrote, 'We should pay special attention to the organisation of cinemas in the countryside and in the east, where they are novelties and where, therefore, our propaganda will be particularly successful.'[23] For the time being his words were not matched by deeds.

In December 1921, on Lenin's suggestion, a commission had been established to examine the structure of the industry and consider the possibility of reorganising it along more centralised lines. The commission's proposals were accepted in December 1922 and led to the creation of Goskino, a centralised cinema organisation with a monopoly of distribution rights throughout the Russian Federation which retained the right to lease or rent equipment, studios, theatres, etc. to other organisations, both state-owned and private, which could then continue with the production and exhibition of their own films. This form of organisation was chosen to enable Goskino to amass capital for the reconstruction of the Soviet cinema under state control at a later date. It was, in other words, an application of the rationale of the New

Economic Policy to the world of the cinema. But many of the smaller organisations, like Proletkino (which served the network of workers' clubs) and Mezhrabpom-Rus (a mixed company with strong German connections) issued their own newsreels, produced their own feature films, and arranged their own imports and local distribution networks over which Goskino had no control. Hence the new organisation could not hope to accumulate the capital with which to pay for its own production and it therefore attempted to cover its own costs by profiting from these other organisations. It surrendered its distribution monopoly to various local organisations, taking between 50 per cent and 70 per cent of their turnover in return. In this way it hoped to finance its own further development but its policy led to a further increase in seat prices and to a fall in attendances, forcing local distribution organisations to expand outside their own areas. Thus state organisation began to compete with state organisation. Goskino could not even supply films to its own theatres and began to import from Germany and the USA. Other Soviet film enterprises did the same and the unbridled competition forced prices up and undermined the financial position of the Soviet film industry even further.[24] In July 1923 *Pravda* pointed out:

Although we are short of both means and personnel, we could nevertheless do many times more than we are doing at the moment if we were to work in an agreed and friendly manner, according to a single plan worked out to correspond exactly to the available resources of manpower and materials.[25]

Following further complaints the Council of People's Commissars, meeting in September 1923, set up a commission of enquiry headed by V.N. Mantsev.[26] The death knell for Goskino had been sounded less than a year after it had first come into existence.

In the meantime the old vicious circle continued. In Moscow in 1923 Goskino owned only five cinemas; fifteen were run by other state-controlled film organisations, while the remainder, between fifty and sixty, were in private hands.[27] By 1924 in some areas of the Soviet Union only one fifth of the cinemas that had been in operation in 1917 were still functioning.[28] In the months that followed the establishment of the Mantsev Commission there was a flood of public criticism of Goskino: it was attacked in the columns of *Pravda* as 'the nationalised property of the cinematographic bourgeoisie'.[29] In the same issue it was claimed that Soviet films were poor, both ideologically and technically,

and that foreign films now accounted for 99 per cent of the total
distribution figures. 'Distribution', the writer asserted, 'is in a state of
complete anarchy and . . . cinemas . . . are dying out in this country'.[30]
A report on the state of the cinema in the region surrounding Rostov-
on-Don, published under the rather lurid title 'The Cinema's Ulcer Can
Be Cured', confirmed this view: 'the theatres exist exclusively from the
occasional picture which is supplied by private dealers'.[31] Of the 140
films available for distribution in the region only four had any
appreciable revolutionary content. Goskino had completely failed to
solve the problems of the Soviet cinema and was itself 'the heaviest,
most absurd and senseless tax on theatres . . . The cinema, which in our
hands can and must become a most powerful weapon for the spread of
knowledge, education and propaganda, has been turned into a weapon
for the corruption of adolescents.'[32] It was in this context that Stalin
not surprisingly observed that, 'Things are going badly in the cinema.'[33]

    In December 1924 the Council of People's Commissars decided to
establish a new all-Union cinema company to be known as Sovkino. The
new company was to have an initial capital of one million roubles and
shares in it were to be held exclusively by Soviet governmental organs.
There was to be a separate exclusive monopoly of distribution in each
republic of the union; in the largest, the RSFSR, this monopoly would
be the preserve of Sovkino which would also take over all the existing
cinema organisations with the exception, because of their special
functions, of Proletkino and Mezhrabpom-Rus. Some lessons had been
learned from the Goskino experience: Sovkino, unlike its predecessor,
began with adequate resources, would embrace its potential rivals, and
had no right to sell off its monopoly – and indeed nobody left to sell it
to. The new organisation, which came into existence on 1 January 1925,
was faced with enormous tasks. At the centre it was required on the one
hand to increase the quantity of Soviet film production, so that the
dependence on foreign imports could be first reduced and then elimin-
ated; on the other hand Sovkino was expected to raise the quality of
Soviet films which, in this context, meant ensuring that the actual films
produced were more closely tied to the ideological needs of the Party
than had hitherto been the case. At the same time it was to concentrate
on what were, for one reason or another, deemed to be 'priority areas',
the areas that had allegedly been neglected by Goskino and other Soviet
film organisations. Sovkino was expected to provide cinema facilities
and suitable films for the network of workers' clubs, for the armed
forces and the younger generation, and, above all, for the countryside:
in other words it was to ensure the allegiance of the pillars upon which

the new state and society were supposed to rest. Its weapon was to be 'the only book that even the illiterate can read'.[34] From the Party's point of view the problem was quite simply stated:

> Here in Russia the cinemas are confined to the more or less large centres and aimed almost exclusively at the bourgeois classes. Even our urban workers are far from everywhere and always in a position to enjoy the benefits of the cinema, because the luxurious cinemas of the bourgeois type are inaccessible to them in terms of cost and uninteresting to them in terms of the content of the pictures, which here too are predominantly bourgeois.
>
> The countryside however is completely unable to enjoy the benefits of the cinema.[35]

Yet Lenin had urged that 'we should pay special attention to the organisation of cinemas in the countryside': it was therefore in the countryside that Sovkino faced its most challenging task. The cry went up for the 'cinefication' (*kinofikatsiya*) of the countryside.

The rural areas of the Soviet Union were still remote and primitive. Travelling along the Volga in the agitational steamer *Red Star* in 1919, Lenin's wife, Krupskaya, had encountered people who were apparently not aware of the existence of the Soviet authorities.[36] The situation in many areas had shown little change: in some parts of Siberia, for instance, the peasants had no ready cash and paid for their admission with eggs and other produce[37] but, even more significantly, it is estimated that, in the Volga region that Krupskaya had traversed, over 80 per cent of the village youth in 1921-22 had never seen a film.[38] The Bolsheviks hoped therefore that the spread of the cinema into such regions would, at least in the minds of the peasantry, equate Bolshevism with technology and consequently with the whole process of modernisation and progress. The potential audience in the countryside was too widely scattered to justify the construction of a network of cinema theatres and so the authorities returned to methods that pre-dated the Revolution. They returned to the idea of the mobile projector, but there were two obstacles: first, Soviet industry proved unable to evolve a satisfactory design and put it into production and second, Party workers proved incapable of working what equipment they were given: 'Comrades of the Beryozovsk district . . . lubricated the projector with tar instead of oil and then complained that it was not fit for use.'[39] With comrades like that the Party scarcely needed enemies in its battle to penetrate what had been called the 'areas of darkness and

illiteracy'.[40] It was a daunting task: even at a rate of one projector to
every 10,000 of the population it would need 11,000 projectors to
cover the Soviet Union adequately — and that target would obviously
take many years to achieve.[41]

Three-quarters of the cinema installations in the Soviet Union in
1925 were situated in workers' clubs[42] and since 1923 there had been a
special organisation, Proletkino, to cater for them. It had not however
proved very effective: Bukharin commented that it offered, 'More
words than actions. More "plans" and projects than living practice.'[43]
Just as the Party regarded itself as the vanguard of the workers and the
workers as the vanguard of the revolutionary society, so the workers'
clubs were seen as the vanguard of the attempt to win the active support
of the working masses of the Soviet population in the battle for
socialism. Sovkino therefore offered a preferential rate for film hire to
workers' clubs which almost halved the cost of showing a film: the
proportion of foreign films, expressed as a percentage of the total
number of films shown in workers' clubs, dropped from 79 per cent in
the period from March to October 1925 to 51 per cent in the year from
October 1926 to October 1927.[44] This was no mean feat. In the same
period Sovkino also increased the production of Soviet feature films
from 77 to 122 a year.[45] Whereas a film like *Battleship Potemkin* had
been apparently 'incomprehensible to the millions'[46] these new films
met with greater success. Whereas in the 1926-27 season the box-office
receipts for imported films exceeded those for Soviet films by
2,991,064 roubles, in the following season the income from Soviet
films exceeded that from foreign films by 627,829 roubles.[47] For the
first time in the history of the Russian cinema the native product had
overhauled the import. It was of course quite another question to make
these films ideologically acceptable to the Party.

Sovkino was constantly accused of commercialism and even of a
surrender to bourgeois ideology in order to increase the sales of its
films abroad. Many of the accusations now made against Sovkino had
earlier been made against Goskino and some can be dismissed as mere
polemic. The task of the Soviet cinema was, in one critic's opinion, to
'romanticise everyday life':

> In as far as the new way of life is still an abstract concept, we must
> show it in the process of creation. We must depict the sprouting
> shoots of the new way of life, the new relationships between people.
> We must romanticise the struggle between the birth of the new and
> the death of the old.[48]

As we shall see this is precisely what a whole series of films made in the Soviet Union in the later 1920s set out to do. In other words the Soviet film industry was, ten years after the Revolution, beginning to produce in quantity the kind of films that the Party required. But there was still a long way to go: until deprived of the opportunity, Soviet audiences still preferred Chaplin, Keaton, Fairbanks and Pickford to tractors and the history of what was, after all, supposed to be their Revolution. Lunacharsky's contribution to *The Kiss from Mary Pickford* underlines this dilemma: people preferred escapism to realism, however unreal that realism might in fact have been. The Soviet government was however aware of the problem. In an attempt to link audiences more closely with the cinema industry, the People's Commissariat for Internal Affairs (NKVD) had in July 1925 set up a new mass organisation called the Society of Friends of the Soviet Cinema (ODSK).[49] Its first head was Felix Dzerzhinsky, former head of the secret police. In his speech of acceptance he outlined the tasks facing the society:

> The cinema can and must become a powerful tool for the cultural elevation of our workers' and peasants' country. We are tired, uncultured, illiterate, but we have given ourselves the very difficult task of becoming in a short time the most progressive, the most cultured, the most literate country. The first successes in the development of our economy and the prospect of a further rapid growth in our industry and in our economy furnish a strong base for the cultural development of the masses of workers and peasants. In this cause the cinema must play an important role.[50]

ODSK was to be organised on a 'non-bureaucratic' basis, that is, membership cells were to be allowed to grow up in places like factories and offices rather than being established by government or Party fiat. It was to be composed of strong local organisations with only a guiding and co-ordinating central control. At the same time it was expected to undertake the daunting task of supplying the countryside with projection equipment and films and to provide training courses for those who were to show the films. It was required to maintain close links with the local branches of the Party and to supplement its income by producing local newsreels. Finally it was suggested that ODSK should operate in workers' clubs and should in fact take over the management of the film sections of these clubs. It was supposed to do all this without falling into the trap of 'bureaucratism' that had hitherto ensnared every Soviet film organisation.[51] The task of ODSK, and the task of the Soviet

cinema in general at the end of its first decade, were neatly summed up
by a contemporary writer:

> The cinema, more than any other field of our work, needs public
> support. The cinema is not merely a medium of agitation and prop-
> aganda, but it is a powerful and a key factor with the aid of which
> we shall raise the masses to a higher cultural level. The tasks which
> face the cinema in this respect are so great and so complex that
> without public assistance they would not be possible. ODSK is the
> only organisation which has formed around the cinema that can
> help it to pave the way and that in addition should do much to
> transform the cinema into a real weapon for the cultural influencing
> of the masses.[52]

In short, the cultural revolution that was to accompany the First Five-
Year Plan was at hand. The cinema was to become a 'weapon of class
enlightenment for the proletariat'.[53]

The general change in attitude that heralded the onset of the 'proletarian cultural revolution' was heralded by the resolution adopted by
the Central Committee of the Party on 18 June 1925 concerning Soviet
literature: 'leadership in the field of literature belongs to the working
class . . . There is not yet a hegemony of proletarian writers.'[54] The exact
nature of this revolution was to be decided in a series of Party conferences on the arts.[55] The last of these conferences was that on the
cinema, held in Moscow after some delay from 15 to 21 March 1928.[56]
The conference was preceded by a prolonged press campaign directed
against Sovkino and its policies and marked a watershed in the development of the Soviet cinema. One of Sovkino's most radical critics was
Adrian Piotrovsky. He started from the premiss that the cinema, unlike
the theatre and literature, had no classical tradition: the existing, or
'bourgeois' cinema was the product of the 'militant bourgeoisie'. For
this reason Soviet film makers should reject the past completely and
start again from scratch:

> The cinema was born among the bourgeoisie as the last of the arts
> and the first art of socialism . . . [The conference] should take a
> categorical stand *for* the specifically Soviet and socialist tendencies
> and directions in our cinema and *against* halfheartedness, *against*
> the 'academicism' of the past, *against* attempts to turn the Soviet
> cinema into an ideological colony of bourgeois cinematography,
> which is socially harmful and formally reactionary . . . So let us be

clear: there is no place in our cinema for halfheartedness, for complicated tacking manoeuvres. Here we can and must be maximalists. Here we can and must stake everything on the socialist art of the cinema and, perhaps, on the socialist industry of the cinema. Here we must speak with one voice, with the voice of the Five-Year Plan, a voice that speaks of industrialisation and the electrification of our country.[57]

This was an extreme statement of a theme taken up in all the film journals. Another critic attacked Sovkino's alleged preoccupation with '90% commerce – 10% ideology' and urged: 'The Soviet cinema must look for commercial success in new Soviet themes, in ideology. It must help the Party and Soviet power to carry out the cultural revolution, the transformation of our way of life, and socialist construction.'[58] The Conference engaged in an exhaustive study of the weaknesses of the Soviet cinema, even placing some of the blame on the Party itself. Delegates from the villages complained about the situation there, delegates from the workers' clubs complained about the situation there, and similar complaints were heard from people concerned with the provision of films for children. The cinema was, as one delegate dryly observed, in a 'state of civil war'.[59] Probably the most important report read to the Conference came from A.I. Krinitsky and was entitled 'the results of the construction of the cinema in the USSR and the tasks of Soviet cinematography'. His views of the functions of the cinema in the Soviet Union were clear:

As Comrade Bukharin has said, 'We are emerging from the cells of "chamber" culture on to the city streets and squares and we are sending the heralds of culture into the villages and the countryside'; we are creating a 'great mass cultural movement', we are 'calling into life the vast, broad and profound flow of mass cultural construction' ... The mass aspect of all forms of art, and especially of the cinema, the force of example and great conviction, the capacity for influencing profoundly the most outmoded strata of society – all this transforms art into one of the most powerful instruments of the struggle for cultural improvement, an enormous factor in the cultural revolution and the socialist transformation of the country ... The cinema must be a weapon for the *organisation of the masses* around the task of the revolutionary struggle of the proletariat and socialist construction, and a means of *agitation* for the current slogans of the Party.[60]

These views were reiterated in the resolution passed by the Conference
on Krinitsky's report:

> The cinema, 'the most important of all the arts', can and must play a
> large role in the cultural revolution as a medium for broad educa-
> tional work and communist propaganda, for the organisation and
> education of the masses around the slogans and tasks of the Party,
> their artistic education, and their wholesome relaxation and enter-
> tainment.
> The cinema, like every art, cannot be apolitical. The cinema must
> be a weapon of the proletariat in its struggle for hegemony, leader-
> ship and influence in relation to the other classes, it 'should be, in
> the hands of the Party, the most powerful medium of communist
> enlightenment and agitation' (in the resolution of the 13th Congress
> of the Communist Party).[61]

The cinema had then reached a turning point: this time the words were
to be translated into actions. The cinema was at last to be harnessed to
the purposes of the Party. As Piotrovsky observed: 'Now we are
witnessing an organic transformation of our cinema, which is entering,
one might say, the period of its reconstruction . . . Our cinema is still
being constructed as a socialist art.'[62]

On 11 January 1929 the Central Committee of the Party took the
first practical step towards realising the Conference resolution: it issued
a decree 'On the strengthening of the cadres of the cinema'.[63] Its aim
was to strengthen not so much the cadres themselves as the Party's
ideological control over them and it was based on the current assump-
tion that the economic, social and cultural revolution associated with
the Five-Year Plan would provoke a sharpening of the class struggle, thus
necessitating greater vigilance on the part of the proletariat and its
advance guard, the Party:

> The heightening of the class struggle on the ideological front cannot
> fail to evoke from petit bourgeois groups the desire to influence the
> most important lever for the cultural improvement and education of
> the masses. The task of the Party is to use all measures to strengthen
> its leadership of the work of the cinema organisations and, by pre-
> serving the ideological consistency of the films produced, to combat
> decisively the attempts to bring the Soviet cinema nearer to the
> ideology of the non-proletarian strata . . . Party, professional,
> Komsomol, social and scientific organisations should play a more

active part in the work of the cinema.[64]

Four months later, Lunacharsky, speaking to the 14th Congress of Soviets, admitted that the pace of developing the Soviet cinema as an effective propaganda weapon had been too slow, but now, 'at last, great steps have been taken'.[65] The most important step, the transformation of the films themselves, was of course still to come. There had been much debate in the second half of the 1920s, culminating in the 1928 Conference, over the need for films that were 'comprehensible to the millions'. This debate began as a reaction to the more extreme experiments of film makers such as Eisenstein but it soon developed into a euphemism: 'comprehensible to the millions' came to mean 'in accordance with the Party line'. That line was of course itself in the process of transition and the tolerance that had been extended to various groups in the 1920s was giving way to the cultural straitjacket of the 1930s. This change is exemplified in the call by Petrov-Bytov, another leading critic, for 'comprehensible' films:

When we talk of the Soviet cinema we wave a banner on which is written: *Strike, Battleship Potemkin, October, Mother, The End of St Petersburg* and we have recently added *New Babylon, Zvenigoa, Arsenal. Do 150 million workers and peasants march beneath this banner? I know very well that they don't* . . . The people who make the Soviet cinema are 95% alien, aesthetes or unprincipled . . . *You will not lead with 'Octobers' and 'New Babylons', simply because people do not want to watch these pictures. Before you lead the masses behind you, you must either be of the masses yourself, or have studied them thoroughly, and not just studied, but also experienced what the masses experience* . . . I repeat, we must speak in their own comprehensible, native language. Our heart and mind must be in it. We must not look down on the masses from above, but the artist himself must think and feel fundamentally and positively at one with the masses and be in the vanguard . . . *Every picture must be useful, comprehensible and familiar to the masses, otherwise neither it nor the artist who made it are worth twopence* . . . With the help of art that is not separated from the masses we shall fight all the base aspects of life so that not only art but life itself will become beautiful.[66]

The discussions and arguments of the 1920s were giving way to the slogans and polemics of the 1930s. What better warning could there be than Petrov-Bytov's last sentence? 'With the help of art that is not separated from the masses we shall fight all the base aspects of life so that not only art but life itself will become beautiful.' What better prelude could there be to the ideals of socialist realism?

Apart from the complex task of propagating the Cultural Revolution that was to accompany the Five-Year Plan, the Soviet cinema was beset by a new technical challenge that affected the cinema throughout the world — the advent of sound. The prospect of sound had haunted the cinema ever since the early days of the silent film and before the First World War there had been attempts to link sound and vision through somewhat primitive machines with exotic names like the Photochromoscopograph, the Kinemerephone and the Chronomegaphone.[67] These attempts were short-lived. It was not until 1925 that the theoretical and practical implications of 'radio-cinema' for agitation and propaganda began to attract serious discussion.[68] But it was some time before the prospects for the new invention were generally recognised. As late as May 1928 a manifesto calling for changes in the Soviet cinema, and signed by all the leading Leningrad directors, including Trauberg, Kozintsev and Ermler, made no mention of the sound film.[69] The most common reaction of those who did recognise the possibilities that sound offered was a hostile one. They feared that the new technique would be used exclusively as a novelty, just as the silent film had been exploited in its early days, and that this would mean that all the progress that the cinema had made in the ensuing thirty years would be thrown to the winds. This view was best expressed in the statement, signed by Eisenstein, Pudovkin and Alexandrov, that was published on 5 August 1928:

We who work in the USSR recognise that, with our technical capabilities, we shall be unable in the near future to move towards the realisation of the sound film in practice. Nonetheless we consider the time ripe to state a number of principal premisses of a theoretical nature, especially as the accounts of the new invention that we have received suggest that people are trying to use the new cinematographic invention in an incorrect way. At the same time a misunderstanding of the potentialities of the new technical discovery could not only slow down the development and perfection of the cinema as an art form, but also threatens to destroy all its present formal achievements . . .

Sound is a double-edged invention, and it is most probable that its use will proceed along the line of least resistance, i.e. along the line of *the satisfaction of simple curiosity.*

In the first place there will be commercial exploitation of the most saleable merchandise, *talking films.* These will be films in which the sound recording proceeds on a naturalistic level, corresponding exactly to the movement on the screen and creating a certain 'illusion' of talking people, audible objects, etc.

The first period of sensations will not harm the development of the new art, but it is the second period that is terrible: it will accompany the loss of the virginity and innocence of a first perception of new technical possibilities and will replace it by an assertion of the epoch of its automatic exploitation for 'high cultural dramas' and other photographed performances of a theatrical kind. [70]

The signatories to this statement wanted to ensure that the principles of montage were preserved in the era of the sound film: sound should not merely illustrate the film image, it should contrast with it in an 'orchestral counterpoint'. Thus, 'The new technical discovery is not a chance moment in the history of the cinema, but an organic escape for the cultured cinematic avant-garde from a whole series of blind alleys which have seemed unavoidable.' Ironically enough, it was Dziga Vertov, who had not signed the statement and who had spent much of the 1920s engaged in polemical argument with its authors, who was the only film maker to realise the ideal of 'orchestral counterpoint' in his film *Enthusiasm* in 1931. Thorold Dickinson has related the stunning effects of the showing of this film to a London audience the following year:

When Vertov attended the presentation of his first sound film, *Enthusiasm*, to the Film Society of London on November 15, 1931, he insisted on controlling the sound projection. During the rehearsal he kept it at a normal level, but at the performance, flanked on either side by the sound manager of the Tivoli Theatre and an officer of the Society, he raised the volume at the climaxes to an ear-splitting level. Begged to desist, he refused and finished the performance fighting for possession of the instrument of control, while the building seemed to tremble with the flood of noise coming from behind the screen. [71]

Eisenstein's first sound film, *Alexander Nevsky*, was not completed until 1938. Pudovkin came to terms with the new invention more quickly. True to his view on 'orchestral counterpoint' he wrote in 1929 that the merely 'talking film has no future'[72] and in *Deserter*, made in 1933, he was able to realise some of his ideas.

The theoretical debates about the consequences of sound paled into insignificance in comparison with the awesome prospect of re-equipping the Soviet film industry to cope with sound. When the first Soviet sound film, Abram Room's *Plan for Great Works*, was released in March 1930 there were only two cinemas in the whole of the Soviet Union that were equipped to show it, one in Moscow and one in Leningrad. Although important Soviet silent films like Mikhail Romm's *Boule de Suif* were still being made as late as 1934, by the following year almost all the films made in the USSR were made with sound. In five years areas that had just been equipped for silent films, and areas that had not yet been equipped for anything, had to be provided with new equipment, and all this on top of the ideological tasks that had been set for the cinema by the Cultural Revolution and the Five-Year Plan. Faced with these enormously increased requirements the Soviet authorities decided that the time had come to reorganise the film industry once more.

On 13 February 1930 a government decree established Soyuzkino, a combine that was to exercise supreme control over all aspects of the film industry, including for the first time the production of equipment and film stock, and throughout the USSR, rather than just in the Russian Federation.[73] Shvedchikov, the former chairman of Sovkino, the lesser organisation that Soyuzkino was replacing, justified the move: 'The existence of a large number of independent film companies in the Soviet Union has made it impossible thus far to work out a Five Year Plan for the industry. As a result of this situation the normal film requirements of the RSFSR are being only half met.'[74]

The chairman of the new organisation was to be Boris Shumyatsky, who has become famous largely for the obstacles that he placed in Eisenstein's way in the course of the 1930s. Shumyatsky survived a further reorganisation on 11 February 1933, when Soyuzkino became GUK, the Main Administration of the Cinema and Photographic Industry, a body with quasi-ministerial powers.[75] He was also appointed to a leading position on the new Committee on Art Affairs, established on 17 January 1936[76] to 'raise the cultural level of the working people'. But this was precisely the task that the cinema had been set before the Cultural Revolution. Clearly it had failed and there would have to be a scapegoat. Shumyatsky had entertained grandiose plans for the construction of a Soviet Hollywood on the shores of the Black Sea which would produce 300 films a year. He had dealt brutally with anything that seemed to stand in his way: in March 1937 he halted the production of Eisenstein's *Bezhin Meadow* after two million roubles had been spent in its production.[77] Despite his plans the Soviet cinema failed to produce the requisite films for the twentieth anniversary of the Revolution in 1937 and this was a crucial error: if, at the height of the purges even success was punished, then failure did not stand a chance. In January 1938 *Pravda* revealed that in 1935 only 43 of the planned 120 films had been released and that in 1937 this figure had fallen to 24. In 1936 the average film had taken fourteen months to produce, while Shumyatsky's planning had left directors idle and in 1937 alone around five million roubles had been wasted:

The Soviet cinema can work better and produce far more films than it is now doing. It needs a complete overhaul of its whole method of working and the immediate eradication of all traces of the sabotage that has put down deep roots in cinema organisations.[78]

Shumyatsky, the 'captive of the saboteurs', was within a week being described as the 'former manager'.[79] On 23 March 1938 GUK was replaced by a new Committee on Cinema Affairs which was completely separate from the Committee on Art Affairs and was directly responsible to the Council of People's Commissars.[80] This was a virtual ministry and indeed in March 1946 it was in turn transformed into the Ministry of Cinematography.[81] When Stalin died in March 1953 this was the structure of the film industry that was bequeathed to his successors. In 1924 he had said: "The cinema is the greatest means of mass agitation. The task is to take it into our own hands.'[82] By the outbreak of the Second World War that task had finally been accomplished.

Notes

1. G. Boltyanskii, *Lenin i kino* (Moscow, 1925), pp. 16-17.
2. G.V. Plekhanov, *O zadachakh sotsialistov v bor'be s golodom v Rossii* (Geneva, 1892), p. 58.
3. V.I. Lenin, *Collected Works*, Vol. 5 (Moscow, 1961), pp. 409-10.
4. Ibid., p. 410.
5. Plekhanov, *O zadachakh*, pp. 57-8.
6. F. Shipulinskii, 'Dusha kino', in *Kinematograf. Sbornik statei* (Moscow, 1919), p. 20.
7. P. Poluyanov, *Gibel' teatra i torzhestvo kino* (Nizhny Novgorod, 1925), p. 35.
8. P. Poluyanov, 'Kino i teatr – vragi', *Novyi zritel'*, 19 February 1924, 9-10.
9. Ivan Mosjoukine the actor, Vladimir Starevich the animator, and Yakov

Protazanov the director were among those who went to Paris. Vladimir Sokoloff became a prominent actor in German silent films (*The Love of Jeanne Ney*, for instance) and Rouben Mamoulian became a leading Hollywood director. Of these, only Protazanov returned to Russia, in 1923.

10. L. Forest'e, '*Velikii nemoi*'. (*Vospominaniya kinooperatora*) (Moscow, 1945), p. 98, and N.F. Preobrazhenskii, 'Vospominaniya o rabote V.F.K.O.', *Iz istorii kino*, 1 (1958), 88.

11. *Mir ekrana*, 26 April 1918, 1.

12. *Izvestiya V.Ts.I.K.*, 2 September 1919.

13. *Izvestiya V.Ts.I.K.*, 18 September 1919.

14. H. Carter, *The New Theatre and Cinema of Soviet Russia* (London, 1924), p. 240.

15. For a more detailed treatment of the agitational trains, see: R. Taylor, A medium for the masses: agitation in the Soviet Civil War', *Soviet Studies*, 22 (1971), pp. 562-74.

16. Lenin was shot on 30 August 1918 and the film was made on 16 October. See: A.A. Lebedev (ed.), *Kinokamera pishet istoriyu* (Moscow, 1971), pp. 34-5; M. Polyanovskii, *My vidim Il'icha* (Moscow, 1969), pp. 13-17; A.M. Gak *et al.* (eds), *Lenin. Sobranie fotografii i kinokadrov* (2 vols., Moscow, 1970-2), vol. 2, pp. 28-97.

17. *Kino*, 1923, no. 1/3 (January).

18. *Pravda*, 19 June 1923.

19. L. Aksel'rod, 'Dokumenty po istorii natsionalizatsii russkoi kinematografii', *Iz istorii kino*, 1 (1958), 36; N. Lebedev, 'Kino', *Pravda*, 3 January 1923.

20. In 1926-7 income from the distribution of Soviet films within the USSR was 2,991,064 roubles less than the income accruing from the distribution of foreign films. In 1927-8 income from Soviet films exceeded that from foreign films for the first time, by 627,829 roubles: E.G. Lemberg, *Kinopromyshlennost' SSSR: Ekonomika sovetskoi kinematografii* (Moscow, 1930), p. 71.

21. L. Trotskii, 'Vodka, tserkov' i kinematograf', *Pravda*, 12 July 1923, reprinted in *Voprosy byta. Epokha 'kul'turnichestva' i eë zadachi* (Moscow, 1923). The English translation is from Chapter Three, 'Vodka, the Church and the Cinema', of *Problems of Life* (London, 1924), pp. 37-9.

22. A.M. Gak (ed.), *Samoe vazhnoe iz vsekh iskusstv. Lenin o kino* (2nd edn, Moscow, 1973), p. 42. Goebbels pursued a similar formula, quoting the Soviet example: E. Leiser, *Nazi Cinema* (London, 1974), p. 10.

23. Gak, *Samoe vazhnoe*, p. 42.

24. A.M. Gak, 'K istorii sozdaniya Sovkino', *Iz istorii kino*, 5 (1962), 131.

25. *Pravda*, 14 July 1923.

26. Gak, 'K istorii', pp. 140-1; *Deyatel'nost' Goskino – Tsentral'nogo Gosudarstvennogo organa Narkomprosa R.S.F.S.R. Okt. 1923-Okt. 1924* (Moscow, 1925). p. 3.

27. *Pravda*, 14 January 1923.

28. Gak, 'K istorii', p. 136.

29. N. Plastinin, 'Da dokole zhe?', *Pravda,* 16 February 1924.

30. 'Dela kinematograficheskie', *Pravda*, 16 February 1924.

31. A. L'vov, *Kinematograficheskaya yazva izlechima* (Moscow, 1924), p. 8.

32. Ibid., p. 9.

33. *Trinadtsatyi s"ezd R.K.P. (b). 23-31 maya 1924 goda. Stenograficheskii otchët* (Moscow, 1924), p. 132.

34. *Pskovskii nabat*, 3 July 1924, quoted in A. Goldobin, *Kino na territorii SSSR* (Moscow, 1924), p. 64.

35. *Kino*, 1923, no. 4 (June/September).

36. N.K. Krupskaya, 'Po gradam i vesyam sovetskoi respubliki', *Novyi mir*, 1960, no. 11, pp. 113-30.

37. I. Trainin, *Kino-promyshlennost' i Sovkino* (Moscow, 1925), p. 21.
38. V. Vainshtok and D. Yakobzon, *Kino i molodëzh'* (Leningrad, 1926), p. 57.
39. A. Katsigras (ed.), *Kino-rabota v derevne* (Moscow, 1925), p. 44.
40. Goldobin, *Kino na territorii SSSR*, p. 64.
41. Vainshtok and Yakobzon, *Kino i molodëzh'*, p. 60.
42. B. Filippov, *Kino v rabochem klube* (Moscow, 1926), p. 6.
43. *Proletarskoe kino*, 1 February 1925, 3.
44. Lemberg, *Kino-promyshlennost' SSSR*, p. 93.
45. Ibid., p. 39.
46. See, for instance: P. Petrov-Bytov, 'U nas net sovetskoi kinematografii', *Zhizn' iskusstva*, 21 April 1929, 8.
47. Lemberg, *Kinopromyshlennost' SSSR*, p. 71.
48. V. Nedobrovo, 'Romantika byta v kino', *Zhizn' iskusstva*, 14 December 1926, p. 5.
49. L.M. Sukharebskii, *Nauchnoe kino* (Moscow, 1926), p. 45.
50. Quoted in the obituary for Dzerzhinsky in *Novyi zritel'*, 27 July 1926, 5.
51. K. Mal'tsev, *Na pomoshch' sovetskomu kino* (Moscow, 1927), *passim*: I. Potëmkin, 'O blizhaishikh zadachakh O.D.S.K.', *Zhizn' iskusstva*, 6 April 1926, 5; G. Boltyanskii, 'Kino i sovetskaya obshchestvennost'', *Zhizn' iskusstva*, 7-10 November 1925, 15.
52. Mal'tsev, *Na pomoshch' sovetskomu kino*, p. 6.
53. Boltyanskii, 'Kino', 15.
54. N.A. Lebedev, *Ocherk istorii kino S.S.S.R. Nemoe kino (1918-1934)* (Moscow, 1965), p. 261.
55. S. Fitzpatrick, 'Cultural revolution in Russia 1928-32', *Journal of Contemporary History*, 9 (1974), 33-52.
56. The proceedings of the conference were published in B.S. Ol'khovyi (ed.), *Puti kino. Pervoe Vsesoyuznoe partiinoe soveshchanie po kinematografii* (Moscow, 1929).
57. A. Piotrovskii, 'Budem maksimalistami!', *Zhizn' iskusstva*, 13 December 1927, 4.
58. P. Blyakhin, 'K partsoveshchaniyu', *Novyi zritel'*, 13 December 1927, 14.
59. Savitsky, the delegate from the state film school, also emphasised the need for active ideological guidance from the workers and peasants and alleged that there was a surfeit of aliens in the film industry; as evidence of this he cited seventeen recent arrests in the Mezhrabpom studios: Ol'khovyi, *Puti Kino*, pp. 92-3.
60. Ibid., pp. 19-25.
61. Ibid., pp. 430-1.
62. A. Piotrovskii, 'Kino 1928 goda', *Zhizn' iskusstva*, 4 November 1928, 9.
63. 'Ob ukreplenii kadrov kino' in N.A. Lebedev (ed.), *Partiya o kino* (Moscow, 1939), pp. 82-5.
64. Ibid., p. 82.
65. *XIV Vserossiiskii s"ezd sovetov. Stenograficheskii otchët* (Moscow, 1929), Part 12, p. 11.
66. Petrov-Bytov, 'U nas net sovetskoi kinematografii', 8.
67. A.A. Khanzhonkov, *Pervye gody russkoi kinematografii. Vospominaniya* (Moscow, 1937), p. 18.
68. A. Fevral'skii, 'Tendentsii iskusstva i "Radio-glaz" ', *Molodaya gvardiya*, 1925, no. 7, pp. 166-8.
69. 'Otkrytoe pis'mo kino-rezhissërov', *Zhizn' iskusstva*, 27 May 1928, 9.
70. S. Eizenshtein, V. Pudovkin, G. Aleksandrov, 'Zayavka', *Zhizn' iskusstva*, 5 August 1928, 4-5.

71. T. Dickinson and C. De La Roche, *Soviet Cinema* (London, 1948), p. 23, note 1.
72. V.I. Pudovkin, 'K voprosu zvukovogo nachala v fil'me', *Kino i kul'tura*, 1929, no. 5/6 (June), 3. Cf. 'Vremya krupnym planom', *Proletarskoe kino*, 1932, no. 4 (April), 30-2.
73. *Sobranie zakonov*, 18 March 1930, p. 298.
74. Quoted in P. Babitsky and J. Rimberg, *The Soviet Film Industry* (New York, 1955), p. 28.
75. *Izvestiya*, 12 February 1933.
76. *Izvestiya*, 18 January 1936.
77. Babitsky and Rimberg, *Soviet Film Industry*, p. 42.
78. *Pravda*, 9 January 1938.
79. *Sovetskoe iskusstvo*, 16 January 1938.
80. *Sobranie postanovlenii i rasporyazhenii*, 11 April 1938, pp. 216-20.
81. *Vedomosti Verkhovnogo Soveta SSSR*, 1946, no. 10.
82. *Trinadtsatyi s"ezd R.K.P.(b).*, p. 132.

5 RUSSIA: THEMES AND VARIATIONS

> With us 'art' is not a mere word. We look upon it as only one
> of many instruments used in the battlefronts of the class
> struggle and the struggle for socialist construction. Art is in the
> same category as the metallurgical industry, for example.
>
> Sergei Eisenstein, 1930[1]

Every cinema has its stereotypes of good and evil, personified in the
archetypal hero and villain. In the Hollywood Western, the detective
film or the spy thriller the eternal battle between 'goodies' and 'baddies'
has reflected the basic social, political and even economic attitudes both
of the film-makers themselves and of the society in which they live. The
emergence of the American negro or the Red Indian in films of recent
years as central figures in the drama, rather than merely touches of local
colour like the period costumes, is ample demonstration of this, and of
the changes that have taken place in America itself. Until recently, the
American cinema has tended to support the existing order and it has
done this out of conviction and economic self-interest, rather than
because of direct political control by the American government, even in
war-time. In the early 1920s, especially in films such as *Strike*, *The
Unusual Adventures of Mr West in the Land of the Bolsheviks* or *The
Little Red Devils*, Soviet film makers similarly projected a revolutionary
message out of spontaneous enthusiasm and genuine conviction,
political and artistic. It was only later, as the government and Party
exerted increasingly effective control over the machinery for production, distribution and exhibition, without which the films could not be
made, that the film-makers were compelled to toe the Party line,
regardless of their individual convictions. As Eisenstein wrote in 1930:

> In the Soviet Union art is responsive to social aims and demands.
> One day, for example, all attention is centred on the village; it is
> imperative to raise the village from the slough of ancient custom and
> bring it into line with the Soviet system as a whole; the peasant must
> learn to see the difference between private ownership and individual-
> istic survivals on the one hand, and co-operation and collective
> economy on the other.
> S.O.S.!

The seismograph of the Party apparatus notes a vacillation in this section of Soviet life. At once, all social thought is directed toward it. Throughout the country the press, literature, the fine arts are mobilised to ward off danger. The slogan is: 'Face the Village!' The smitchka, the union of proletarian and poor peasant, is established. Opponents of Soviet aims are ousted. The strongest propaganda guns are put into action; there begins a bombardment on behalf of socialist economy. Here the cinema plays a big role.[2]

To effect the desired transformation, and in particular to force through the Cultural Revolution that was deemed to be a necessary corollary to the First Five-Year Plan, the structural reorganisation of the cinema industry was in itself not enough. Film content too had to be controlled. In this control, and in the films that it permitted and encouraged, we can see the image of Soviet Russia that the authorities wanted to project, both to their own citizens and to the world. We can also see, from the manner in which the themes and their treatment varied, the way that official attitudes changed to meet new circumstances: we can see the seeds, and the fruits, of the doctrine of socialist realism.

The propagandist, to be most effective, must establish in the minds of his audience a clearly defined tension between the opposing forces of 'good' and 'evil', or 'us' and 'them', and preferably both. The audience can then identify *with* the forces that the propagandist represents *against* the forces to which he is opposed. The establishment of such simple, if not simplistic, stereotypes had in any case been dictated by the technical limitations of the silent cinema as a medium on the one hand, and by the particular agitational needs of the Civil War and early Soviet period on the other. Once foreign films had effectively been excluded, and Soviet audiences therefore *had* to watch the films produced by their own cinema industry, the tendency to compete by striving for new and more exciting forms was undermined. Artistic conservatism reigned supreme and the Soviet cinema was slow to shake off the simplicity and straightforwardness of the silent film and its methods of conveying a message. This has of course now changed, so that *Battleship Potemkin* now appears as crude and obvious to a contemporary Soviet audience as it would to a Western one. But until well into the 1940s, the Soviet sound film was still indulging in the same technique of propaganda through stereotype that had characterised its silent predecessor.

It would be sensible to look first at the positive stereotypes projected by the Soviet cinema in the 1920s and 1930s, and at the ideological assumptions that dictated and underpinned them, for only an understanding of the positive image of Soviet society and the Revolution that created it will properly illuminate the rationale behind the creation of its antithesis, the negative stereotype of the villain, scapegoat and enemy. As a class-based ideology, Soviet Marxism-Leninism demanded a class-based image of itself, denying in particular the legitimacy, or even sometimes the possibility, of alternative allegiances. This doctrinaire intolerance led to a hero who fell clearly into an ideologically respectable category, be he worker, peasant, soldier, sailor, revolutionary or Party worker, while the villain included all potential sources of dissent or opposition, being characterised (and frequently caricatured) as capitalist, bourgeois, landowner, kulak, priest, officer, spy or counter-revolutionary. The conflict between good and evil is underscored by a contrast between the community and the individual. The enemy is usually a self-seeking individual, whereas the hero is, implicitly or explicitly, a member of a larger group, a representative ultimately of the mass. In some of the earlier Soviet films this point is emphasised by the employment of non-actors to play the leading roles, as for instance in Eisenstein's *Strike*, *Battleship Potemkin* or *The Old and the New*. Another method of depersonalising and universalising the conflict is to give the characters generic names like 'worker', 'sailor', 'mother', as in Pudovkin's *Mother*. In this film the broader nature of the struggle is further underlined by a sequence bringing the mother into contact with a mother breast-feeding her own son: her particular fight thus becomes part of the general struggle, a fight on behalf not just of herself, or indeed of those committed to the cause, but a fight on behalf of *all* mothers *everywhere*. Vertov uses the same technique in the mourning sequences in *Three Songs of Lenin*. The mother/son imagery also emerges at the heart of *Battleship Potemkin*, in the Odessa Steps sequence: a small boy is shot and his mother turns to climb the steps to the spot where he lies dying. But the panic-stricken crowd is rushing down the steps: tension is created, not merely by the opposing movement of the mother and the crowd, but also by the strong emotional bond that ties the mother to her son and separates her from the crowd. The sacrifice of the small boy, like the sacrifice of the son in *Mother*, stimulates the elderly schoolteacher into action, bringing her, as it were, off the fence and on to the barricades. The tension is heightened as the mother, carrying her dead son, walks up the steps to confront the descending troops until she too is shot dead. This time, however, we know that in spirit at least the crowd is with her. The sequence that follows involves a younger mother and her baby in a pram. She is killed, separated from her child as the pram bounces down the steps, carrying the baby to its death. The imagery here is calculated to cause a sense of emotional outrage in the audience at the callous brutality of the tsarist army, a feeling echoed on the screen by the schoolteacher and a student. The following scene makes it clear that the sacrifice has not been in vain: the marble lion appears to stand up, just as the Russian people will now rise up in revolt and revolution. This sequence on the Odessa Steps provides an excellent example of the power of the propagandist's imagery, and of the way in which that imagery depends for its effect on a particular context, in this case the context of the events depicted in the film itself, of the history of Russia, and of the predispositions of the audience and its emotions. The image itself has no inherent value, but acquires its value, and therefore also its effect, when seen in that context.

The most important single hero figure in the Soviet cinema has been the worker, for it was after all the worker who was in the vanguard of the successful revolutionary movement. The worker is portrayed in what we have come to regard as the traditional heroic mould: upright, even when downtrodden, calm and courageous in adversity, compassionate and self-sacrificing. Physically the worker is strong, clean-limbed and muscular, as for example are the sailors sleeping in their hammocks in *Potemkin.* He is cheerful, although not as cheerful as the happy smiling peasants harvesting the grain in the newsreels of the 1930s. He is rarely seen alone, and is certainly never lonely, but is usually depicted, directly or indirectly, as a member of a group. Sometimes that group is a family (*Strike, Mother*), sometimes it is based on the workplace (the battleship in *Potemkin*, the factory in *Strike*, the eponymous store in *New Babylon*), sometimes the group becomes the mass itself (*The End of St Petersburg, October*). In films depicting life in the countryside the peasant too is part of an almost organic group, be it the village or the collective (*The Old and the New, Earth, Bezhin Meadow*). In Room's *The Ghost that Never Returns* the entire film recounts the prisoner-hero's struggle both for political freedom and for the right to return where he belongs, to his family. The hero then belongs – to his family, his workmates, his village: he is above all part of a community, with which he enjoys a relationship of mutual responsibility. In the unity expressed between the individual and the community lie both their economic solidarity and their political strength. When the workers act together in *Strike* or *Mother* or *New Babylon*, or the peasants in *The Old and the New* or *Earth*, or the sailors in *Potemkin*, then they are

assured of eventual victory, even if they suffer a temporary defeat.
Here the propagandist was able to rely on subsequent historical developments: by depicting pre-revolutionary manifestations of unsuccessful
revolutionary activity, and linking them with the ultimate success of
October 1917 (as, for instance, in the closing sequence of *Mother*), the
film maker was able to imply that present difficulties and setbacks
would be similarly overcome (as, for instance, in *The Old and the New*).
The Soviet Union was, at least by implication, favourably compared
with other countries in such films as *The Unusual Adventures of Mr
West in the Land of the Bolsheviks* and *The Ghost that Never Returns*,
while in Protazanov's *Aelita*, almost a science fiction fantasy, a futuristic
revolution takes place on Mars. The Soviet Union was, of course,
constantly compared too with tsarist Russia: the personal tragedy of
inhuman laws was demonstrated in *The Living Corpse*, and the
injustices of the autocracy explored in numerous films, including *Strike*,
Potemkin and *Mother*, but also *The End of St Petersburg*, *October*,
The Fall of the Romanov Dynasty, *Lev Tolstoy and the Russia of
Nicholas II* and countless others. The mood of triumphant pride that
soon soured into self-congratulatory complacency was further
encouraged by a spate of films celebrating the progress that the Soviet
Union had already made. Among these films are *Fragment of Empire*,
The Great Way, *Turksib* and Vertov's documentaries: *Forward, Soviet!*,
A Sixth Part of the World, *The Eleventh Year*, *The Man with a Movie
Camera*, *Symphony of the Donbass* and *Three Songs of Lenin*. It was
Vertov who put the task of Soviet film makers in a nutshell:

> Only in the USSR, where the cinema is a tool in the hands of the
> state, can and should the battle against the blinding of the popular
> masses begin, the battle for sight . . .
> *To see and show the world in the name of the world proletarian
> revolution – that is the simple formula of the Cine-Eye.*[3]

Under the name of socialist realism, it was to become the simple
formula for all Soviet film-makers: not 'life as it is', but 'life as it ought
to be'. Even in the 1920s the few films that touched upon contemporary
social problems were expected to have a positive outlook and an
optimistic conclusion. Room's *Bed and Sofa* was heavily criticised
because it fell short on both counts.[4]

As the Party tightened its control over the Soviet cinema, so the
requirements it laid down became more rigid: the cinema was, after all,
'the most important lever for the cultural improvement and education

of the masses'.[5] Film content reflected these changes, and nowhere more so than in the depiction of the hero. We can see the seeds of this change too in the films of the 1920s, particularly in the emergence of a specific leader figure as hero. Eisenstein's *October* marks the first depiction by actors[6] of Lenin and the other Soviet leaders, or at least some of them, on the screen. Here the revolutionary movement is, also for the first time, personified, not in the ordinary anonymous worker stereotype, but in an identifiable individual leader with almost super-human qualities. The cult of Lenin and of Leninism emerged after his death for quite specific political reasons connected with the rise of Stalin: in writing *Foundations of Leninism* Stalin ensured himself the mantle of Lenin and, as a result, direct praise of Lenin became in effect indirect praise of Stalin. In *October* Stalin is clearly visible as one of Lenin's fellow conspirators: Trotsky has almost disappeared, and in any case his appearance is so similar to that of Antonov-Ovseyenko and an unnamed Menshevik that his actual role in the events of October 1917 is completely blurred. In films of this period people with pointed beards and pince-nez should never be trusted anyway. By the time Mikhail Romm came to make *Lenin in October* and *Lenin in 1918* a decade later, Trotsky had become a non-person and Lenin was made to say of his right-hand man, 'Comrade Stalin is right'. In between *October* and *Lenin in October* the 'cult of personality' was growing. Vertov's *Three Songs of Lenin* is ample evidence of this. In this film Lenin is elevated to Christ-like status: 'He gave us all he had'. What was implied in *October*, where it is only when Lenin appears at the Finland Station that the Revolution is assured, is now made explicit: Lenin is the saviour of the downtrodden masses, and the context tells us that Stalin has stepped into his shoes. Marc Ferro has already amply demonstrated the manner in which the ideology of Stalinism is reflected in *Chapayev*, made in 1934 and set in the Civil War.[7] *Peter the First* implied a direct historical parallel between Stalin and Peter the Great: both of them had pulled Russia up by its own bootstraps, persuading it that it had to modernise at all costs and, where necessary, forcing it to do so. In 1931 Stalin had announced, 'We are fifty years behind the advanced countries. We must make good this lag in ten years. Either we accomplish this or we shall be crushed.'[8] What St Petersburg had been to Peter the Great, the hydro-electric power stations were to Stalin: a gateway to the future. Lenin himself had proclaimed the slogan for the Soviet government's electrification programme: 'Socialism is Soviet power plus the electrification of the whole country'. It is small wonder that the Dneprostroi project features so prominently in the later films of Vertov:

electrification was the key to industrialisation and the mechanisation of agriculture. And for most of the film makers of the 1920s the machine was the new God.

The manifesto of the Eccentrics (Kozintsev, Yutkevich and Leonid Trauberg), published in 1922, proclaimed '*The pace today: the rhythm of the machine*',[9] while the Cine-Eye group around Vertov announced in the following year:

I am the Cine-Eye. I am the mechanical eye.
I, the machine, show you the world as only I can see it.[10]

In most of their films the machine is a force for progress, as are the trains in *Turksib*, the tractors in *Earth* or the cream separator and the idealised village co-operative in *The Old and the New*. Eisenstein even used mechanical similes in his writings, comparing the process of montage with 'the series of explosions of the internal combustion engine'.[11] But, even so, the hints of the dangers of machine worship were there for those who wished to see them: the conveyor belt sequence of slaves in *Aelita* is an early example that must surely have influenced Fritz Lang's *Metropolis*. In *October* the machine, a heavy press, is clearly used as a metaphor for the crushing oppression of the workers, while *Springtime*, made by Vertov's brother Mikhail Kaufmann, contains a disturbing sequence of phantom tree chopping. The ideological consequences of excessive adulation of the machine were made manifest in an article on the Cine-Eye group that was published in 1929: 'The machine, like a work of art, is higher and more important than the master who has made it. Man is only an engineer, a pilot directing it.'[12]

But on the whole, like their fellows in other countries, the theorists and practitioners of the Soviet machine age did not concern themselves overmuch with the consequences of their obsessions: they were 'for allowing technology to run its course, and believed that they understood where it was going, even without having bothered to acquaint themselves with it very closely'.[13] They were, in short, content to worship at the temple of the new God:

The cinema is a new outlook on life.
The *cinema* is the triumph of the machine, electricity and industry.
The *cinema* alone can compel us to live with the wonders of technology at an ever more feverish pace. The latest cars, Canadian locomotives and ocean-going liners can rush furiously across the

screen, and mills, machines, pistons and levers can work at a fantastic
pace.
THE CINEMA IS THE POWER OF THE MACHINE.[14]

And the cinema was also, in their eyes, the 'art of the future'.[15]

We have seen how the positive stereotype was produced and what it
consisted of. From the ideological point of view every film made had to
have a positive outcome, a happy ending. It is small wonder, therefore,
that there were constant complaints of a chronic shortage of films on
contemporary themes. There could be no dramatic interest in a film if
there were no tensions or conflicts to be resolved in the development of
the plot. It was difficult, if not dangerous, to depict such tension and
conflict in contemporary society: both Room's *Bed and Sofa* and
Eisenstein's *The Old and the New* attempted to grapple with a contemporary problem − the housing shortage in the one and the modernisation
of agriculture in the face of the conservatism of the peasantry in the
other − and both films ran into trouble. Both Room and Eisenstein had
attempted to tackle contemporary social issues (which, in such a highly
politicised society, were also political problems) with a degree of
realism, but not perhaps with sufficient attention to the embryonic
tenets of socialist realism. Eisenstein was particularly unfortunate. He
had begun making his film about agriculture, *The General Line*, when
he was called upon to make *October* for the tenth anniversary of the
Revolution. He returned to it only after completing *October*, but by
this time the 'general line' of the Party had changed. Parts of the film
therefore had to be amended, and the title altered to *The Old and the
New.* There was, however, one way around the difficulty of making
films on contemporary themes, and that was to find a scapegoat for the
ills afflicting Soviet society, a negative stereotype.

The Bolsheviks and their supporters were able to conjure up a large
number of such scapegoats of varying provenance. Some of these, like
the landowners or the capitalist, had had their property sequestrated
after 1917, and thus had been effectively emasculated in political terms:
they were a hangover from the pre-revolutionary struggles and served
the propagandist as a means of reminding his audience of the bad old
days. Some, like the priest or the bourgeois, were perceived, for ideological reasons, to be inherently hostile to the workers' movement:
because their influence could not be eradicated overnight, they still
represented a threat in post-revolutionary Soviet society. Others had
only emerged as a threat after October: they included the nepmen,
kulaks, spies and, later, saboteurs − all denounced as counter-

revolutionaries. All these categories were interrelated, they overlapped, and all of them were collectively designated as 'enemies of the people'. As such the negative stereotype had certain common characteristics, be he bourgeois or kulak, landowner or capitalist, priest or spy. In Soviet films, as in Soviet posters, he lived off the fat of the land, and off the honest toil of the workers, peasants and soldiers. He was therefore almost always fat, or at least well built, wining and dining in smoke-filled rooms (*October*), in seedy taverns (*Mother*), or in complete isola-tion (*Strike*, where there is a direct contrast between the factory owner, alone and isolated, and the worker, surrounded by his family). In short, the enemy of the people leads an artificial, abnormal, unhealthy, even parasitic existence, and he merely exists, while the hero lives, or attempts to live, life to the full. He is often cold, cruel and heartless, like the police officer in *Mother*, played by Pudovkin himself, the medical officer who inspects the maggot-ridden meat in *Potemkin* and declares it fit for human consumption, the bourgeois woman who stabs a Bolshevik with her umbrella in *October*, or the Master of the Teutonic Order in *Alexander Nevsky*. Sometimes the enemy is sinister and two-faced, like Owl in *Strike*, the judge in *Mother*, who sketches horses while mouthing platitudes about the principles of justice, or Shuisky, who is to *Ivan the Terrible* what Trotsky was to Stalin. Occasionally the negative stereotype is weak, spineless and indecisive: the archetype of this character is Kerensky in *October*, who lives in a limbo world somewhere between his ambitious fantasies and the steadily encroaching forces of reality. In a sense the depiction of Kerensky fits the assump-tion that he was merely a puppet of the forces of reaction, for it matches the standard characterisation of the lackeys and lickspittles of capitalism: the footman in *October* who bows low as he presents on a silver platter the Provisional Government's decision to continue the war and 'honour its obligations to its allies' is but an echo of Kerensky's role. The policeman outside the court-house in *Mother* provides yet another symbol of oppressive authority: he is photographed from below to enhance his stature, as is the enemy soldier in *Zvenigora*. The enemy of the people maintains his position by manipulation and exploitation and, if necessary, by the force depicted in *Strike*, *Mother* or *Potemkin* or in the mechanised prison in *The Ghost that Never Returns*. In the latter film there is a rare element of the grotesque in the portrayal of the ape-like prison governor. There is an even rarer element of humour in the depiction of the negative stereotype in Kuleshov's *The Unusual Adventures of Mr West in the Land of the Bolsheviks*, which combines the use of grotesques with a large number of slapstick jokes..In the first

film by the Eccentrics, *The Adventures of Oktyabrina*, there is an
extravagant portrayal of a capitalist stooge with the remarkable name
of Coolidge Curzonovich Poincaré, thus combining attacks on the
United States, Britain and France! But these humorous characterisations are the exception rather than the rule, for the enemy was seen to
pose a sufficiently important threat to be taken seriously in both senses
of the phrase.

The enemy is then a lifeless and unpleasant character, lacking all the
human warmth projected by the hero, be he worker, peasant or soldier.
He is usually isolated too, although it is always understood that like the
worker he represents a class. There are occasions however when the
enemy is depicted *en masse* and then the stress is laid on his faceless
inhumanity: this is particularly clear in the scenes involving the
Teutonic Knights in *Alexander Nevsky*, whose actual faces are covered
in elaborate helmets, and in the massacre on the Odessa Steps in
Potemkin. In this latter sequence the victims are clearly identified as
individuals, even though they still represent a type: the mother and her
son, another mother and her baby, the schoolteacher whose glasses are
smashed in the charge. As the victims scatter and die, the solid impersonal phalanx of the troops moves remorselessly down the steps,
destroying the life that lies in its path: the contrast between life and
death, right and wrong, good and evil, could not be clearer. The
effectiveness of these images lies not necessarily in their accurate portrayal of the realities of a particular depicted situation, but more in
their appeal to underlying psychological predispositions and fundamental human values. It is perhaps a sign of insecurity to require an enemy
to fight against and a scapegoat to blame, or — at the other end of the
spectrum — a hero to worship, but such symptoms of political
immaturity are by no means confined to the Soviet Union in its forma-
tive period: indeed one could argue that the Soviet Union in the
1920s and 1930s was undergoing such fundamental and far-reaching
changes that there was some necessity for the projection of such
simplified stereotypes. It cannot be denied that these stereotypes were
enormously effective, even, or perhaps especially, outside the Soviet
Union: the phenomenal success of *Potemkin* in Berlin, and the attempts
to ban it both there and elsewhere, are ample evidence of this.

Why were Soviet films so popular abroad? Clearly the answer lies in a
combination of hope and ignorance: the Soviet Union in the period
under discussion was to that generation what Cuba and China have been
for later generations disillusioned with the excesses and the faults of
Western liberal democracy and the capitalist system that underpins it.

It was a faraway country of which they knew little, but from which they expected a great deal: the grass is always greener on the other side of the hill, especially when you cannot see the weeds. The Soviet Union offered the hope of a new direction for mankind, a direction that involved a liberation from the travails of the existing order of society and an exciting and unique combination of planning and experimentation. Soviet propaganda films thus had an exotic appeal combined with a social conscience that seemed to be missing from, say, the Hollywood film. But it is in this last continuing characteristic that the continuing appeal of the Soviet cinema can be found. The stereotypes that I have discussed in this chapter, and the themes that are examined in subsequent chapters, all appeal to values that are not the exclusive prerogative of convinced Communists[16] and are indeed to be found in many Christian tracts: their lynchpin is the emancipation of the oppressed and the creation of a paradise on earth. As time goes by, that paradise seems increasingly utopian: it was not so perceived in the 1920s.

Film is above all a visual medium. The Soviet cinema, from *Strike* to *Ivan the Terrible* and beyond, has created a visual poetry of unforgettable images to convey its message of the liberation and resurrection of mankind, of which the Odessa Steps sequence in *Potemkin* and the storming of the Winter Palace in *October* are the most famous. The most important thing is not to have talked or written about the films, but to have seen them. As Winifred Bryher observed half a century ago: 'For the moment the battle is to the spectator'.[17]

Notes

1. Eisenstein, quoted in: J. Freeman, J. Kunitz and L. Lozowick (eds), *Voices of October: Art and Literature in Soviet Russia* (New York, 1930), p. 231.

2. Ibid.

3. D. Vertov, 'Kino-glaz', *Pravda*, 19 July 1924.

4. It did not go down too well with at least one member of the British intellectual élite either. When it was shown at the London Film Society on 7 April 1929, A.W., writing in *Close Up*, May 1929, 58-60, overheard the following snatch of conversation:

She: What a disgusting picture!
He: Yes, darling. If I had known it would be like this I would not have brought you here.

5. From the Central Committee decree 'On the strengthening of the cadres of the cinema' (Ob ukreplenii kadrov kino), dated 11 January 1929 and reprinted in: N.A. Lebedev (ed.), *Partiya o kino* (Moscow, 1939), p. 82.

6. Though the parts were taken by actors, they were not necessarily professional actors: the part of Lenin was played by a worker called Nikandrov.

7. M. Ferro, 'The fiction film and historical analysis', in: P. Smith (ed.), *The*

Historian and Film (Cambridge, 1976), pp. 80-94. See also: S. Crofts, 'Ideology and form: Soviet socialist realism and *Chapayev'*, *Essays in Poetics*, vol. 2, no. 1, 43-59.

8. Quoted in: T.H. von Laue, *Why Lenin? Why Stalin?* (London, 1966), p. 212.

9. *Ekstsentrizm. Sbornik statei* (Petrograd, 1922), pp. 3-4, partially translated by R. Taylor in: I. Christie and J. Gillett (eds), *Futurism/Formalism/FEKS. 'Eccentrism' and Soviet Cinema 1918-1936* (London, 1978), pp. 10-13.

10. D. Vertov, 'Kinoki. Perevorot', *Lef*, 1923, no. 3, 140-1.

11. S. Eizenshtein, *Izbrannye proizvedeniya*, vol. 2 (Moscow, 1964), p. 291.

12. N. Kaufman, 'Kinoki', *Sovetskii ekran*, 18 January 1929, 8-9.

13. R. Banham, *Theory and Design in the First Machine Age* (London, 1960), p. 329.

14. I. Sokolov, 'Skrizhal' veka', *Kino-Fot*, 25/31 August 1922, 3.

15. G. Boltyanskii, 'Iskusstvo budushchego', *Kino*, 1922, no. 1/2, 6-7.

16. See the documents collected in: N. Harding (ed.), *Marxism in Russia: Key Documents* (London, 1980).

17. Bryher, *Film Problems of Soviet Russia* (Territet (Switzerland), 1929). p. 133.

6 MOTHER

> The picture was a sincere one. It was an attempt to master
> or, in my own words, to come to love the Revolution.
>
> Pudovkin, 1935[1]

Pudovkin's first feature film, *Mother*, was made in 1926 in response to
Eisenstein's *Battleship Potemkin*. In its subject matter *Mother* recalls
Strike rather than *Potemkin*, just as Pudovkin's next film, *The End of St
Petersburg*, parallels *October*. The film is set in pre-revolutionary Russia
and the hardships that befall its principal characters serve, for Pudovkin,
as a necessary justification for the October Revolution: the downtrodden and oppressed masses of Russia rebel, rise up and cast off their
chains of bondage, and only Soviet power can guarantee their liberty,
their security and their dignity.

Mother is loosely based on Gorky's novel of the same name. In his
writings on the film Pudovkin constantly reiterates the difficulties
involved in transferring a literary work to the screen.[2] He concludes
that:

> The theme is almost always the most that one can take from a
> literary work in changing it into a screenplay.
> The development and treatment of the plot of a literary work
> (especially in the hands of a great master) are the result of purely
> literary methods. Their translation to the screen is quite impossible.[3]

If the power of a literary work was achieved by literary means, the
strength of a film lay in its use of cinematographic means: 'The work of
the film actor should be only the raw material, while the pathos is
achieved by specifically cinematographic methods.'[4] Although this
remark sounds like an echo of Eisenstein, Pudovkin's examples serve to
illustrate the different balance in their respective approaches. Pudovkin
continues:

> For instance, *Potemkin*. The ship or the life-belt cannot be com-
> pelled to act. Photographed in a certain way they acquire enormous
> and striking significance. That's how I treated actors.
> An example: the shattered and exhausted mother. Her exhaustion

81

is underlined by photographing her from above so that *it looks as if
this exhaustion is driving her into the ground*. Light was used in the
same way. The father, an enormous man, takes hold of a fragile
object – the clock. Illuminated from below, he casts an enormous
shadow, and *this produces the necessary effect*.[5]

Clearly Pudovkin, like Eisenstein, was willing and able to use the
cinema's unique methods and techniques but equally clearly, and unlike
his contemporary and great rival, Pudovkin was more interested in his
characters as people rather than as ciphers or symbols. He himself later
observed, 'I think perhaps there was in me a strong instinctive attraction
towards living man, whom I wanted to surround with the camera and
inside whom I wanted to "climb" in the same way that Eisenstein had
climbed inside the battleship.'[6] Eisenstein, however, rejected living man
as an obstacle 'on the path to the intellectual cinema': 'Comrade
"living man"! I cannot speak for literature. Nor for the theatre. But you
have no place in the cinema. To the cinema you are a "rightist deviation".'[7]

Despite his tribute to the power of *Potemkin*, Pudovkin regarded
Mother as a break with Eisenstein's method:

Mother was my first independent work . . . First and foremost in
this picture I stubbornly fought with all my strength against
Eisenstein and much of what Kuleshov had given me. I could see no
chance of finding a place for myself with my organic need for
excitement (more precisely in my case a 'lyrical excitement') in that
dry and peculiarly contemporary form that Kuleshov was then
teaching. My attitude towards Eisenstein was roughly the same.[8]

Mother was then to be a *Pudovkin* film.

The film opens with shots of trees silhouetted against the evening sky,
the moon shining through the clouds. The next shot shows a policeman
standing in the middle of a square: the contrast heightens our sense of
anticipation. We see the illuminated windows of a tavern. The door
opens and the shadowy figures of two drunkards are ejected. One drags
himself to his feet and stumbles off into the darkness: it is Vlasov, the
father. The scene changes to the Vlasov house. The mother, downtrodden,
is bent over the sink, washing clothes. The son, Pavel, is asleep. Vlasov
staggers in, his eyes searching for something that he can sell to buy
more to drink. He climbs on to a stool to take down the wall-clock.
The mother restrains him. He falls to the floor and the clock smashes to

pieces beside him. He tries to strike his wife, but she is protected by
Pavel. Vlasov is astounded that his authority has been questioned in his
own home, and he leaves.

The first scene thus sets out the triangular family relationship that,
with its wider political implications, lies at the heart of the whole film.
Vlasov, the father, represents the old ways: tyranny, brutality, autocracy. Pavel, the son, symbolises the new world still to come: a world
of freedom, equality and justice, but a world that has still to be fought
for. The mother stands between them. Hers is the pivotal role: if she
follows the emotional bond that this first scene clearly implies between
her and her son, then the downtrodden masses will be free, but if she
succumbs to her fear of her domineering husband, they will remain
enslaved. The choice is clearly stated in the incident with the clock and
it is this scene that Pudovkin is referring to in the statement quoted
above. It was one of the basic truths of pre-revolutionary Russian
Marxism that the proletariat could only emancipate itself through the
consciousness of its own condition. The story of this film is the story
of the mother's path towards that consciousness.

The next scene makes the underlying class conflict more explicit.
Vlasov is in the street but the doors of the tavern are wide open and
inviting. Inside, the workers are relaxing after a hard day. A small group
is feasting in another room: they are members of the Black Hundreds,
an extreme reactionary group of *agents-provocateurs*. They are plotting
to stir up trouble amongst the workers in order to crush them. Vlasov
enters and offers the barman a flat-iron in exchange for a drink, but the
barman refuses. In his desperation, Vlasov is a clear candidate for the
attentions of the Black Hundreds. Their leader remarks: 'VLASOV IS
THE MAN WE NEED . . . WE MUST ENTICE HIM.' The task is simply
accomplished by offering him a drink. There are a few whispers and the
possibility of money is mentioned: Vlasov has sold his soul to this
particular devil. Several shots of the tavern serve to underline its place
in the lower depths.

Back at home Pavel and his mother are asleep when a young woman,
Anna, taps at the window. She has a package that she wants Pavel to
hide from the police. Moving carefully, he conceals it under the floor-
boards. His mother, still half asleep, is dimly aware of what is happening:
the basic framework of the plot is now clear and their fate is sealed. The
father has allied himself to the forces of reaction, the son is deeply
involved with the forces of revolution. As yet the mother is, as I have
said, only dimly aware of her future decisive role.

Scenes of daybreak echo those of the previous evening. The natural

calm is disturbed by a cock crowing. The revolutionaries meet in a field
to distribute and conceal about their persons the pamphlets that they
are to smuggle into the factory. The cock crows again and the factory
hooter sounds. Shots of the workers awakening are intercut with scenes
of nature coming to life. Then, in a dark shed, we see the Black
Hundreders preparing for their day's work. Thus, the workers are placed
between the revolutionaries and the reactionaries and seen, at this stage,
as the unwitting object of their confrontation. Next we see inside the
factory. The factory-owners view the scene from an open window.
There is a renewed sense of expectation. The Black Hundreders stand
around waiting for the fray; they are armed with knuckle-dusters, straps
and chains. The strikers enter the factory and the gates are shut behind
them: they are trapped. The leader of the strikers is confronted by one
of the reactionaries. After a pause, they exchange blows, and a general
mêlée ensues. This is designed by the Black Hundreders to give them an
excuse to crush the strikers. Vlasov discovers that Pavel is one of the
ringleaders of the strike. With increasing urgency the Black Hundreders
call on their followers to 'Beat them! . . . BEAT THEM! . . . *BEAT
THEM*!' But the workers in the factory come to the strikers' aid, dis-
tracting the attention of their pursuers at a vital moment and allowing
them to escape. This move marks the first glimmerings of the activation
of the working mass, the beginnings of the self-consciousness that must
precede its full participation in the revolutionary struggle. The strikers
are eventually cornered in the very tavern that we have seen before.
Pavel escapes but his companion Misha is trapped and draws a pistol.
Vlasov throws a chair at him as he stands on the bar. Misha loses his
balance and fires the pistol accidentally, killing Pavel's father. That the
shooting is an accident is an essential feature of the plot, for it preserves
the complete innocence of the revolutionaries in the face of reactionary
provocation. Misha is immediately lynched by the Black Hundreders, so
that the bodies of the two opponents are left on the floor of the tavern.
Nature reappears in the shape of barely moving clouds, bushes and birch
trees. There is a close-up of Vlasov's body, followed by further shots of
nature, but this time the clouds, bushes and birch trees are in violent
motion. Pavel is seen running, his figure intercut with that of a policeman, photographed from below to emphasise his stature and authority.
Pavel explains to Anna what has just happened.

The film now returns to the Vlasov household and the mother. She
is praying to an icon for guidance. Confused and despairing, she lifts
the floorboard and opens the package that Pavel has concealed there. It
contains revolvers. Horrified, she returns the package just as someone

enters the house. The Black Hundreders are bringing home the body of
Vlasov. The mother is distraught with silent grief. Her neighbours wail
and weep. A roll of drums heralds another change of scene. The army is
marching in to the factory to restore law and order. The factory owners
look on, as before, from their window. Their objective has been accomplished, and the soldiers are doing their dirty work for them. We return
to the mother; one of her neighbours warns that Pavel will get himself
and others into trouble. The mother is haunted by the memory of the
concealed revolvers. The soldiers round up the strikers from their homes.
The mother sits by Vlasov's body until Pavel returns. Shocked, he asks
who killed his father. Her reply is simple: 'Your men killed him. The
strikers.' In the corner of the room a dripping tap marks the slow pas-
sage of time. Pavel rises and walks across the room. The bier covers the
vital floorboard beneath which the package is concealed. His mother
struggles with him, shouting, 'Don't dare. Don't dare . . .', echoing the
words he used in the opening scene to protect her against his father.
'They will kill you too.' There is the sound of hammering at the door.
One of Pavel's comrades has come to warn him that the soldiers are on
their way. Alone on the floor in the middle of the room the mother
stares blankly and uncomprehendingly into the distance.

The police enter. Their officer, played by the director Pudovkin
himself (a mark of the importance he attached to the role of the
actor), polishes his glasses slowly as the tension increases. He takes out
his notebook and asks for Pavel Vlasov. Pavel's comrade, Vesovshchikov,
pretends to be the wanted man, but Pavel pushes him aside and identifies himself. The witnesses obediently confirm his identity. The officer
asks for the leaflets and arms, warning him that concealment will only
make his situation worse. The mother is clearly worried by this threat
and her concern is increased by Pavel's stubborn insistence that he
knows nothing. The soldiers are ordered to search the house. Meanwhile
the officer nonchalantly lights a cigar. But the soldiers, to his surprise,
do not find what they are looking for. The officer takes his white gloves
and prepares to leave, telling Pavel menacingly, 'This time you have got
off lightly.' The mother is relieved, although still only dimly aware of
the full significance of what is going on. The police party moves outside,
where a policeman reports that nothing suspicious has been found in
the yard either. Angry, the officer orders Pavel's arrest. They return inside, where the mother is picking things up off the floor. Pavel is
seized. His mother clings to him, asking why. The officer explains that
Pavel is being arrested because he has not confessed: 'If he confesses,
we shall pardon him for everything.' Dazed, the mother promises that

Pavel will confess. She turns to him imploringly. When he does not
react, she lifts the floorboard and takes out the incriminating package.
In trying to help her son, she has helped only to condemn him. The
officer is now beside himself and strikes Pavel, drawing blood. Pavel and
Vesovshchikov are dragged away. The mother throws herself at the
officer's feet but to no avail. She is left alone, lying on the floor in the
middle of the room, surrounded by her scattered possessions. This is
her moment of realisation and awakening: the old world has been
revealed in its true colours and it dawns on her that a new world can
only be achieved through her own efforts and those of the class that she
represents. In her degradation therefore are the seeds of her regenera-
tion.

    In the literary scenario for *Mother* this sequence is followed by six
short scenes that serve to underline the mother's final realisation of her
situation. These have been omitted from the finished film, which passes
straight to the day of Pavel's trial, taking as read the mother's conversion to the revolutionary cause. The sun rises over a snow-covered
landscape. The monolithic buildings of the court-house are shown in
close-up. Then we see a policeman, again photographed from below to
emphasise his authority. The horses bring the prison carriage and Pavel
steps out, blinded by the light to which prison has made him
unaccustomed. He is marched into the courtroom. The mother sits,
dazed with grief, waiting for the trial to begin. Close-up shots of the
tsar's bust and the imperial coat-of-arms identify the whole system of
autocracy with the trial that is about to take place and condemn the
verdict in advance as the product of class justice. The judges are seen in
chamber admiring a picture of a race-horse: clearly the animal has
greater significance, greater reality for them than Pavel and the workers'
cause. The period of waiting and anticipation comes to an end when the
judges enter the courtroom. Intercut with the faces of the judges are
the ironical titles: 'The court is just . . . quick . . . and merciful.' The
charge is read out. The camera shows Pavel, the mother, the judges,
members of the general public. From time to time Pudovkin picks out
members of the bourgeoisie in the audience: for them the trial that is so
vital to the workers' cause is but an entertainment spectacle. In deliberate
contrast to this, and to underline the view that actions speak louder
than words, the titles repeat the jaded and received truth: 'Look,
mother, the presiding judge is very kind.' The first obstacle to the
defence rapidly becomes apparent: the lawyer from the capital is too
busy to defend Pavel and Vesovshchikov. A woman examines the
defendants through her lorgnette as if they were caged animals in a zoo.

The prosecutor demands that people like Pavel should be wiped out: the woman with the lorgnette is amused by the spectacle. The mother weeps. The defence counsel's pleas are dismissed by the presiding judge as empty phrases. Another judge examines his watch to see how much more of his time is going to be wasted by this case. The third judge draws a horse. Such is the attention paid and the importance attached by these men of justice to the case and the cause that they are required to judge. They retire to pass judgement. Outside the crowd wait to hear the judgement. The image is carefully composed: in the foreground a large policeman, behind him another on horseback and beyond him the working mass at the bottom of the court-house steps. Other images show the mounted soldiers photographed from below and then we see the title: 'Sentence'. Inside the courtroom the judges return to pass judgement and sentence. In this sequence Pudovkin shows: the three judges in medium-range shot, the bust of the tsar, then close-ups of the mother, Pavel and Vesovshchikov, and finally the three judges again. We therefore see all the actors and the forces that they represent: on the one hand, authority (the tsar and his judges), on the other, the accused as representatives by implication of their class. As the presiding judge reads the sentence the same images flash before our eyes again. This time the presiding judge is photographed so that the double-headed eagle, the emblem of the tsarist autocracy, appears like a crown on his head. The sentence – to penal servitude – outrages the mother and brings her to her senses and to her feet, shouting, 'Where's the truth?' Her question goes unanswered. The judges, disrobing in their chambers, have more important matters to discuss: they return to the pressing subject of horses. Outside, Pavel is led away to the prison carriage. His mother begs him for forgiveness: she struggles with the guards but is symbolically overwhelmed by the shadows of the departing horsemen and the wheels of the carriage.

The trial sequence marks the turning point of the film, for it is the trial proceedings, and the verdict and sentence, that bring the mother from passive acquiescence in the old world to active participation in the struggle for the new. It is that participation that provides the backbone for the final part of the film. This part opens in the Vlasov household. The mother takes up the floorboard and hands to Anna and a man the leaflets that she has been hiding there. Immediately we realise that she too is now active in the common struggle: she had not only attained class consciousness, she had acted on it as well. The next scene takes place in the prison visiting room. Pavel and his mother are separated by an iron grille but she none the less manages to pass a message to him when the guard is not looking. As he is led out, Pavel turns and thanks her: their reconciliation and their political solidarity are now complete. This is to be their last meeting, but in death they will be united. Outside, spring is in the air. The parallel between nature and the inner emotions of the characters, and the prospects for their political struggle, is now explicit. Whereas the trial sequence was introduced with wintry snow-covered landscapes, now the ice is melting and the ice floes on the river are breaking up. The old order is beginning to crack. The mother walks along by the flowing river and watches the children playing on its banks: life begins anew. Inside the prison, Pavel surreptitiously reads the note his mother has smuggled in to him: 'Everything is ready for your escape. Tomorrow you will be free . . .' The title 'Tomorrow' alternates with close-up shots of Pavel's face and images of rushing water. Delighted, he hammers on the door. The occupants of the common cells dream of the outside world. A peasant muses over his horses and the ploughing that he would now be doing in the outside world. The word passes round that there is to be a large demonstration in the morning aimed at freeing the prisoners. It will be timed to coincide with the morning break when the prisoners will be in the yard. In the factory and in the town the same news is being circulated. The film cuts to the corridors of power, where the governor orders, 'Don't spare the cartridges!' There is to be a bitter confrontation, a struggle to the death.

Tomorrow comes. The guards patrol while in his cell Pavel reads further instructions: 'The lamp-lighter will place his ladder against the wall. The horses will be waiting round the corner at exercise time, twelve o'clock.' The prisoners arm themselves with stones and iron bars. Outside, the workers and townspeople gather for the demonstration. The mother meets a younger woman breast-feeding her small child. This encounter with another mother and son effectively universalises her struggle: she is fighting not just for herself and her son but for all mothers and sons. The column marches towards the prison; the ice breaks; the prison bell rings for the morning break. Pavel peers eagerly out of his cell window, ignoring the warder's orders to move away. For this he is punished by being deprived of his exercise period. He is distraught, as his chance of escape seems to have disappeared. The other prisoners exercise in the yard: they are ordered to walk faster, and then the police chief decrees that the break should be brought to a premature end. The demonstrators proceed towards the bridge over the river that separates the prison from the town. The army is ordered out to stop them. There follows another of Pudovkin's lyrical sequences in which shots of the bridge, the melting ice, the marching demonstrators, the mother, the workers' banner and the bridge are intercut with one another. Inside the prison the men refuse to return to their cells before time and a fight breaks out, with the prisoners using stones and bars against the rifles of the guards. Inside the prison building the men break out of their cells and escape over the prison gate. The guards open fire and many prisoners fall, wounded. Pavel is shot as he climbs over the prison wall and he too falls, wounded. Vesovshchikov escapes on a cart. Pavel drags himself to the river and clambers on to the ice. A soldier takes aim and shoots him. He falls motionless on an ice floe which drifts slowly away: man and nature are finally united. Meanwhile the demonstrators approach the bridge where the cavalry are waiting for them. Pavel, who is not after all dead, manages to climb up to the embankment to witness the confrontation. As the cavalry approach there are scenes of joyful reunion with the escaped prisoner. But the soldiers open fire on the crowd and the standard-bearer falls to the ground. Pavel dies in his mother's embrace. As she wipes the blood from his face the demonstrators flee in panic from the cavalry. To stem the tide the mother raises high the banner of the demonstrators, which becomes the banner of the revolutionaries. Clutching the banner to her she faces the oncoming cavalry. The editing contrasts the two opposing forces in an accelerating process of montage until the moment of impact: the mother screams in pain as the cavalry ride over her. Several shots show the cavalry chasing and rounding up the remaining demonstrators: the pace of the film slows down and we see the body of the mother lying in the mud. As the ice breaks, the film concludes with double exposure shots of factories merging into the Kremlin walls. The final shot in the film shows the Red Flag flying over the House of the Soviets in the Moscow Kremlin. Whatever the cost to the leading characters in the film, Pavel and his mother, their struggle has not been in vain. The flag flutters in the sun. The existence of the workers' state in Russia represents a hope for all toiling and oppressed mankind.

Mother was released on 11 October 1926 to general acclaim. Writing in a Leningrad film journal one critic remarked:

> The film *Mother* can be compared with *Potemkin*. The *Battleship*, the first film of general significance produced by the Soviet cinema, is a creative triumph for the director and the cameraman. In this picture Eisenstein was able to demonstrate astonishing mastery in directing the mass and in the magnificent art of montage. In the picture *Mother*, in addition to these achievements, the triumph of the actors deserves just as much attention: they have been employed

by the director to the full extent of their creative ability.
All this propels the new film into the ranks of the cinema's
achievements of world importance.[9]

This reviewer makes it clear that Pudovkin had not merely distinguished
himself in *Mother*, but also distinguished himself from Eisenstein. While
using the montage sequences that Eisenstein elevated to a dogma,
Pudovkin also uses the techniques of the actor as part of his raw
material. The characters in *Mother* are archetypes, they represent their
class in its historical struggle, but they are also individuals, with
individual relationships and individual human emotions. They have individual names (in the literary scenario even the mother has a name —
Nilovna); they are individual human beings caught up in a historic
human struggle. It is true that in *Potemkin* the dead sailor has a name —
Vakulinchuk — but that name is the only sign of his individual human
existence for, like most of the characters in Eisenstein's silent films,
Vakulinchuk is no more than a cipher for the mass. Discussing *Battleship
Potemkin* at the time of its release, Pudovkin observed: 'As far as the
performances in the different roles are concerned, everything is bad,
apart from the almost static moments of people who are not acting.
This is partly the fault of the director who has not mastered his human
material.'[10]
Pudovkin manages to combine his individual characters successfully
with the mass: his characters are both human and universal. For this
reason it is perhaps easier for the audience to identify with the figures
in a Pudovkin film than with the symbols in an Eisenstein one, and it is
at least partly for this reason that Pudovkin retained his popularity with
audiences and authorities alike longer than did Eisenstein. It was, after
all, Pudovkin rather than Eisenstein who was decorated as the doyen of
Soviet film directors in January 1935. There was never any question of
claiming that a Pudovkin film was 'incomprehensible to the millions'.
One of their fellow film directors, Ilya Trauberg, made a prophetic
observation in his review of *Mother*:

The Soviet cinema is taking two paths: one path involves the conquest
of the box office — *The Three Million Trial* and other similar films.
The other path involves the conquest of the viewer — *Battleship
Potemkin* and *Mother*. A comparison between these two recent films
is not superfluous. If *Potemkin* is our pride, *Mother* will become our
pride.[11]

Notes

1. From a speech to the First All-Union Conference of Creative Cinema Workers, reprinted in N.A. Glagoleva (ed.), *Mat'* (Moscow, 1975), p. 191. I have used this edition of the Russian screenplay for my analysis. As well as an illustrated frame-by-frame breakdown of the film the book contains the literary scenario by Natan Zarkhi which is available in an English translation by Gillon R. Aitken in *Two Russian Classics: 'Mother' and 'Earth'* (London, 1973).

2. V.I. Pudovkin. 'Mat'', *Kino*, 24 August 1926; 'Mat'', *Sovetskii ekran*, 31 August 1926; 'Pervaya fil'ma', *Kinogazeta*, 24 September 1932; 'Novaya fil'ma', *Novyi zritel'*, 7 September 1926.

3. Pudovkin, *Sovetskii ekran*, 31 August 1926.

4. Pudovkin, *Kino*, 24 August 1926.

5. Ibid.

6. From the speech quoted in note 1; Glagoleva, *Mat'*, p. 190.

7. S.M. Eizenshtein, 'Perspektivy', *Iskusstvo*, 1928, no. 1/2.

8. Glagoleva, *Mat'*, p. 190.

9. B. Filippov, 'Mat'', *Kino*, 26 October 1926.

10. *Kino*, 2 February 1926, quoted in A. Karaganov, *Vsevolod Pudovkin* (Moscow, 1973), p. 61.

11. I. Trauberg, 'Mat'', *Rabochii teatr*, 1926, no. 43, quoted in Glagoleva, *Mat'*, pp. 213-14.

7 OCTOBER

After *Battleship Potemkin, October* is bad.

Soviet critics, 1928[1]

October is without doubt a film of great revolutionary and artistic importance. It is good in its revolutionary content, good in its execution.

Krupskaya, 1928[2]

These two comments are typical of the reception that greeted Eisenstein's third film and typical of the arguments that surrounded the film maker's career as a whole. Eisenstein was commissioned to make a film of the revolutionary events of 1917 to commemorate the tenth anniversary of the Revolution: similarly Pudovkin was commissioned to make *The End of St Petersburg* and Shub made *The Fall of the Romanov Dynasty* and *The Great Way*. Eisenstein had already completed *Strike*, which had been attacked for its experimental nature and its obscure symbolism, and *Battleship Potemkin* which, despite its immense popularity in Berlin, had failed to move Soviet audiences in large numbers, probably for similar reasons. When approached to make the film that was to become *October*, Eisenstein was already engaged in filming *The General Line*. He deferred this project to make his revolutionary film. He had little choice, and there is no evidence to suggest that he had any doubts; none the less it was a decision that was to have serious consequences for his career. *October* (if we allow for the earlier start on *The General Line*) was Eisenstein's last silent film, and the last film he was to complete for over ten years. After *October* Eisenstein was always on the defensive: in 1929, for instance, he announced that *The General Line* was 'an experiment comprehensible to the millions'.[3]

October was made in a hurry. Filming began in mid-April 1927 and did not finish till October. Editing began in September and a preliminary version of the film was shown to a selected audience in the Bolshoi Theatre, Moscow, on 7 November, the actual date of the tenth anniversary of the October Revolution.[4] The film was then re-edited, some of the more 'intellectual' sequences were removed,[5] and it was given a general release on 14 March 1928.[6] Like *Potemkin, October* was shown in Berlin, where it was re-titled *Ten Days that Shook the World*, after

John Reed's famous account, to increase its popular appeal. Neverthe-less, *October* never achieved the fame or notoriety of *Potemkin* and never attracted the same degree of political acclaim outside the USSR. Inside the Soviet Union its reception was, as we have seen, mixed. On the one hand it was attacked for being obscure: one of the speakers at the first Party Conference on the Cinema in March 1928 remarked:

> In the countryside many films are not understood . . . And it must be said that the more widely the Soviet cinema develops, the greater will be the percentage of films that are completely incomprehensible to the peasantry. I am talking about a film like *October*.[7]

On the other hand, Krupskaya, Lenin's widow, felt that *October*, despite its faults, marked a turning-point in the development of Soviet film art: 'Now an art is emerging that is near to the masses, that depicts the fundamental experiences of the masses. This art has a colossal future. The film *October* is a fragment of this art of the future.'[8]

I am inclined to agree with Krupskaya, although for different reasons: despite its weaknesses *October* is of fundamental importance, both in the Soviet context in terms of the transition from artistic pluralism to the straitjacket of socialist realism, and in the general con-text in terms of the development of the propaganda film, especially in the field of the heroicisation of reality.

Almost no film exists of the October Revolution or of the most important event of the February Revolution, the abdication of the Tsar.[9] The reality of the Revolution does not therefore exist on film and it was thus necessary to create it. The Bolsheviks had to establish a basis of historical legitimacy for their regime and the absence of ade-quate documentary evidence gave Soviet film makers a golden oppor-tunity for the re-creation of the realities of Russian history, and for some improvement on them. Eisenstein was in the forefront of the projection of this revolutionary realism at the expense of the actual historical reality. In *Battleship Potemkin* he had highlighted the oppression of the masses by inventing the episode on the Odessa Steps. In *October* he was to present the Bolshevik view of the elemental nature of the October Revolution, culminating in the storming of the Winter Palace. Ironically enough, the very absence of documentary material which made this possible has also meant that subsequent histo-rians and film makers have turned to *October* as their source material, and Eisenstein's fictional re-creation of reality has, because of its very realism, acquired the legitimacy of documentary footage. That is a measure of its success as a propaganda film.

October[10] begins with a sequence showing the toppling of the statue of Tsar Alexander III, the symbol of the worst aspects of autocracy, who ruled Russia from 1881 to 1894 after Alexander II, emancipator of the serfs in 1861, had been assassinated. Alexander III epitomised the depths of reaction and repression and the massive machinery of tsarist oppression is conveyed by his immense statue. In his hands he holds the traditional symbols of power, the orb and sceptre, while the pedestal is adorned with eagles. The film shows these symbols in close-up. To us the meaning of this sequence may be abundantly clear, but a Soviet peasant in the 1920s would have found the symbolism incomprehensible, and the necessary process of explanation (which was attempted with this and other 'difficult' films) would have destroyed much of the vivid effect of the film: it was for this type of relative obscurantism, for the 'intellectual cinema' in which he so fervently believed, that Eisenstein was constantly criticised. Workers rush up towards the statue, echoing the Odessa Steps sequence in *Potemkin*: but on that occasion they were mown down by the Tsar's soldiers, whereas this time they will, ultimately, gain their revenge. They erect a ladder against the statue's head and tie ropes around the Tsar: autocracy is doomed and helpless. The film then cuts to a crowd of peasants angrily wielding their scythes: the peasantry too is in revolt and, by implication, in alliance with the workers and soldiers in the overthrow of the *ancien régime*. The first title appears: 'FEBRUARY'. For those of us in the know, this is a warning, but only if we do know the subsequent history of the Revolution. The statue is toppled hesitantly and in parts: first the head, then the arms and legs, with the orb and sceptre, and finally the throne itself. The workers', soldiers' and peasants' Revolution is apparently accomplished, the autocracy is overthrown. But then Eisenstein's warning is made explicit: the Revolution is greeted by the bourgeoisie and blessed by the Church. It is *their* Revolution, although it was effected by the masses. As such, February is but a prelude to the *real* Revolution, that of October, and the aptly named Provisional Government is more provisional than even it anticipated.

From the Revolution the masses expect land, peace and bread, fundamental human demands that date back to the Old Testament and beyond. The soldiers at the front abandon their rifles and fraternise with the 'enemy': we see an Asiatic Russian soldier trying on a German helmet, while the German tries on his fur cap. The solidarity of the international working class is thus underlined, the artificiality of the concept of patriotism in an imperialist war emphasised. Then, suddenly, the tsarist eagle is intercut with the abandoned rifles: the threat to the Revolution is now direct. A lackey crosses a tiled floor, bows low and proffers a silver platter with the government's note: 'THE PROVISIONAL GOVERNMENT HONOURS ITS OBLIGATIONS TO ITS ALLIES.' There is a violent shellburst, the war is resumed, the working class betrayed. In the cities bread rationing is introduced. We see women and children queuing for bread in heavy snow. As the ration is gradually reduced, Eisenstein introduces a metaphor: we see a press being lowered as if to squeeze the workers. Finally their situation becomes intolerable, they are desperate – but a saviour is at hand.

The scene switches to the Finland Station. Searchlights flash frenetically across the roof, the crowd is turbulent, a sense of eager anticipation prevails. The tension reaches its climax with the heroic, liberating arrival of: 'ULYANOV . . . LENIN.' There is a storm of enthusiasm and Lenin speaks from an armoured car. Flags and banners fluttering dramatically in the background and the flickering searchlights increase the sense of urgency. He denounces the Provisional Government and pledges a socialist Revolution: he offers the masses hope in their hour of utmost trial. None the less, despite this elaborate heroicisation, Lenin does not appear in *October* as an individual but as an embodiment of the elemental power of the mass, of the collective will. Eisenstein was severely criticised by many of his contemporaries for the portrayal of Lenin in this film: the poet Mayakovsky attacked the superficiality of the characterisation: 'It is revolting to see someone striking poses and making movements like those of Lenin, when behind this exterior you can feel complete emptiness, the complete absence of life.'[11]

The Soviet critics quoted at the head of this chapter also had their doubts about the characterisation of Lenin:

> Lenin has turned out badly. The audience is faced with a rather brisk and fidgety little man. Ilyich's characteristic dash and liveliness have given way to an improbable fussiness. Antonov-Ovseyenko grows into the gigantic figure of the leader of the whole uprising.[12]

The part of Lenin was played by an unknown worker by the name of Nikandrov. Eisenstein was averse to the use of professional actors, at least as far as his silent films were concerned, feeling that greater realism was to be achieved by using ordinary workers and peasants. In the case of Lenin, having the part played by a worker emphasised the revolutionary's role as representative of the mass. It was perhaps inevitable

that, if Lenin were to be portrayed in this impersonal way, he would
fail to come alive for audiences as a human being: his function is as a
leading symbol in a film full of symbols. Indeed Krupskaya conceded
that if the film had a fault, it lay in the director's use of symbolism that
would not in fact be 'comprehensible to the millions':

> In the film *October* there is a great deal of symbolism. There is some
> symbolism that is accessible and comprehensible to the mass: the
> toppling throne, the idols from St Basil's, etc. These symbols are
> very good: they help the viewer to make sense of the film, they
> provoke him to thought. But in the film there is much symbolism
> that will be little understood by the masses, and this is particularly
> true of the symbolism embodied in the statues – all the Napoleons
> and so on. The following symbol is probably also incomprehensible:
> a sea of scythes that appears before the toppling of the thrones. To
> someone who had not seen pictures and sculptures that symbolise
> the mass peasant movement by scythes this image would probably
> be incomprehensible and it would pass right over him.[13]

Krupskaya was thus agreeing with the implied criticism of other re-
viewers that Eisenstein was, in effect, producing a pedant's film for a
peasant audience.

The symbolism however was only just beginning. The action of the
film moves now to July 1917. Workers and soldiers are seen streaming
across a bridge bearing placards and banners calling for: 'ALL POWER
TO THE SOVIETS!' The Provisional Government loses its nerve and
the demonstrators are machine-gunned. Bolsheviks are denounced,
attacked and beaten up. There is a particularly gory sequence of a
young worker being stabbed to death by bourgeois ladies in their
finery using their umbrellas as offensive weapons. Their hatred is quite
clear, as is the nature of their allegiance to the Revolution. We then see
a functionary of the government speaking on the telephone. The order
is given to raise the bridges, thus cutting off the workers' quarters from
the centre of the city. The martyrdom of the working class is symbolised, rather sentimentally, by the images of the dead girl and the dead
horse, both lying across the middle of the bridges, both in a sense torn
apart by the decision to raise them. The horse eventually drops into the
river, thus linking with the next scene, where the bourgeoisie are
throwing copies of *Pravda*, the Bolshevik paper, into the same river, the
Neva. The banners of the demonstrators are also seen floating down the
river: the Revolution is being literally washed away.[14] The First

Machine-gun Corps is 'disarmed for solidarity', the Bolshevik Party headquarters is ransacked. The Revolution would seem to be in ruins.

Then for the first time we see inside the Winter Palace. Kerensky climbs the stairs. He is in fact climbing the same flight of stairs over and over again, but the sequence is filmed to imply that he is climbing a single endless staircase, metaphorically speaking as well, for his ascent is interspersed with titles proclaiming his different positions: 'DICTATOR/SUPREME COMMANDER/AND SO FORTH . . . AND SO FORTH . . . KERENSKY.' Finally, both metaphorically and actually Kerensky reaches the Tsar's apartments. His figure is overshadowed by a statue holding a crown, and he is attended by the Tsar's footmen. We are shown his elaborate boots and gloves: he is fascinated by the external trappings of power. By contrast with Lenin, Kerensky is a dilettante, playing at revolution, alone and isolated from the mass. Whereas Lenin has been shown in an active and decisive posture, Kerensky vacillates. At this point Eisenstein introduced another of his 'intellectual' metaphors: a golden peacock, a gift from Tsar Nicholas to his wife Alexandra, preens itself. Kerensky hesitates again and then enters the Tsar's apartments.

To underline the contrast with Lenin the scene then switches to the latter's thatched hideout in the misty marshes near Razliv. There could be no greater contrast. Back in Petrograd Kerensky broods now in the Tsarina's apartments. Eisenstein uses the caption 'ALEXANDER FYODOROVICH IN THE APARTMENTS OF ALEXANDRA FYODOROVNA': by playing on the fact that Kerensky's first name and patronymic share the same root as those of the Tsarina he is able to imply a continuity and a close resemblance. This resemblance goes beyond the shared imperial heritage, for in showing Kerensky in the Tsarina's bedroom, surrounded by all her finery, he is also able to suggest a degree of unmanly weakness and indecisiveness both on the part of the Prime Minister and his government. His one decisive action is a reactionary one, the reintroduction of the death penalty. This action leads into the scene criticised by Krupskaya. We see first Kerensky, then a statuette of Napoleon. To an audience that knows its history the inference is clear: Kerensky is a second Napoleon and, like his mentor, he will usurp and betray the ideals of the Revolution. His intentions are symbolically clarified as he plays with a set of decanters, moving them into different positions and finally bringing them into place, fixing them together with a stopper that is shaped like a crown. Kerensky, like Napoleon, wishes to be emperor. But he is not alone in this ambition. A factory hooter sounds a warning: 'THE REVOLUTION

IS IN DANGER!' While Kerensky busies himself changing the mono-
gram on the Tsar's bed from A III (representing the autocrat whose
statue has been toppled in the opening sequence of the film) to A IV,
thus confirming his own imperial ambitions, General Kornilov is app-
roaching the city with British tanks, French aeroplanes and the
notorious 'Wild Division' of Cossack horsemen. He stands 'FOR GOD
AND COUNTRY'. His values are expressed through a sequence of
religious images from the Russian Orthodox through the Muslim and
Buddhist back to primitive tribal masks. This sequence served partly
to indulge the director in one of his particular artistic interests but in
the context of the film it has a more immediate importance in demonstrating that the significance of the appeal to religion is a universal one,
just as the significance of the Revolution will be universal. Further, the
universal appeal of religion, even in its diversity of forms, serves to
point up the universal appeal of patriotism in its diversity of forms.
Both religion and patriotism are, in the Marxist terminology, opiates
of the people, both are spurious focal points for popular allegiance:
only the Bolsheviks represent the true demands and needs of the mass
for bread, peace and land. The religious masks fade into epaulettes and
military decorations: the Tsar's statue is restored by montage and the
nadir of the Revolution's betrayal has been reached.

Kornilov and Kerensky are compared with two statuettes of
Napoleon: both are traitors and counter-revolutionaries, both megalo-
maniacs. The one, Kerensky, lies motionless and helpless face down-
wards on a couch, not knowing what to do: he has the trappings of
power but not the power itself. The other, Kornilov, advances on revolutionary Petrograd. The Provisional Government, in the hands of the
ineffectual Kerensky, is powerless to defend the city and this task is left
to the Soviet. For the first time we see the Bolshevik headquarters at
Smolny. Arms are being distributed to the proletariat, agitators
harangue the fighting men by the light of bonfires and torches. The
darkness enhances the sense of anticipation. The camera cuts to
Kornilov's Wild Division: a close-up tells us that their swords are inscribed with the motto 'God is with us'. Bolshevik agitators arrive,
distribute leaflets and address the 'enemy': they offer bread, peace,
land. The Cossacks sheath their swords, dance and fraternise: the Wild
Division has changed sides. Kerensky takes refuge under the Tsarina's
cushions as his power ebbs away.

Eisenstein then indulges in an effective piece of trick photography.
In a series of stills a rifle is assembled from its constituent parts.
Symbolically this sequence denotes the need for proletarian self-help:

the mass must make the best of the materials it has available, it must literally forge its own weapons to defend the Revolution that nobody else will save. The next title reiterates this: 'PROLETARIAT, LEARN TO USE ARMS.' We see the serried ranks of the Petrograd Soviet training on a makeshift parade ground. The scene shifts again, to the smoke-filled room in which the Bolshevik leaders are deliberating. With Stalin at his side[15] Lenin designates 25 October as the date for the seizure of power. The deadline for the victory of the Revolution has now been established: progress can be measured against that deadline and the tension that leads to the climax of the film can therefore be created.

Eisenstein then intersperses a shot of the cruiser *Aurora* which is to fire the shot that signals the storming of the Winter Palace. The bridges reappear: they are raised, then lowered. The functionary on the telephone is beside himself. Kerensky is desperate: he phones for the Cossacks but the phone is answered by a Bolshevik sympathiser and his message is not passed on. He flees to Gatchina in a car flying the US flag. The comparison with Napoleon is continued by the stance that Kerensky takes in the car, and by his gestures. As the captain leaves his sinking ship, the gates of the Winter Palace are closed on the outside world. The Provisional Government is now completely isolated, devoid of outside support, and the final confrontation is drawing near. The Palace itself is defended by a remarkable group of rather Brechtian women called the Shock Battalion of Death. They are largely drunk and disorderly. There are shots in which the women admire a Rodin statue of an embracing couple and another sculpture of a mother and child: by these devices Eisenstein suggests that the Shock Battalion of Death has been driven to its reactionary political stance by sexual frustration. The scene switches to Smolny, a complete contrast, a hive of frenzied activity as the Bolsheviks enthusiastically report for duty, while the Mensheviks spy on them treacherously. The darkness of the surroundings serves to heighten the tension: the storm clouds are gathering.

The Second Congress of the Soviets is in session. If the seizure of power is not effected soon, the Mensheviks, Social Revolutionaries and Constitutional Democrats will gain control and the Bolsheviks will have lost their historic opportunity. Lenin waits in the corridor, disguised as a man with toothache: there is a tension-heightening diversion as we wonder whether he has been recognised by his enemies. Meanwhile Kerensky's car speeds towards Gatchina and the Provisional Government sits waiting, the Prime Minister's chair conspicuously empty. The contrast of extremes between Lenin and Kerensky, Soviet and government, is once more underlined by the juxtaposition of the imagery. *Aurora* appears again: it represents the new element that will upset decisively the present balance of authority between the two. The Congress of Soviets, like the government, waits and tension mounts. The Bolshevik appeal is distributed, the Red Army surrounds the Winter Palace and presents an ultimatum. The government still waits. Some of the women soldiers defending the Palace lay down their arms and join the Revolution, while others remain undecided. Their indecision is echoed by the owl clock that moves its head first one way and then the other. Bolshevik agitators penetrate the Winter Palace, sailors arrive on the roof. The Bolsheviks take over the Congress of Soviets, their banner adorns the platform as the Revolution gathers its momentum. A messenger enters: 'THE CYCLE CORPS IS WITH US!' There is a montage of cycle wheels, accelerating in tempo and heightening the tension still further. Sailors drop a grenade through the Palace roof, breaching its defences. The government sleeps as history slips beyond its reach. At the Congress a Menshevik speaker urges caution: a montage of harps suggests that these tired arguments have been heard once too often. A Bolshevik takes the rostrum and announces: 'THE TIME FOR TALK IS PAST.' Action, not words. The guns open fire on the Palace, now virtually undefended The Provisional Government is like the emperor without his clothes. Eisenstein makes this visual comparison by showing the ministers' empty suits.

This is the climax of the film *October* – the storming of the Winter Palace. It is midnight on 24-25 October 1917. Crowds of workers, soldiers and sailors stream across the square and up the stairs. This time they will be victorious, this time they will avenge *Potemkin* and the betrayal of February. When this vanguard of the masses penetrates the Palace, when ordinary workers and soldiers see the ornate splendour of the royal bedchamber and the size and scope of the royal wine cellars, they are amazed. Their amazement soon turns to something less passive and they begin to loot the Palace. But property, especially royal property, is theft and the sailors take disciplinary action. To prevent the looting of the wine cellars, they start to smash the bottles. This time the liquid that flows across the screen is not the workers' blood but the Tsar's wine. In the bedroom soldiers find religious images, Fabergé eggs and a box containing thousands of the medals that have been used to reward bravery at the front. The truth of the imperialist war finally dawns on them: 'IS THIS WHAT WE FOUGHT FOR?' The hollow façade of imperial power is then underlined by a shot of a small boy sitting on the Tsar's throne, swinging his legs. The soldiers, led by

Antonov-Ovseyenko, burst into the Cabinet Room and arrest the Provisional Government. The film quotes Lenin's declaration that the government is overthrown. A series of clocks indicates this historic moment in the different time zones of the world: Petrograd, Moscow, London, Berlin, Paris, New York and other places. The boy on the Tsar's throne is asleep: history has passed him by and made the throne irrelevant. The Congress of Soviets applauds Lenin's declaration and the montage of clapping hands merges into a montage of the clock faces. Finally, Lenin speaks to the Congress. Again he is bursting with vitality and movement — a leader, but of and with the mass: 'THE WORKERS' AND PEASANTS' REVOLUTION IS ACCOMPLISHED. LONG LIVE THE WORLD OCTOBER.' The victory that had been thwarted in *Strike* and *Battleship Potemkin* is now finally assured.

October, as I have already shown, had a mixed reception. One leading critic insisted that the film should be re-edited.[16] Another, describing the film as 'not easily accessible', conceded that, 'In spite of all its defects, *October* is undoubtedly the best film that we have of the history of the October Revolution.[17] The discussions provoked by the film in the columns of the journal *Zhizn' iskusstva* were perhaps most fairly summed up in the following words:

> *October* is unusual in theme and execution. It requires interpretation, careful preparation for its comprehension and the explanation of the enormous work and the enormous material which it contains. It deals with the great events of the proletarian revolution in a new cinema language, aimed not merely at the contemporary cinema audience, but also at the audience that will appear in the near future as the cultural level of the broad working masses improves. And we are entitled to say that, with all its particular and separate faults, *October* is our great achievement, preparing the way for the creation of a great Soviet cinema art.[18]

But even this praise did not save Eisenstein from his critics. In June 1928 a rather unpleasant caricature of the film director appeared in the pages of *Sovetskii ekran*[19] and Eisenstein's career never really recovered from *October*. It is ironic that one of the supreme examples of cinematic myth-making should have caused its creator to be denounced for obscurantism by the very people whose ideology he was attempting to popularise. However, when Pudovkin saw the film, he remarked, 'How I should like to make such a powerful failure.'[20]

Notes

1. A. Kamigulov, I. Skorinko, M. Chumandrin, 'Posle *Potëmkina* – *Oktyabr'* plokh', *Zhizn' iskusstva*, 27 March 1928, 12.

2. Nadezhda Krupskaya, Lenin's widow, had since the Revolution, like Lenin himself, shown a particular interest in the use of the cinema for propaganda purposes. During the Civil War of 1918-21 she had been in charge of the Extra-mural Department of the People's Commissariat for Enlightenment and had travelled with the agit-steamer *Red Star* down the River Volga. Her account of the journey was first published only forty years later in 'Po gradam i vesyam sovetskoi respubliki', *Novyi mir*, November 1960, 113-30. This quotation is from an article that appeared in the Party newspaper: 'O fil'me *Oktyabr'* ', *Pravda*, 9 February 1928.

3. S. Eizenshtein, G. Aleksandrov, 'Eksperiment, ponyatnyi millionam', *Sovetskii ekran*, 5 February 1929, 6-7.

4. Until February 1918 Russia had been on the Julian Calendar, whereas the rest of Europe had already adopted the Gregorian. This left Russia thirteen days 'behind' the rest of Europe: the Bolshevik Revolution occurred on 25 October 1917 in Russia, which was 7 November elsewhere. Hence the anniversary of the October Revolution is now celebrated in November.

5. See J. Leyda (ed.), *Eisenstein: Three Films* (London, 1974), p. 85. Although containing some minor errors of translation, this book includes the most authentic text of the shooting script for *October*. It is translated from: S.M. Eizenshtein, *Izbrannye proizvedeniya v shesti tomakh*, vol. 6 (Moscow, 1971), pp. 65-86. A far less reliable translation is available in French in the series *L'Avant-Scène du Cinéma*, no. 74, October 1967.

6. *Sovetskie khudozhestvennye fil'my. Annotirovannyi katalog*, vol. 1 (Moscow, 1961), pp. 215-16.

7. Comrade Meshcheryakov in his report 'The cinema and the countryside', printed in the stenographic report of the conference: B.S. Ol'khovyi (ed.), *Puti kino* (Moscow, 1929), p. 256.

8. Krupskaya, loc. cit.

9. V. Listov, *Istoriya smotrit v ob"ektiv* (Moscow, 1973), p. 51.

10. This analysis follows the 16mm silent print available from the British Film Institute, London.

11. Quoted in: N.A. Lebedev, *Ocherk istorii kino SSSR: Nemoe kino (1918-1934)* (Moscow, 1965), p. 323.

12. Kamigulov et al., 'Posle *Potëmkina'*.

13. Krupskaya, loc. cit.

14. There is a detailed analysis of this sequence in: P. Sorlin and M.C. Ropars, *Octobre: Ecriture et idéologie* (Paris, 1976).

15. Although not as obviously as in Mikhail Romm's *Lenin in October*, made in 1937, in which Stalin is clearly Lenin's right-hand man and is even honoured with the leader's accolade, 'Comrade Stalin is right'.

16. A. Piotrovskii, '*Oktyabr'* dolzhen byt' peremontirovan', *Zhisn' iskusstva*, 27 March 1928, 12.

17. T. Rokotov, 'Pochemu malodostupen *Oktyabr'*?', *Zhizn' iskusstva*, 10 April 1928, 17.

18. '*Oktyabr'*. (Itogi diskussii)', *Zhizn' iskusstva*, 27 May 1928, 8.

19. 'Vsyakii sam sebe Eizenshtein', *Sovetskii ekran*, 19 June 1928, 6-7.

20. V. Shklovskii, *Zhili – byli* (Moscow, 1966), p. 489.

8 THREE SONGS OF LENIN

> The movement of thoughts and the movement of ideas take
> many paths but a single direction, leading to a single goal. The
> thoughts rush from the screen and penetrate the consciousness
> of the audience without being translated into words.
>
> Dziga Vertov, 1934[1]

Dziga Vertov had been the leading experimental newsreel and documentary film maker of the 1920s. Founder and leader of the Cine-Eye
group, he had proclaimed the cinema's creation of a new reality: 'I am
the Cine-Eye, I create a man more perfect than Adam was created . . .
through montage I create a new, perfect man.'[2] For Vertov as for
Eisenstein montage was the key to the new reality but its use was
incompatible with his other fundamental belief in what he termed 'life
caught unawares'. This he saw as the decisive advantage of the documentary over the fiction film. In 1924 he wrote: 'We shoot only facts
and bring them through the screen to the consciousness of the workers.
We consider that to explain the world as it is is our principal task.'[3] He
went on to assert that 'the very term "art" is essentially counter-revolutionary'. In the following year he issued a comprehensive denunciation
of the fiction film and its methods:

> The film drama is the opium of the people. The film drama and
> religion are a fatal weapon in the hands of the capitalists. The screen-
> play is a fairy-tale thought out by literature for us . . . Down with
> bourgeois screenplay fairy-tales! Long live life as it is![4]

In this context the documentary film, and in particular the Cine-Eye
group, had a special responsibility:

> Only in the USSR, where the cinema is a tool in the hands of the
> state, can and should the battle against the blinding of the popular
> masses begin, the battle for sight . . .
>   *To see and show the world in the name of the world proletarian
> revolution – that is the simple formula of the Cine-Eye.*[5]

But, as one of his contemporary critics remarked, 'Montage deforms

facts. The rearrangement of pieces changes their sense.'[6] Reality in
Vertov's formula was not then 'life caught unawares' or 'life as it is'
but 'life as it ought to be', and that formula contained the germ of
socialist realism.

Vertov had been active in the film teams sent out with the agit-trains
during the Civil War, but he first came to prominence in the early 1920s
with his *Kinopravda* newsreels, which were intended to be the cinema's
equivalent of the Party newspaper *Pravda*, 'cine-truth' as opposed to
'truth'. Vertov's early feature films (*Forward, Soviet!*, *A Sixth Part of
the World*, *The Eleventh Year* and *The Man with the Movie-Camera*),
while consisting of film material of 'life caught unawares', are none the
less organised through montage and it is this organisation that gives
them rhythm and direction. Life may have been caught unawares, but
the director is concerned to make life more aware of itself. Viktor
Shklovsky attacked Vertov's concept, stressed the importance of both
context and content and suggested that Vertov was not in fact following
his theories in practice:

> Montage of life? Life caught unawares. Not material of world
> importance. But I think that newsreel material in Vertov's treatment
> is devoid of its soul – documentary quality.
>
> A newsreel needs titles and dates.
>
> There is a difference between an idle factory and the
> Tryokhgorny workshops idle on 5 August 1919.
>
> Mussolini talking interests me. But a straightforward plump and
> bald-headed man who talks can go and talk behind the screen. The
> whole sense of a newsreel is in the date, time and place. A newsreel
> without this is like a card catalogue in the gutter . . .
>
> He takes newsreel as material. But we must admit that the very
> frames of Vertov are more interesting than what he has found in the
> newsreel. There is a director there. There is aesthetic consideration
> and invention.[7]

To some extent Vertov took note of these criticisms in making *Three
Songs of Lenin*; some of the material – such as the shots of Lenin's
funeral – is familiar, but the rest is given its significance by association
with this familiar material, and all the sequences in the film are clearly
labelled. This was a step away from *The Man with the Movie-Camera*
and *Enthusiasm*. Writing in 1934, partly reflecting the modification in
his own opinions and partly underlining the changed political and artistic
climate, Vertov advocated: 'Not "cine-eye" for "cine-eye's" sake, but

the *truth* through the methods of the "cine-eye" – that is "cine-truth".[8] At the same time he regarded *Three Songs of Lenin* as the culmination of his previous work:

> To remove all falsity, to achieve the simplicity and clarity that the critics have noted in *Three Songs of Lenin*, required editing of exceptional complexity. In this respect the experience of *The Man with the Movie-Camera*, *A Sixth Part of the World*, *Enthusiasm* and *The Eleventh Year* rendered great service to our production group. These films have turned out to be 'films that beget films'.[9]

Three Songs of Lenin was made to commemorate the tenth anniversary of Lenin's death. It is, like all Vertov's films, a peculiarly difficult film to describe in writing because of its particular combination of image and word, or image and sound, its uniquely *cinematic* quality. Vertov once remarked, 'I work in the field of the poetic documentary film.'[10] Elsewhere he wrote, 'I am a cinema writer. I write not on paper but on film.'[11] *Three Songs of Lenin* is a superb example of these techniques. On the other hand, as Vertov's biographer, Nikolai Abramov, has pointed out, it is also 'an outstanding work of socialist realism in the documentary cinema . . . a classic of Soviet cinema art'.[12] But, despite the accuracy of these descriptions the film can still be regarded as a development of the experimental tradition of the 1920s.[13]

Three Songs of Lenin is, as the title suggests, conceived in three parts, each part being constructed around a particular song by which the peasants of Soviet Central Asia commemorate the dead leader. Vertov wrote at the time:

> Together with the other themes there runs through the whole film *Three Songs of Lenin* the image 'Lenin is Springtime'.
>
> This theme, like the others, is represented in the film, not through the medium of words, but by other means – through the relationship between sound and image, through the combined effect of many media . . .
>
> *Three Songs of Lenin* is a production with many facets. But its basic strength lies in the fact that it is rooted in the images of popular art, in images created by the art of the emancipated popular masses. The giant Lenin and beloved Ilyich, close friend and great leader, and 'Lenin poured his blood into every one of us' – that is how the image of Lenin appears to the emancipated Turkmen and Uzbek, that is how he appears to the woman of the Soviet east, who has

been emancipated two and three times over.[14]

The three songs around which the film is built are: 'My face was in a
dark prison'; 'We loved him'; 'In the great stone city'. There is a brief
prelude before the first section of the main part of the film.

The film starts with the titles: 'Three Songs of Lenin, of the leader
of the oppressed of the whole world'. The background to the film is
explained: 'In the different corners of the globe, in the countries of
Europe and America, in the countries of Africa and beyond the Polar
Circle people sing songs of Lenin, of the friend and saviour of all those
who are enslaved.'[15] The songs for this film are confined to three from
the Soviet east: 'These are songs: of the woman who has abandoned the
veil; of the lamp that reaches into the village; of the water that attacks
the desert; of the illiterate, who have become literate; of what ILYICH-
LENIN *is*.' The titles grow larger: 'These are songs of the October
Revolution and of what ILYICH-LENIN *is*.' Finally, in even larger
letters: 'This is a song of the war for a new, happy life, of what ILYICH
. . . *LENIN* is.' Then the film moves to images of Gorki, the estate
outside Moscow where Lenin spent his last years and where he died in
January 1924. We see the house, the room where Lenin died, the park
and then the bench on which he used to sit. It is empty. The sequence
ends with a photograph of Lenin sitting on his bench, a shot which has
become very famous and which gains in power by contrast with the
shot of the empty bench that has preceded it.[16] The scene is set for the
first song, 'My face was in a dark prison'.

We are in Central Asia and a woman with a black veil appears on the
screen; we see a mosque and then the title of the song: 'My face was in
a dark prison'. There is Asian music on the sound track, a blind and/or
drunken girl staggers across the screen: 'My life was blind'. A prayer
wall precedes the next caption: 'Without light and without knowledge,
I was like a slave without chains.' Then we see beasts of burden – human
beasts of burden – and the atmosphere of degradation is intensified.
But the saviour is at hand: 'But then came the ray of truth – the dawn
of the truth of LENIN.' The Russian word for truth, *pravda*, is of
course also the name of the Party newspaper of which Lenin was the
first editor. The mention of Lenin's name changes the scene completely:
we see Young Pioneers, members of the Party's youth movement, then
a girl unveiling herself in a symbolic act of liberation. There is a general
view of a Central Asian town; a girl leaves her house with a book under
her arm. She is off to the school, one of the fruits of the Revolution,
which doubles as a clinic. A smiling child is being weighed: the Revolution

looks after the physical as well as the spiritual health of the people. A
literacy class is being held: musical instruments are being played and
we see the works of Lenin on the desk. The screen goes dark while music
is played: 'We never saw him once . . . We never heard his voice.' On the
wall of the schoolroom there is a portrait of Lenin as a youth: 'But he
was close to all of us, like a father . . . and more!' This remark is then
amplified: 'No father ever did as much for his children as LENIN did
for us.' Lenin is about to be deified; what he has given to the emancipated masses of Central Asia will be seen in contrast to the 'dark
prison' of the opening shots of this part of the film, the life of the
woman veiled and wrapped in slavery and superstition. We begin with a
close-up of a woman's face unveiled and the caption: 'MY collective
farm.' This is illustrated by shots of tractors and combine harvesters
against a bright and open sky, a complete and deliberate contrast to the
'dark prison'. There is stirring martial music. An unveiled girl feeds a
large flock of hens, a young girl marches into the future, aircraft fly
over the tractors: woman now has a role in society and public life and is
participating fully in the processes of mechanisation and modernisation:
'MY country'. A family ride in a car, there are more shots of aircraft
and tractors, and literature is distributed. A bicycle and a camel, the
new and the old, are ridden off into the distance. We see a group
reading newspapers, another tractor. After centuries of isolation, Soviet
Central Asia is being brought into contact with the outside world and is
beginning to benefit from that contact: 'MY land'. Women drive
tractors and receive military training; this is another part of their
enhanced role in Soviet society. The radio brings a direct relay of
Lenin's funeral from Red Square. One woman mourns, another switches
on the light in her hut. At this point Lenin achieves his apotheosis: 'If
he saw darkness he created light, from the desert he created a garden,
and from death -- life.' A woman rides a bicycle through a vineyard, the
garden that has been created from the desert. A group of girls are
talking: 'MY university'. The sunlight streams down on their unveiled
faces and we hear a song of happiness: 'MY factory'. A modern building,
a cotton mill, cotton-spinning machinery, camels, a mechanical loom
worked by women, all give way to a shot of a camel and a tractor, the
old and the new: 'MY collective farm'. This sequence has in effect
provided a breathing space, reiterating the themes of the old and the
new, tradition and modernisation; the film now moves to a new
crescendo. Women march through the farm to the fields where they
pick cotton; one woman feeds her child at the breast. In simple, almost
biblical imagery Lenin's role is recalled in the words of a peasant song:

He persuaded the weak and the poor
That a million grains of sand make a hill
That a million grains of corn make a sackful
That a million of the weak make a great force!

The peasants, men and women, are digging in the fields; an emancipated
girl peers through a microscope; a woman embraces her child: 'MY
family'. The women harvest the cotton: 'MY hands'. There is a close-up
shot of their hands: 'Hands of STEEL'. Just as the earlier use of the
word *pravda* was significant, so too is the use of the word *stalny*, 'of
steel'; Lenin's successor had after all chosen for himself the name
Stalin, 'man of steel'. But hands of steel can also be mechanical and we
see again a woman driving a tractor, ploughing the fields; the military
music emphasises the effort of organisation that has made this possible
and introduces the caption: 'MY party'. As this first part of the film
draws to its conclusion we return to the figure of Lenin. Using a
newsreel sequence of May Day 1920, Vertov shows us the lost leader
speaking to a mass demonstration at the laying of the foundation stone
for a monument in Moscow to emancipated labour.[17] Then we return
to the photograph seen earlier of Lenin sitting on his favourite bench at
Gorki: 'He gave us all he had: his brain, his blood, his heart.' The first
song closes with images that we have seen already: a close-up of the
unveiled woman's face, the house and park at Gorki, and finally the
empty bench.

The purpose of the first song is to demonstrate the effect that the
October Revolution and the ideals of Soviet socialism, as personified by
Lenin, have had on the life of Soviet Central Asia. The twin themes are
thus those of emancipation, exemplified by the unveiling of women and
the spread of literacy, and modernisation, represented by the machinery
we see depicted on the screen: tractors, aircraft, radio and electric light,
cotton-spinning machinery and mechanical looms. The implication is
clear: Central Asia has been transformed, the peasantry have come from
their 'dark prison' into their own. The relationship between image and
word is not a straightforward one. In part, of course, the images
illustrate the titles, but in another sense the titles are a part of the
image structure itself and give it a sense of organisation and coherence.
Each title performs a dual function: it serves to explain and justify the
imagery that has preceded it and to introduce the imagery that follows.
In addition much of the imagery is repeated throughout the song
sequence, individual frames acting like the individual notes in a piece of
music, bringing different parts of the visual argument together. The titles

themselves thus mark neither a sudden break nor a sudden change of direction, but a smooth transition from one part of this visual argument to the next. To illustrate this, let us look at one of the short sequences outlined above, taking as our starting and finishing points the two quasi-biblical comments on Lenin's role:

> *Title:* If he saw darkness he created light,
> From the desert he created a garden,
> And from death — life.

The first line has just been illustrated by a shot of a woman switching on the light in her hut; the second line is followed by a shot of another woman riding a bicycle through a vineyard. Bicycles have been seen before alongside camels, contrasting the new with the old. The last line of the title takes us back to the opening sequence of the film and the scenes of Gorki, and thus also anticipates the final sequence of this first song of Lenin. The vineyard scene gives way to that of the women talking and the next title: 'MY university'. We have, in this song, already seen the women of Central Asia unveiling themselves and reading; now they have gone on from literacy classes and school to university. The combination of a facial close-up and the music lead to the next title: 'MY factory' and to the buildings and machinery that illustrate the theme of modernisation and mechanisation. The machines are intercut with camels and tractors, symbols of tradition and change again. The camels lead us to the next title: 'MY collective farm'. Then we see the women peasants again, but this time they are harvesting the cotton that we have just seen being spun; hence the concept of cotton bridges the title and brings the two sequences together. These scenes, intercut with the mother feeding her child ('And from death — life'), culminate in the title: 'He persuaded the weak and the poor . . . That a million of the weak make a great force!' Thus Vertov conveys the message of his film by intertwining word, image and sound. Through montage he arranges individual sequences of 'the world as it is' in order 'to see and show the world in the name of the world proletarian revolution — that is the simple formula of the Cine-Eye'. That is also the explicit purpose of this film.

The second song, 'We loved him', is altogether calmer and more elegiac. It begins with the face of the unveiled woman once more. This is followed by the title voicing her thoughts:

We loved him as we love our steppes.
No - more than that!
We should give up all our huts and steppes,
We should give up our lives,
If only we could bring him back!

Chopin's Funeral March is heard and we see more mourning faces:
'Neither we nor the grandchildren of our grandchildren shall ever forget
him!' Then we see Lenin's body at the lying-in-state, newsreel shots
that Vertov took at the time for his *Lenin Kinopravda*. These shots are
interspersed with film of the Gorki estate under snow and close-ups of
mourning women of Asia; the sequence marks the transition from the
scenes of the first song to the newsreel material that constitutes the
major part of the second song. The titles underline Lenin's political
importance: 'He founded our party of steel . . . He built it year in year
out . . . He trained and forged it in ceaseless and persistent struggle . . .'
Next we see the funeral cortège that brought Lenin's body from Gorki
to Moscow. The train passes through villages and towns, where the
track is lined with mourners; the Red Flag is dipped in homage. The
train arrives in Moscow; Clara Zetkin, the veteran German Communist,
is among the crowd of mourners. Then, by contrast, Vertov shows us
scenes of Lenin while still alive: reading, smiling, talking and speaking.
The titles inform us that: 'He was untiring in his work . . . His eyes were
full of irony, shining with intelligence . . . Here he gives a welcoming
smile . . . Here he speaks with passion, inspiring the masses . . .' Next
Lenin speaks at the unveiling of a monument to Marx and Engels and
Vertov places him in his historical and ideological context: 'THE
FOUNDER OF THE COMMUNIST INTERNATIONAL'. He speaks
to the Comintern itself: 'LEADER OF WORLD COMMUNISM'.
Close-up shots lead us to: 'THE LOVE AND PRIDE OF THE INTER-
NATIONAL PROLETARIAT . . . THE BANNER OF THE DOWN-
TRODDEN EAST . . . THE HEAD OF THE WORKERS' DICTATOR-
SHIP IN RUSSIA'. In contrast to Lenin the leader and symbol we then
see Lenin the man: 'He was simple and direct in manner . . . and the
Russians called him simply ILYICH.' A smiling Lenin confirms the
message of the titles. The next shots are of Razliv, on the Gulf of
Finland, where Lenin went into hiding in 1917. The title 'In October
Lenin led us into battle' introduces a series of shots of the early revolu-
tionary days: banners, demonstrations, meetings, armies, leading up to
the reappearance of Lenin as leader. Successive titles read:

> Through devastation . . . but they march.
> Through the cold . . . but they march.
> Through starvation . . . but they march.
> Through fire . . . but they march.
> They are led by ILYICH-LENIN.

The climactic image of Lenin speaking in Red Square is accompanied on the soundtrack by a recording of one of his speeches: the sound is none too clear and so the words roll up on the screen as if on a fluttering banner: 'Stand together . . . Go forward bravely against the enemy . . . Victory will be ours . .'

The next sequence is constructed along dialectical lines:

Title: LENIN
Image: Lenin speaking at the stone-laying ceremony for the monu-
           ment to emancipated labour (as in the first song).
Title: But he doesn't move.
Image: Lenin's corpse.
Title: LENIN
Image: Lenin smiling and waving.
Title: But he is silent.
Image: Lenin's corpse.
Title: THE MASSES
Image: People filing past Lenin's coffin at the lying-in-state.
Title: They move.
Image: People filing past.
Title: THE MASSES
Image: Lenin's corpse.
Title: They are silent.

To the accompaniment of funeral music the masses and the Soviet leadership file past Lenin's open coffin: we can identify his widow, Krupskaya, his successor, Stalin, the Red Army commanders, Budyonny and Voroshilov, a wreath from Maxim Gorky in exile, the Commissar for Enlightenment, Lunacharsky. Above the shrouded chandelier a banner reads: 'Lenin is dead but the Communist Party he created remains. Let us close our ranks even more around it.' There follow shots of peasants, sailors workers; across the screen their thoughts are superimposed in writing: 'Your legacy and your task have been fulfilled.' Marching mourners carry a banner inscribed 'Lenin is our immortality'. others carry a black flag with his head emblazoned in

the middle. Their thoughts are encapsulated in the next two titles: 'How
many times here on Red Square . . . have we seen the LIVING Lenin!'
That is the last title in the sequence devoted to the second song: the
rest of the song is composed of images of Lenin's funeral intercut with
the faces of the unveiled women of Central Asia, the snow-covered
estate at Gorki, the desert sands and the industry that has come to a
halt as a mark of respect. This section of *Three Songs of Lenin* concludes by returning to the Chopin Funeral March and the empty bench
and finally to the eyes of the unveiled woman.

The third song in the film is entitled 'In the great stone city' and it
brings together the personal grief of the first song and the mass mourning of the second into a triumphant affirmation of hope for the
future. The sequence opens with views of Moscow — the river, buildings,
bright lights, the Kremlin — interspersed with the titles: 'In Moscow . . .
in the great stone city . . . in the square there is a tent . . . in it lies
LENIN.' From the mausoleum the scene changes to Central Asia:
desert, rocks, sand, mourning women, a mother and child and the
titles: '. . . and if you have great sorrow . . . go to this tent and look
upon Lenin and your sadness will flow away like water.' Back in
Moscow we see the mausoleum and the long queue of people waiting
to see the dead leader. Searchlights flash across Red Square; there is a
montage of a gymnastics display for which the material is taken from
various parts of the Soviet Union. The Leningrad gymnasts form into a
star: the sense of mourning and sadness flows away: '. . . and your
grief will float away like leaves in a ditch . . .' After the image of a
ditch we see an Asian mother and child, water flowing and children
singing while martial music fills the soundtrack: '. . . our life has
become cheerful and joyous - our Leninist path is the true one . . .'
But this is almost the last we see of Central Asia in the film, for the
scene switches to the world of industry, modernisation and mechanisation, the world of tomorrow. There is a montage sequence of factories,
trains, a steel furnace, aircraft, machines, and amongst them the cap-
tions: '. . . and on every section of the front . . . inch by inch . . . we
are winning our great country for socialism . . .' The culmination of
this sequence is a silhouette of Lenin superimposed upon the water
flowing over the Dneprostroi dam: it is a shot from Vertov's earlier
film *The Eleventh Year*. It leads us straight into a set piece in which a
Ukrainian woman worker on the Dneprostroi project, Maria Belik, tells
a radio audience how she came to be awarded the Order of Lenin for
overfulfilling the plan. Her speech is followed by a repetition of the
image from *The Eleventh Year* and by other scenes of the Dneprostroi

project: flags, new housing, flags again, a clock, workers' faces, rushing water, scaffolding, the turbines – all these images in quick succession culminate in a shot of a clock superimposed on a view of the control room. The chief engineer, who has also received the Order of Lenin, speaks of the political significance of the project: his voice, like that of the woman shock worker before him, is carried on the soundtrack: 'These very complex installations, the hydro-electric power station and the dam, are the best monument to the great builder of communism, the first electrifier in the Soviet Union – Comrade Lenin.'

This is followed by a further montage sequence of images related to the project: rushing water, a statue of Lenin set against scudding clouds, the electricity grid, the dam, the power lines. The caption that acts as the concluding theme of the film then appears for the first time: '. . . if only LENIN could see our country now!' We then see a series of images that emphasise the progress of the processes of mechanisation and modernisation in both industry and agriculture that the October Revolution has brought in its wake: Lenin speaking in Red Square, power lines, tractors, a collective farm. One of the farm workers tells how he increased the yield of the land and urges other farmers to do the same. There follow images of a grain silo, the statue of Lenin against the sky again, aircraft, a parachute drop: '. . . if only LENIN could see our country now!' A woman farm worker, chairman of the Lenin collective farm, repeats the exhortation to greater productive effort: there are more aircraft and parachutists; the aircraft spell out the letters CCCP, the Russian initials for USSR. The next caption shows how the Soviet government is developing the country's natural resources: 'OUR oil'. The sense of individual liberation in the first song has now become a sense of communal property: we see shots of the sea and oil rigs and Lenin's statue again. The next caption, 'OUR coal', is followed by scenes of coal mining and the caption 'OUR metal', by shots of a blast-furnace: '. . . if only LENIN could see our country now!'

Vertov now shows us what the Soviet Union has done with its increased supply of these basic raw materials: Lenin points the way and we see the network of canals that has been constructed, the sequence culminating with: 'Our Magnitostroi'. Then we see the project under construction, trains and the Moscow metro, an ice-breaker forging ahead. This brings the film to the Soviet polar expedition, and to shots of Lenin's books that have inspired them. There are shots of the expedition and of the welcome afforded them on their return to Moscow: '. . . if only LENIN could see our country now!' The ticker-tape welcome is intercut with shots of marching columns and these give

way to film of the celebration of May Day in different countries: the
USSR is a beacon for the workers of the whole world, and Lenin is the
light that will liberate them just as he liberated the oppressed peoples of
the Soviet east. The film ends with another montage sequence: armed
columns march through Red Square as Stalin takes the salute, an
enormous statue of workers, Lenin, aircraft. We see the mausoleum in
Red Square with a profile of Lenin's head and the word 'October' in
neon lights superimposed upon the image. The third song, and the film
itself, end with a shot of Lenin as he speaks on the sound track: 'Stand
firm. Stand together. Go forward bravely against the enemy. Victory
will be ours.'

Three Songs of Lenin was given a general release in the Soviet Union
on 1 November 1934[18] but was suddenly withdrawn from exhibition,
at least in Moscow, shortly afterwards: this caused Vertov to reflect, and
to comment, rather bitterly in his diary on the powers of the petty
bureaucrat:

> I was appalled at the thought that some petty and stupid official
> here could take a film off the screen because of his own personal
> taste or other considerations and at the same time spit with impunity
> in the face of the entire Soviet public.
>
> What do *Pravda*, the Comintern, the Congress of Writers mean to
> him! What is the opinion of academics, artists or political activists to
> him! He has his own little 'taste', his own little 'considerations', his
> own hypocritical little thoughts . . .[19]

Despite this initial setback the film went on to triumph. It was shown
at the first Soviet International Film Festival in 1935 and was awarded
a prize at the Venice Film Festival in the same year. It is rather surprising that a Soviet film praising Lenin and his achievements should
have received such an accolade in Fascist Italy and this is perhaps a
tribute to the power of the film. At home, despite the obvious adulation
of Lenin in the film, Vertov's work never quite escaped the suspicion
that surrounds all innovatory and experimental works of art, and the
accusation that had haunted Eisenstein in the 1920s — that his films
were 'incomprehensible to the masses'. It was after all the official view,
expressed in Lenin's words that, 'Art belongs to the people',[20] and
that 'of all the arts for us the cinema is the most important'.[21]

Notes

1. D. Vertov, 'Bez slov', *Rot-Front*, 14 August 1934, reprinted in S. Drobashenko (ed.), *Dziga Vertov. Stat'i. Dnevniki. Zamysli* (Moscow, 1966), p. 132.
2. D. Vertov, 'Kinoki. Perevorot', *Lef*, 1923, no. 3 (June/July), 140-1.
3. D. Vertov, 'Otvet na pyat' voprosov', *Kino-gazeta*, 21 October 1924.
4. D. Vertov, 'Kino-glaz', in *Na putyakh iskusstva* (Moscow, 1925), p. 220.
5. D. Vertov, 'Kino-glaz', *Pravda*, 19 July 1924.
6. I. Sokolov, 'Shestaya chast' mira', *Kino-Front*, 1 February 1927, 9.
7. V. Shklovskii, 'Kuda shagaet Dziga Vertov?', *Sovetskii ekran*, 10 August 1926, 4.
8. D. Vertov, 'Kinopravda', *Sovetskoe kino*, 1934, no. 11/12 (November/ December), quoted in Drobashenko, *Dziga Vertov*, p. 143.
9. D. Vertov, 'Khochu podelit'sya opytom', written in 1934 but published for the first time in Drobashenko, *Dziga Vertov*, p. 136.
10. D. Vertov, 'Eshchë o Mayakovskom', *Iskusstvo kino*, April 1957, 119.
11. D. Vertov. 'Fil'my o zhenshchine', *Iskusstvo kino*, April 1957, 123.
12. N. Abramov, *Dziga Vertov* (Moscow, 1962), p. 143.
13. Vertov specifically denied that *Three Songs of Lenin* represented a rejection of the principles of the 'cine-eye' movement: Drobashenko, *Dziga Vertov*, p. 142.
14. D. Vertov, 'Poslednii opyt', *Literaturnaya gazeta*, 18 January 1935.
15. The translations are my own from the screenplay published in *Tri pesni o Lenine* (Moscow, 1972). This edition was prepared by Vertov's widow, E. Vertova-Svilova, and V. Furtichev.
16. A.M. Gak *et al.* (eds), *Lenin. Sobranie fotografii i kinokadrov* (2 vols., Moscow, 1970-2), vol. 1, pp. 366-7.
17. Ibid., vol. 2, pp. 314-39.
18. *Tri pesni o Lenine*, p. 122.
19. Diary entry for 9 November 1934, quoted in Drobashenko, *Dziga Vertov*, pp. 181-2.
20. K. Tsetkin, *Vospominaniya o Lenine* (Moscow, 1966), p. 11.
21. G. Boltyanskii, *Lenin i kino* (Moscow, 1925), pp. 16-17.

9 ALEXANDER NEVSKY

'Patriotism is my theme' was the thought immediately in my
mind and in the mind of everyone in our creative collective
during the shooting, the sound recording and the editing.

Sergei Eisenstein, 1939[1]

Alexander Nevsky, made in 1938, marks a watershed in the development of Sergei Eisenstein as a film director. After completing *October*
in 1927, in time for the celebration of the tenth anniversary of the
October Revolution, Eisenstein returned to the studio to finish *The
General Line*, his film statement on the problems confronting Soviet
agriculture. Unfortunately, during the time he had spent making *October*
the Party Line on agriculture had changed: for this reason *The General
Line* had to be altered, and then re-titled as *The Old and the New*. He
was then sent abroad on a delegation to investigate the possibilities of
sound and stayed in the United States and Mexico to shoot *¡Que Viva
México!* This project ran into difficulties and Eisenstein returned to the
Soviet Union. But the Soviet film industry was now under the control
of Boris Shumyatsky, who proved to be unco-operative towards the
director's proposals for a film involving Paul Robeson or one based on
Marx's *Das Kapital*. Eventually, in 1935, Eisenstein was allowed to
begin shooting *Bezhin Meadow* which dramatised the problems of
collectivisation in a conflict between the generations. In March 1937
however, after two million roubles had been expended on the film,
Shumyatsky ordered a halt to production, alleging that Eisenstein was
wasting the resources that he had been given. Ironically enough, when
Shumyatsky was dismissed in January 1938 these same charges were
made against him and he was accused especially of squandering money
by cancelling films like *Bezhin Meadow*.[2]

It was Shumyatsky's dismissal that opened the way for Eisenstein
to finish a film. *Alexander Nevsky* was to be his first completed film
since *The Old and the New* in 1929 and his first completed sound film
— the first opportunity therefore for the public to measure the practical
application of the principles of 'orchestral counterpoint' enunciated by
Eisenstein, together with Pudovkin and Alexandrov, in their statement
of August 1928, in which they had inveighed against the use of sound
for ' "high cultural dramas" and other photographed performances of a

theatrical kind'.[3] In his own writing Eisenstein made the political purpose of *Alexander Nevsky* abundantly clear:

> The theme of patriotism and a national rebuff to the aggressor is the theme that permeates our film. We have taken a historical episode from the 13th century when the forerunners of the present-day fascists – the Livonian and Teutonic knights – waged a systematic struggle for the conquest and invasion of the east in order to subjugate completely the Slavs and other peoples in the same way that contemporary fascist Germany is seeking to subjugate them with the same frenzied slogans and the same fanaticism.[4]

The film then was to be an allegory, a projection of present events on to the past, an appeal to the example offered by Russian history:

> Reading the chronicles of the 13th century and alternating them with contemporary newspapers, you lose all sense of the difference in time, for that murderous fear spread by the conquering orders of chivalry in the 13th century is almost the same as that which is being spread in Europe today.
>
> And so the picture, telling of a completely historical epoch, of completely historical events, was made and is seen, according to audience testimony, as a completely contemporary picture, so close are the feelings that inspired the Russian people in the 13th century in repulsing the enemy to the feelings that inspire the Soviet Russian people now, and doubtless to all the feelings that inspire all those towards whom the grasping claw of German aggression is spreading.[5]

This historical precedent was to be used to strengthen the resolve of those inside and outside the Soviet Union who were engaged in the struggle against fascism, to transform their passive opposition into active resistance:

> We want our film not only to mobilise those who are in the thick of the fight against fascism on a world scale, but also to give heart, courage and conviction even to those parts of the world population to whom fascism appears as invincible as the orders of chivalry appeared in the 13th century. Let them not cringe before fascism, let them not kneel before it without protest, let them stop the unending policy of concession and appeasement towards this insatiable monster. Let the sceptics remember that there is no force

of gloom and darkness that could stand against the combined efforts of all that is best, healthiest, most progressive and forward-looking in mankind.[6]

These words were written early in 1939; like the film itself they were to fall foul of the Nazi-Soviet Pact of August 1939 and be temporarily suppressed in the Soviet Union. They do however confirm that *Alexander Nevsky* was both conceived and executed primarily as a work of political propaganda: the artistic considerations were therefore secondary.

In terms of both its content and its style *Alexander Nevsky* marks a break with Eisenstein's previous films and looks forward to his last film, *Ivan the Terrible*. The differences are only partly attributable to the advent of sound, for they also reflected developments in Eisenstein's technique and the changes that had occurred in the political life of the Soviet Union. His silent films had all been characterised by a use of free and rapid montage. This in itself had a dehumanising effect on the characters in the drama and underlined the director's deliberate policy of making the mass, rather than an individual, the hero of his work. The introduction of sound slowed the pace of visual montage even for a more experimental director like Dziga Vertov; it also enabled individual characterisations to be more fully developed on the screen for the characters could now voice their thoughts as well as demonstrate their actions. Instead of the workers in *Strike* or *October* or the sailors in *Battleship Potemkin*, we have the figure of *Alexander Nevsky* himself. Admittedly Eisenstein had also used an individual characterisation for the figure of Marfa Lapkina in *The Old and the New*: she came to symbolise the progressive peasant, just as Alexander was to symbolise the spirit of Russia and its resistance to the invader. However, Lapkina's limited individualism is the only trace of that characteristic in the film: *Nevsky*, on the other hand, also offers us the characters of Gavrilo Olexich and Vasili Buslai and their rivalry in love and war. It is in their characterisation above all that we see the break: for the first time in an Eisenstein film we see characters who display signs of individual human emotion and motivation, who behave as the audience might behave, rather than as symbols. This is also true of Vasilisa, whose ferocious participation in Alexander's army is inspired by the Germans' torture and execution of her father during the sacking of Pskov. It is of course true that the degree of individualism permitted by Eisenstein in *Alexander Nevsky* is no greater than that employed by Pudovkin in *Mother* twelve years earlier and in this sense he may be reacting to the criticisms levelled at his films in the late 1920s. However, in the emphasis given in the film to a powerful leader figure, Eisenstein is following in the steps of other directors of the 1930s. In the 1920s the mass themselves had been the hero of the Soviet cinema, but now the mass had acquired a leader. Marc Ferro has amply demonstrated the function of *Chapayev*, made in 1934, in propagating the ideology of Stalinism,[7] but other examples of the powerful and charismatic leader figure abound: Petrov's *Peter the First*, Pudovkin's *Minin and Pozharsky*, Dovzhenko's *Shchors* (made in response to Stalin's request for a Ukrainian *Chapayev*), even Vertov's *Three Songs of Lenin*, and films like *A Great Citizen*, *Baltic Deputy* and later *Bogdan Khmelnitsky* and *Ivan the Terrible*. But perhaps the simplest and most instructive comparison can be made between *October* and films like *Lenin in October* or *Lenin in 1918*: in the latter the role of the individual, and the role of Stalin in particular, is much enhanced.

It is against this background then that we must see *Alexander Nevsky*. When Stalin had distributed honours to the Soviet film industry in January 1935 Eisenstein had been ignored. In February 1939 both he and Nikolai Cherkasov, who played Alexander, were awarded the Order of Lenin. *Alexander Nevsky* was the film that rehabilitated its director: it also marked his major contribution to the Soviet war effort.

The screenplay for the film was written in collaboration with Pyotr Pavlenko and a first draft, under the title *Rus*, the name for mediaeval Russia, was published in December 1937.[8] Several alternative titles were considered – *Lord Great Novgorod* and *Battle on the Ice* among them – but eventually *Alexander Nevsky* was chosen; in the light of Stalin's 'personality cult' the choice is in itself significant. Filming began on 5 June 1938 and finished on 7 November. Eisenstein was determined to show that he could produce a film quickly if necessary, to rebut Shumyatsky's criticisms of *Bezhin Meadow*. He succeeded beyond his wildest expectations. The film divides into three major sequences: the first depicts the Russians uniting in the face of common danger. This sequence further divides into seven scenes: (1) on the shores of Lake Pleshcheyevo Alexander encounters the Mongols; (2) Gavrilo and Vaska rivals in love; (3) the Novgorod assembly debates its response to the German attack; (4) the sacking of Pskov; (5) emissaries from Novgorod come to Pereyaslavl to ask Alexander to lead the Russian forces; (6) a brief interlude showing the recruitment of the peasant army; (7) Alexander assumes command of the Novgorod forces. The second sequence marks the focus and the climax of the film – the Battle on the Ice. The third sequence, with which the film ends, consists of the victorious entry of Alexander's forces into Pskov and the reckoning with the invaders.

The opening scene of the film shows the devastation and humiliation suffered by mediaeval Russia at the hands of foreign invaders. In this case the invaders are the Mongols. It was Eisenstein's original intention to depict a Russia fighting a battle on two fronts — against the Mongols, symbolising the contemporary threat from Japan, and the Teutonic Knights, representing the Nazis. In an early draft of the screenplay Alexander, having defeated the Germans, was to have been poisoned by the Mongols, and his death was to have been avenged by his great-grandson, Dmitri Donskoi, another legendary figure from the history of mediaeval Russia. But a battle on two fronts would have disturbed the simplicity of the story line and lessened the impact of the propaganda message. Eisenstein was therefore content to confine the Mongol presence to this opening episode. The scene is set on the shores of Lake Pleshcheyevo, near Alexander's home at Peryaslavl. It is a scene of peace and harmony, emphasised by the shots of the lake and the sky. Throughout the film there is a close relationship between man and nature and their respective moods. As Eisenstein wrote elsewhere: 'Everywhere the emotional landscape assumes the form of the mutual submergence of man and nature in one another.'[9]

In this scene the sky is open and bright, but the idyll is disturbed by the arrival of Mongol horsemen. They are dark and threatening figures, kicking and lashing the Russian peasants. The khan has sent an envoy to ask Alexander to join the Golden Horde. The contrast between the two men is instructive: Alexander is tall, composed and dignified, a fisher-man and man of the people, a man among men, a Russian among Russians. The Mongol peers from behind a curtain; he is feared by his men and his whole position is unnatural and alien. Alexander refuses the offer: 'We have a saying: die on your native soil, do not abandon it.'[10] The incident brings home to Alexander the plight of his country and its imminent need of his services: 'The Mongol can wait. We have an enemy more dangerous than the Mongol, closer at hand and more evil, one who cannot be bought off by tribute — the German. When we have beaten him we can attend to the Mongol.' This tentative call to arms leads into the next scene.

In a sense the next scene is a light interlude between serious affairs of state. The two characters Vasili Buslai and Gavrilo Olexich are seen together, joking and courting Olga: their friendly rivalry is established. Novgorod is busy and prosperous, with little outward sign of the impending danger. The sets for the Novgorod and Pskov scenes were reconstructed in the studio because the originals, in Eisenstein's eyes, were no longer sufficiently authentic. Over the centuries the old palaces and churches had sunk several feet into the ground and their visual proportions and perspective had therefore altered. Such was Eisenstein's sense of perfection that they were rebuilt in the studio according to their original proportions.[11] But the idyll of Novgorod too is shaken as a bell calls the population to an assembly. We see carts bringing refugees from Pskov and a wounded soldier calls for vengeance. Tension mounts as he tells of the German atrocities and the crowd respond:

> *Soldier*: If they catch you with a sword, they beat you for having it!
> If they catch you with bread, they beat you for the bread! They've
> tortured mothers and wives for their sons and husbands.
> *Crowd*: The German is a beast! We know the German!

There are of course those who argue for compromise and collaboration with the invader, but they are confined to the merchants and the Church, both by now familiar actors in the demonology of Soviet propaganda. There is confusion and shouting, emphasised by the music, but eventually the assembly decides to call on Alexander Nevsky to lead the forces of Novgorod. It seems that Russia may be saved.

The next scene brings us face to face with the confrontation between good and evil that has been hinted at in the opening sequence and the previous scene. The portrayal of the sacking of Pskov is itself a classic example of atrocity propaganda. The characters are all typecast in line with Eisenstein's concept of 'typage', and we revert briefly to the Eisenstein of the silent film era. The Russians are again open, human characters, 'real people'. The Germans are faceless, often hooded and frequently shot in profile, with cruel, animal-like features. In their meanness they are dwarfed by the massive solidity of the Russian buildings that surround them. The contemporary relevance of the film is underlined by a shot of a knight's helmet decorated with the swastika. Otherwise their symbol is the conventional Latin cross of Western Christianity, usually shot from below to increase the sense of its power. Russian Christianity, which obviously played a significant part in the life of the country in the thirteenth century, is represented in the first instance by its buildings. But these are portrayed as an integral, almost a natural, part of the Russian background. The only priests who appear on the Russian side play the part assigned to the monk Ananias, that of a traitor. The Russia presented on the screen is a secular state, religion is only a folk memory; in other words the portrayal reflects the official

view of contemporary Soviet life. But the mayor of Pskov, Tverdilo, is a
Russian who has betrayed his country: his character echoes the accusations of the purges and presages the role of Shuisky in *Ivan the Terrible*.
He is contrasted with Pavsha, the good Russian, who is executed calling
for vengeance. Similarly the traitor-priest Ananias, despatched to
Novgorod to rouse the people there against Alexander, is contrasted
with the beggar Avvakum, whose dying words at the stake become the
clarion call for Russia's resistance:

> Arise, people of Rus,
> To glorious battle, mortal battle!
> Arise, men of freedom,
> For our fair land!

The next scene takes place in Alexander's hut near Pereyaslavl. The
prince is pacing up and down; one of the men voices his thoughts: 'We
ought to be fighting the Germans, not mending nets.' Emissaries from
Novgorod arrive to ask Alexander to lead the army of resistance. He
accepts the challenge with fighting words and plans to raise a peasant
army. The scene changes to show the peasants joining Alexander's army
in large numbers. They are seen largely in silhouette against the sky,
and dominated by it. Again man is closely intertwined with nature: the
Soviet cameraman, Anatoli Golovnya, has observed of this sequence:

> The movement of people is drawn across the bottom of the frame.
> The earth is at times completely absent from the frame and it looks
> as if people are walking across the sky. There is a certain convention
> at the basis of such composition. The white costumes show up
> effectively against a background of grey sky. With its indefinite colour
> the earth would only disturb the purity of the tonal compositions . . .
> A realistic treatment of the action at times involves the sacrifice of
> decorative effect.[12]

In the final shots of this sequence the peasants merge like streams
flowing into one large river; there is something elemental in their urge
to resist the invader.

In the original screenplay for *Alexander Nevsky* there followed a
scene set in Novgorod showing two fighting camps, one supporting
Alexander and the other, composed of merchants, arguing for peace.
The material for this scene was shot at considerable expense but was not
included in the final film. The critic Viktor Shklovsky has explained:

Eisenstein was editing the picture . . . He edited and edited and lay
down and fell fast asleep.

One night there was a telephone call from the Kremlin. They said
Stalin was asking for the film. They did not wake the director but
took the cans and carried them away.

The film was a great success, but one scene had not yet been
edited and the can containing the sequence on the Volkhov bridge
lay apart from the others.

It was not shown. Nobody noticed and they decided not to
mention that they had not shown the complete film, and that is how
it was released. The absence of this sequence was not noticed by a
single critic.[13]

It is not known whether the missing sequence has been preserved in the
archives. Eisenstein however considered the missing scene to be an
integral part of the structure of the film and petitioned Dukelsky,
Chairman of the Committee on Cinema Affairs to have it reinstated. He
was unsuccessful.[14] He described his feelings in his autobiographical
notes:

> The eternal rush of the film world was the undoing . . . of the
> Novgorod bridge in *Alexander Nevsky*.
> On it we filmed the scene of the famous fist-fights between the
> St Sofia and merchants' quarters of the ancient city.
> In terms of the story it is here that Vaska Buslai and Vasilisa have
> their first romantic encounter. And it is here in the midst of the
> scuffle that Vaska first shouts enthusiastically, 'What a fine girl!'
> after Vasilisa has hit him in the teeth.
> I grieve for this lyrical link in the relationship between the two
> romantic heroes. I grieve deeply for those desperate children who
> throw themselves from the bridge into the icy water in October . . .
> But I grieve most of all that this whole scene flew into the bin.[15]

It is ironical that what was in some ways Eisenstein's most successful
film should have been released in a form that he considered incomplete
and unsatisfactory.

The film as released moves straight from the raising of the peasant
army to the assembly where Alexander addresses the people of
Novgorod. The cathedral broods over the proceedings. The orators are
filmed against the sky, their heads on a level with the church cupolas.
Only the doubting merchants are filmed from a higher angle, so that the

buildings rise above and dwarf them. They are out of step with their environment and with the spirit of the times. Alexander calls for the defence of Russia and the crowd follow him, singing what has become their battle hymn, 'Arise, people of Rus!' The spearmakers vie with the smiths in their contributions to the armoury. Ignat distributes chain mail and weapons to all and sundry. Vaska and Gavrilo ask Olga to decide between them: she agrees to give her hand to the one who proves bravest in battle. Ignat is left with a chain-mail shirt that is too small for him: 'This shirt's on the short side!' The scene ends with the battle hymn once more.

The Novgorod scene is full of life and vibrant with activity. The next scene on the other hand, set in the Teutonic camp, reeks of death. In the background is the bishop's tent, adorned with the cross. The knights, with the Master of the Order at their head, are kneeling in prayer. Whereas Alexander, though a prince, is still a man of the people, here there is a clearly defined hierarchy and a remoteness from real life. They hear that Alexander's army is marching through the forest towards them. It is night and the snow weighs heavily on the trees. The Master believes that the Russians can be trapped and orders his men on to their horses.

In the middle of the forest the knights find a detachment of Russians: it is the advance party led by Vaska. Although taken by surprise, they do not run away. Battle is joined and the longest scene in the film begins. All in all the sequence of the Battle on the Ice lasts 37 minutes: it is both the climax and the focal point of the film. It was perhaps typical of Eisenstein that he should decide to shoot the most important scene in *Alexander Nevsky* first. But this desire conflicted with his wish to shoot the film very quickly. He could not wait until the winter of 1938-39 and so a battlefield of artificial ice and snow was created and the scene was shot in the middle of a Moscow heatwave. Shklovsky writes:

Winter scenes are very difficult to shoot, because winter is a gloomy season. They decided to reconstruct winter. They constructed it without icicles, without steam, and without snow-covered trees. They constructed not winter but a battle. They felled a cherry orchard, dug up the roots, ploughed up a vast field and covered it with asphalt.

Then they put a mixture of chalk and naphthalene on it. They dressed the Russian army and the Teutonic army and started filming.[16]

But before we come to the actual Battle on the Ice there is a period of
tense waiting. The sounds of battle are heard in the Russian camp,
while Alexander and Gavrilo await the return of Vaska's detachment.
Ignat entertains them with a story. The tension mounts. The tale of the
hare and the vixen is an allegory for the fate that awaits the Teutonic
knights on the field of battle. It is this tale that galvanises Alexander
into action: the German troops are heavier and less mobile and he
therefore decides to fight them on the ice of Lake Peipus, rather than
on Russian soil. Just as the vixen in Ignat's story is trapped between
two trunks because she is too fat, so the knights will be trapped on the
breaking ice because they are too heavy. The plan is reminiscent of
Kutuzov's strategy of allowing Napoleon deep into Russia, only to be
worn down by the rigours of the winter climate. It is also a warning to
the potential contemporary aggressor that he too will have to cope with
the Russian winter, and it is a warning that Hitler and his generals
ignored at their peril. One of the strengths of this pre-battle scene lies in
the fact that the enemy is unseen and the tension is increased by the
prolonged anticipation of their appearance. Here Prokofiev's score plays
a very important part, although the relationship between the music and
the visual image remains significant throughout the film. Viktor
Shklovsky wrote of the composer's part in *Alexander Nevsky*: 'For a
long time music has remained on the fringes of the cinema. Now the
cinema breathes music.'[17] This particular segment of the film, the scene
leading up to the appearance of the invading army on the screen, has
been analysed by Eisenstein in the fourth chapter of the collection of
essays published in English as *The Film Sense*. Writing generally of the
relationship between the director and the composer in this film and
dealing in particular with the question of which of the two has the
leading role, he observes:

> It makes no difference whether the composer writes music for the
> 'general idea' of a sequence, or for a rough or final cutting of the
> sequence; or, if procedure has been organised in an opposite
> direction, with the director building the visual cutting to the music
> that has already been written and recorded on sound-track.
>
> I should like to point out that in *Alexander Nevsky* literally all
> these possible approaches were employed. There are sequences in
> which the shots were cut to a previously recorded music-track. There
> are sequences for which the entire piece of music was written to a
> final cutting of the picture. There are sequences that contain both
> approaches. There are even sequences that furnish material for the

anecdotists. One such example occurs in the battle scene where pipes and drums are played for the victorious Russian soldiers. I couldn't find a way to explain to Prokofiev what precise effect should be 'seen' in his music for this joyful moment. Seeing that we were getting nowhere, I ordered some 'prop' instruments constructed, shot these being played (without sound) *visually*, and projected the results for Prokofiev – who almost immediately handed me an exact 'musical equivalent' to the visual image of pipers and drummers that I had shown him.[18]

Eisenstein goes on to explain how individual frames, and individual notes, achieve their power because of the uniqueness of their particular position in the sequence and their combined effect:

The *farewell embrace* between Vaska and Gavrilo Olexich in *Alexander Nevsky* . . . could only occur at one *precise* point in the musical score, in the same way that the close-up shots of the German knights' helmets could not be used before the point where they were finally employed in the attack sequence, for only at that point does the music change its character from one that can be expressed in long shots and medium shots of the attack to one that demands rhythmic visual beats, close-ups of galloping and the like.

Alongside this, we cannot deny the fact that the most *striking* and immediate impression will be gained, of course, from *a congruence of the movement of the music with the movement of the visual contour* – with the graphic composition of the frame; for this contour or this outline, or this line is the most vivid 'emphasiser' of the very idea of the movement.[19]

I would refer the reader to *The Film Sense* for the more detailed analysis of the 'dawn of anxious waiting' sequence with which Eisenstein justifies his statement that 'The audio-visual aspect of *Alexander Nevsky* achieves its most complete fusion in the sequence of the "Battle on the Ice" . . . The method used in it of audio-visual correspondence is that used for any sequence in the film.'[20]

The Russian forces wait. Alexander stands above the lake on Raven Rock, peering into the distance, against a background of open sky and storm clouds. There is little movement. At the base of the rock the Russian army waits; shots of its massed ranks are intercut with close-ups of Ignat and Vasilisa. The conflicting angles of pictorial composition add to the tension created by the music. Suddenly and almost

ILLUSTRATIONS

The Film Maker

1. Leni Riefenstahl
2. Sergei Eisenstein

Lenin: The Reality and the Fiction

3. Lenin arriving at the Finland Station, from Eisenstein's *October*, made in 1927. The part of Lenin is played by an amateur actor, the worker Nikandrov.
4. Maxim Strauch as Lenin in *The Man with the Rifle*, made by Yutkevich in 1938.
5. Lenin walking in the Kremlin, 16 October 1918. This newsreel was taken after Fanya Kaplan's assassination attempt to scotch rumours that Lenin was dead.
6. Boris Shchukin as Lenin in Mikhail Romm's *Lenin in 1918*, made in 1939.

The Führer Prototype: The Use and Abuse of History

7. Paul Hartmann in Wolfgang Liebeneiner's *Bismarck*, made in 1940.
8. Horst Caspar as Herbert Maisch's *Friedrich Schiller*, also made in 1940.
9. Otto Gebühr as Frederick the Great in Veit Harlan's *The Great King*, made in 1942.
10. Horst Caspar as Gneisenau in Harlan's *Kolberg*, released in 1945.

The Hero and his Men

11. *Strike* (USSR, 1925).
12. *Peter the First* (USSR, 1937).
13. *Hitler Youth Quex* (Germany, 1933).
14. *Stukas* (Germany, 1941)

The Enemy

15. The Capitalist: the rich banker in Protazanov's *The Three Millions Trial* (USSR, 1926).
16. The Jew: Werner Krauss in one of his roles in Veit Harlan's *Jew Süss* (Germany, 1940).

17. The vacillating liberal: Vladimir Popov as Kerensky in Eisenstein's *October* (USSR, 1927).
18. The effeminate Englishman: Prince Henry in Carl Froelich's *The Heart of a Queen* (Germany, 1940), before he succumbs to the pox.
19. The inhuman enemy: the faceless Teutonic Knights (i.e. the Nazis) in Eisenstein's *Alexander Nevsky* (USSR, 1938).
20. The inhuman enemy: Andrews Engelman as the Bolshevik commissar Nikolai Boksha, purveyor of chaos and destruction, in Karl Ritter's *GPU* (Germany, 1942).

The Enemy as Oppressor

21. *Mother* (USSR, 1926).
22. *Mother.* There is a very similar sequence in Room's *The Ghost that Never Returns* (USSR, 1930).
23. The headquarters of *GPU* (Germany, 1942).
24. The hypocritical British, distributing bibles to the natives with one one, and rifles with the other in *Uncle Kruger* (Germany, 1941).

The Hero as Victim

25. Tsarist oppression of the workers: the Odessa Steps massacre in Eisenstein's *Battleship Potemkin* (USSR, 1926).
26. The innocent émigrée under interrogation by the *GPU* (Germany, 1942).
27. The man who brought the news from Pskov to Novgorod in *Alexander Nevsky* (USSR, 1938).
28. British oppression of the Irish in *My Life for Ireland* (Germany, 1941).

The Message Translated: *Battleship Potemkin* **and** *Uncle Kruger*

29,30. *Battleship Potemkin* (USSR, 1926).
31,32. *Uncle Kruger* (Germany, 1941).

Retribution

33. The Martian proletariat overthrow their oppressive rulers in Protazanov's fantasy *Aelita* (USSR, 1924).
34. Andrews Engelman meets his end in *GPU* (Germany, 1942).
35. The Teutonic Knights panic as the ice breaks in *Alexander Nevsky* (USSR, 1938).
36. The passengers panic as the Titanic sinks (Germany, 1943).
37. Queen Victoria's deathbed repentance in *Uncle Kruger* (Germany, 1942).

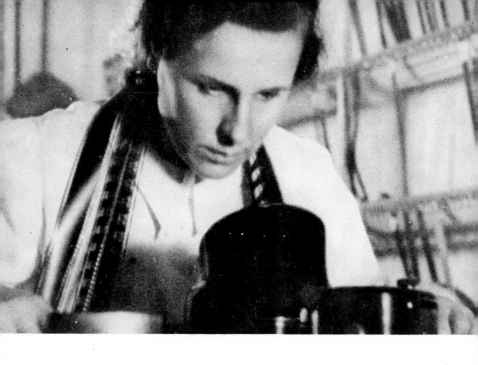

4

5

6

7

8

9

10

11

12

13

14

15

18

19

20

21

22

23

24

25

26

27

29

30

31

32

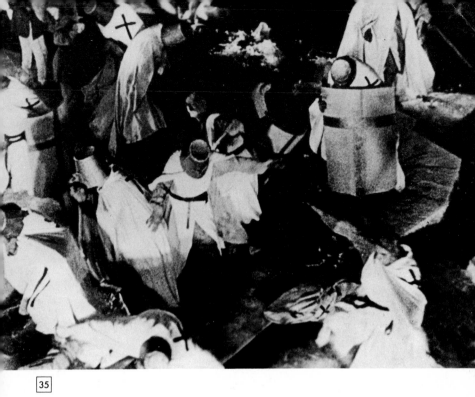

35

36

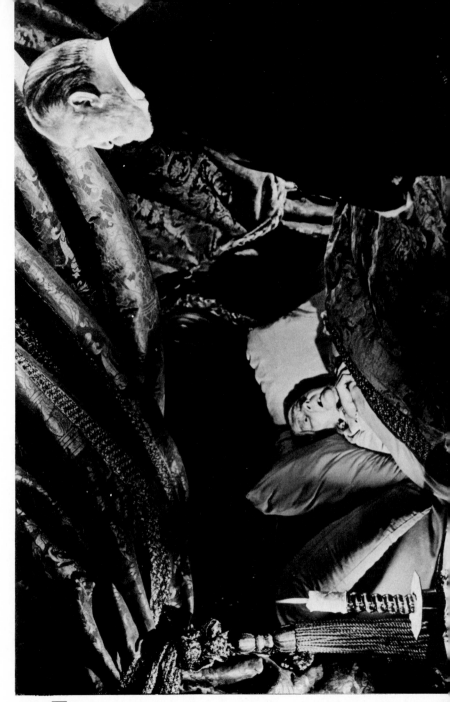

imperceptibly the Germans appear on the horizon, marching across the lake that is to become their graveyard. At last we see the two opposing forces at their full strength. Gradually the camera moves from the Russians to the Germans: it is they who first fill the horizon, then move diagonally across the screen until their movement fills it completely. The final shot in this sequence sets the two armies in immediate confrontation: the camera is raised and the advancing Germans are seen through the heads of the Russian soldiers, through a forest of their spears. The opposing armies meet and the great battle begins.

The Battle on the Ice allows Eisenstein to realise to the full his concepts of montage and an orchestral counterpoint between sound and image. Visually the film cuts from general shots of the advancing armies and the battle to close-ups of the individual participants: Ignat, Vaska, Gavrilo and Alexander himself. The music too is a mixture, combining Russian and German themes until the point in the battle where the tide turns in favour of the Russians: then the Russian themes swamp the German. For much of the scene the music functions in counterpoint to the image, in places sound and vision run parallel, while on two occasions, with the image of the German horns and that of the Russian bugles, the music acts as a direct sound illustration of the image. By this variety of approaches Eisenstein and Prokofiev build up a sense of the confusion and the excitement of the battle. The Russian victory is confirmed by the man-to-man combat between Alexander and the Master of the Teutonic Order, which ends with the Master slipping from his horse. He is led away with a noose round his neck, defeated and humiliated. Vasilisa and Ignat tie up the German bishop, whose prayers for deliverance have remained unheard. Ananias is pursued and killed by Vasilisa. Tverdilo, whose treachery is underlined by his inability to decide whether to cross himself in the Latin or the Russian manner, is captured by Ignat. But at this moment the German war horn sounds, Ignat turns and is stabbed in the back by Tverdilo. He dies muttering, 'This shirt's on the short side!', taking us back to the scene in Novgorod when Alexander took command of the Russian forces. The battle is however won. The Germans crowd round their war horn and the ice covering Lake Peipus begins to crack beneath them. Like Napoleon and Hitler they are to fall victim to the Russian winter. Because of the lack of detailed evidence for thirteenth-century Russian history, Eisenstein was able to use poetic licence in this fashion; indeed it was this freedom that attracted him to the story of Alexander Nevsky.

The next brief scene is known as the 'Field of Death'. It is night and there are corpses everywhere, but Vaska and Gavrilo find one another alive. Olga comes in search of them: each tries to convince her that the other has fought more bravely and the three stumble off into the foggy darkness.

The final scene in *Alexander Nevsky* marks the liberation of Russia and the triumphal entry of Alexander's forces into Pskov. First the dead heroes are brought in, then the captured Germans. Alexander displays his humanity by releasing the foot soldiers and holding only the knights for barter. Tverdilo is left to the mercy of the people he has betrayed. All that remains is for Olga to decide between Gavrilo and Vaska. It is Vaska who makes her decision for her: Gavrilo will take Olga and Vaska will have Vasilisa, the bravest warrior of all. The badinage over, the film comes to its serious conclusion. Alexander addresses his army and the people of Pskov: 'Go and tell all in foreign parts that Rus lives. Let people come to us as guests without fear. But he who comes with the sword shall perish by the sword. On this Rus stands and will stand forever!' His words merge with the shouts of the people and the film ends with the battle hymn:

> Arise, people of Rus,
> To glorious battle, mortal battle!
> Arise, men of freedom,
> For our fair land!

The filming of *Alexander Nevsky* was completed by the deadline that Eisenstein had set himself – 7 November 1938, the twenty-first anniversary of the October Revolution. By 23 November the editing too had been completed and the film had its première. It was released to the general public on 1 December and was an immediate success, capturing, as it did, the spirit of the times. *Alexander Nevsky* brought Eisenstein the official recognition that he had for so long been denied: on 1 February 1939 he was awarded the Order of Lenin, the highest honour that the Soviet government can bestow, and on 15 March 1941 he received the State Prize, First Class. His film was withdrawn from distribution after the Nazi–Soviet Pact had been signed in August 1939, just as anti-Soviet films like *Frisians in Peril* were withdrawn in Germany, but it was released again after the German attack in June 1941. It is perhaps a tribute to the powerful role that the film played in strengthening the Soviet resistance that the government instituted a new battle honour, the Order of Alexander Nevsky.[21]

To Eisenstein himself the success of what he regarded as his least satisfactory film remained an inexplicable mystery. In his archive there is a note, dated 24 December 1938 and entitled 'The Riddle of *Nevsky*':

Nevsky is *brazenly* effective despite *itself. Everyone* can see its defects: its staginess *avant tout*, its length, the rhythmic breaks and failures. *Everyone* can see them, not just the specialists. The persistence with which even those who were dissatisfied the first time go two or three times would make it seem that even the devil would go again if he didn't like it! And it is effective *quand-même*. Why? I think it's a matter of 'Shamanism': it's just like the Shaman's tambourine, there's only a single thought, and *everything* revolves around a *single* thought. There's not a word, a remark, an episode or a scene where the speech and the plot are not concerned with the enemy and the need to beat him: in the shots, designs, reminiscences, the very actions themselves. You do not, of course, have to search so openly for this *single-mindedness* through all the variety (and even diversity) of what is happening. It rivets you hypnotically.[22]

Notes

1. S. Eizenshtein, 'Patriotizm – moya tema', in: *Izbrannye proizvedeniya v shesti tomakh*, vol. 1 (Moscow, 1964), p. 161. (Henceforth *Izbrannye proizvedeniya*.) A translation was published as 'My subject is patriotism', *International Literature*, 1939, no. 2, pp. 90-3.
2. See above, p. 65.
3. See Eizenshtein, V. Pudovkin, G. Aleksandrov, 'Zayavka', *Zhizn' iskusstva*, 5 August 1928, 5. Jay Leyda has translated this and included it as Appendix A to *Film Form* (New York, 1949), pp. 257-60.
4. *Izbrannye proizvedeniya*, vol. 1, pp. 162-3.
5. Ibid.
6. Ibid.
7. M. Ferro, 'The fiction film and historical analysis', in: P. Smith (ed.), *The Historian and Film* (Cambridge, 1976), pp. 80-94.
8. S. Eizenshtein, P. Pavlenko, 'Rus' ', *Znamya*, December 1937.
9. *Izbrannye proizvedeniya*, vol. 3 (Moscow, 1964), p. 394.
10. Quotations are taken from the screenplay published in *Izbrannye proizvedeniya*, vol. 6 (Moscow, 1971), pp. 153-96. Where this differs from the finished film I have amended it to correspond to the 16mm version available for hire from Contemporary Films, London. The translations are my own. The complete screenplay has been translated from the Russian by Diana Mathias and published in *Eisenstein: Three Films* (London, 1974), pp. 89-143.
11. V. Shklovskii, *Eizenshtein* (Moscow, 1973), p. 246; M. Meilakh, *Izobrazitel'naya stilistika pozdnikh fil'mov Eizenshteina* (Leningrad, 1971), p. 254.
12. A. Golcvnya, 'Statika i dinamika v kompozitsii kinokadra', *Iskusstvo kino*, February 1939, p. 41.
13. V. Shklovskii, *Zhili – byli* (Moscow, 1966), p. 499.

14. See the editorial notes in *Izbrannye proizvedeniya*, vol. 6, p. 547.
15. *Izbrannye proizvedeniya*, vol. 1, p. 292.
16. Shklovskii, *Eizenshtein*, p. 247.
17. V. Shklovskii, 'Aleksandr Nevskii', *Kino*, 2 November 1938.
18. S. Eisenstein, *The Film Sense* (London, 1968), pp. 124-5.
19. Ibid., p.135.
20. Ibid., p.136.
21. N. Cherkasov, *Notes of a Soviet Actor* (Moscow, n.d.), p. 103.
22. Quoted in *Izbrannye proizvedeniya*, vol. 6, p. 547. The French phrases were in the original. A Shaman was a kind of Siberian medicine man.

PART THREE: NAZI GERMANY

Art is free and art should remain free, but it must get used to certain norms. In any country other than Germany there would be no need to say this. But in recent years all normal political thought has been stifled.

Goebbels, 1933

There was a time when the artist thought he had a right to create freely, in his own way, without reference to the state. It was a time when people thought they were making a statement of great importance in declaring themselves to be *completely apolitical*.

That time has gone. A new time imperiously demands from each of us a recognition of the great problems and tribulations of the day, and the artist is not excluded. In particular, those of us who are devoted to the cinema have infinitely greater obligations to the people today than ever before because we occupy . . . an important position in the front line.

Hans Steinhoff, 1941

10 GERMANY: THE HISTORICAL BACKGROUND

> We shall never escape from the state of conceptual confusion:
> something new and beautiful has come into being in our life-
> time but, instead of taking it as it is, we try by every possible
> means to fit it into old, unsuitable categories, to deprive it of
> its true sense and value.
>
> Georg Lukács, 1913[1]

> The War has demonstrated the overwhelming power of the
> image and the film as a medium for education and influence.
> Unfortunately our enemies have used the advantage they had
> over us in this field so thoroughly that we have suffered con-
> siderable damage.
>
> General Ludendorff, July 1917[2]

The origins and development of the German cinema until the outbreak
of the First World War in 1914 reflect a pattern common to most
European countries. While the German Empire was more advanced
economically, culturally, socially and possibly politically than the
Russian Empire, the film pursued its path from fairground novelty to
mass entertainment at an only slightly faster pace in Germany than in
Russia. The birth of the cinema was an international phenomenon: the
First World War transformed it into a national resource.

The new invention was in fact demonstrated in Berlin two months
before its first appearance in Paris. The Skladanowsky brothers showed
their 'Bioscope' to the public in the Wintergarten on 1 November 1895[3]
but the films they used appear by all accounts to have been even less
interesting than those produced by the Lumière brothers for their
première on 28 December at the Grand Café. But the French soon had
a virtual monopoly of the German market and it was not until about
1910 that Germany began to develop a significant film industry of its
own. The early years were dominated by films of French, and later
Italian and American origin, just as the Russian cinema had been dominated by them. In Germany too the cinema began as a mobile form of
entertainment, with the projectionist buying his films outright, usually
from Pathé, and taking them from place to place until either the audience
potential had been exhausted or the films themselves had worn out.

These *Wanderkinos*, where the audience sat in a temporary structure
such as a tent, slowly gave way to an increasing number of *Ladenkinos*
(literally, 'shop cinemas'), the direct predecessors of the cinema theatre
buildings that we know today. The films themselves were short,
designed only to attract audiences to the new technical marvel of
movement on a silent screen. In as far as these films had a story, it was
a simple one and sometimes a highly moralistic one; later, morality had
to compete with pornography, a development that led to the establishment of the *Kinoreformbewegung* (Cinema Reform Movement) which
after 1912 began to denounce the film as a medium for the corruption
of the younger generation.[4] *Plus ça change, plus c'est la même chose . . .*
Writing in 1912 a conservative commentator, Dr Duenschmann,
observed:

> The surprisingly rapid development of the cinematograph into a
> picture-house offering serious competition to the theatre has intro-
> duced into our national life a new cultural factor whose influence —
> in both the good and the bad sense — on the population of our
> cities, and in particular on the youth of our large cities, is rightly
> of increasing concern to public opinion. The great daily papers that
> consider the future of our people are primarily concerned with the
> sociopolitical aspect of this burning issue and for this reason most
> of them demand the strongest possible police censorship of films
> before their release.[5]

This writer complained that, 'There is no German national film',[6] and
that Germany was therefore in danger of becoming culturally dependent on other countries, especially France where, he considered, the
government was already using the cinema for its own political ends.[7]
Nowadays this problem would probably be characterised as 'cultural
imperialism' but in 1912 'imperialism' was not yet a dirty word. The
problem however was the same as that faced by world television networks in the 1970s *vis-à-vis* American programmes: the producer is not
necessarily concerned with the political influence exerted by his programmes, but he has a commercial advantage that he is eager to press
home. The political effects of this advantage may be incidental but
none the less they may also be significant, especially when viewed from
the perspective of the receiving nation. It was this kind of effect that
concerned Duenschmann, a fear that Germany's traditions might be
undermined through the over-exposure of her population to an alien
way of life — that of France, where 'we see modern democracy in its

most radical form'.[8] The power of the cinema, in his view (and it was a view later to be developed by Goebbels above all), lay in its dependence on suggestion rather than argument:

> The popular mass is interested in neither reflection nor in powerful logical argument. But it has very vivid powers of imagination: strong impressions, apparently very active personalities, unexpected events, actions and episodes can provoke in it the most powerful emotions. The mass thinks only in images and can only be influenced by images that act through suggestion on its power of imagination.[9]

As long as Germany lacked its own powerful cinema industry its population would be exposed to the suggestive power of the foreign film and this could strike at the very heart of German national life, the family:

> The family life that is depicted in today's cinemas, even when the action purports to take place in Germany, leaves a peculiarly strange impression; seeing it, one often feels as if one had gone on a short trip abroad because there is so little of either German habits or the German family. Should we allow the broad mass of our people henceforth to be surrendered to the suggestive effect of films of foreign origin that are in part deliberately tendentious? It is difficult to understand how anyone could still be blind to the dangers that this holds for our national life.[10]

Censorship alone would not, he felt, solve the problem. A rigid censorship in a Germany surrounded by countries where unbridled licence reigned supreme would be worse than ineffective, for it would also cripple the nascent German film industry and make German films themselves virtually unexportable. Instead Duenschmann advocated that state-supported cinemas should be set up, like state-supported theatres, to function in competition with private enterprise, to attract audiences away from the salacious and the harmful towards the wholesome and uplifting:

> Very recently several German cities (Altona, Stettin) have resolved to fight the 'brutalising influence of sensation-hungry cinemas' on the people, and especially on growing youth, by setting up cinema theatres under municipal management. Should not the state be capable, even more easily than is a city, of intervening in this manner for the common good?[11]

But in Germany, as in Russia, such warnings about the need to harnèss the power of the cinema were to go unheeded by the authorities until it was too late.

What then was the state of the cinema in Germany before the out-break of the First World War? The first German film producer of any note was Oskar Messter who, starting in 1897, produced hundreds of short novelty films.[12] He was also a great experimenter and was the first to introduce the close-up, the use of artificial lighting, animation and the sound film to Germany. Sound was not particularly successful either in Germany or anywhere else at this time: it depended on synchronising the film with a gramophone recording and proved to be expensive as well as awkward. Films were developing naturally without gimmicks like this: above all they were getting longer and by 1910 an increasing number of *Grossfilme* (feature films) were being made and with increasing length came increasing complexity in the story line.[13] It was now possible to film an adaptation of a stage play and this in turn attracted larger audiences for the cinema. By 1910 one provincial theatre reported having lost half its audience for the cheap seats, and audiences for the music hall and the circus were also diminishing.[14] Whereas in 1900 there had been only two cinemas in the whole of Germany, in Hamburg and Würzburg, by 1910 there were 480, and by 1914 the number had reached 2,446, seating over a million.[15] This figure excludes the still considerable number of *Wanderkinos* that were found throughout the country.

The foundation in 1907 of the Projektions-A.G. Union, the first attempt to group together cinema theatres in different parts of the country into a single distribution network marked a decisive turning point. Karl Demeter has pointed out that, even before the First World War:

A newspaper, journal or book is usually published in an edition of thousands or tens of thousands, occasionally hundreds of thousands of copies; and, even if one accepts that each of these copies is read on average by several people, the number of people who read a book or a newspaper reaches, let alone exceeds, a million only in exceptional cases. On the other hand a great modern work of the cinema, when it makes a rather good impression, is seen on average by between five and ten million people.[16]

Elsewhere he explained this by drawing attention to the relative lack of effort required to absorb a film as compared with a book:

But, while the reading of printed matter is a skill that the individual must first learn and is furthermore bound up with the comprehension of the language involved, the film makes direct and sole use of the sensual receptivity of the eye to transmit its content and it is therefore neither checked nor hindered by any educational or linguistic limits in its range of influence.[17]

Cinemas were concentrated, not surprisingly, in the urban areas, where their potential audience was greatest. Cinemas attracted the same kind of people, on the whole, as those who frequented the fairground: indeed Demeter took an even dimmer view of the cinema audience, seeing its only alternative source of pleasure as 'alcohol or even worse forms of drug'.[18] For this reason it proved particularly difficult to make the cinema appear respectable in the eyes of the higher social strata of the population. Established actors were most reluctant to appear on the screen, even though the more excitable theatre owners saw in the cinema a lethal threat to the continued existence of the so-called 'legitimate' theatre — or perhaps because they saw it as a threat. As films grew longer attempts were made to film established plays, but these either bored the public or, like the 1910 film version of Schiller's *Don Carlos*, attracted opprobrium from right-thinking members of the Cinema Reform Movement for straying too far from the original play. But here too the new Projektions-A.G. Union had a significant effect: the head of the organisation, Paul Davidson, made contact with Max Reinhardt and theatrical opposition to the cinema began to fade away. Actors were beginning to realise that the cinema could supplement their income in two ways: it could pay more for a single performance and, in addition, it gave them a wider audience who might later want to see them in person on the stage. In other words, on the eve of the First World War the cinema was on the verge of respectability. New studios were being built in the suburbs of Berlin at Tempelhof and Neubabelsberg; the latter passed later into the hands of Ufa, then became the main production centre for Nazi propaganda films, and are to this day used by DEFA, the state film organisation of the GDR. But, despite this expansion, Germany still produced only a small proportion of the films shown on German screens: it has been estimated that in a two-month period in the autumn of 1912 the German film industry produced only 7 per cent of the films needed to satisfy domestic demand. The other 93 per cent were imported: 35 per cent from France, 29 per cent from the USA and 25 per cent from Italy.[19]

Germany also imported films from Denmark, but Davidson was able, with the promise of a lucrative contract, to lure from the Nordisk firm of Copenhagen their principal star, Asta Nielsen. She was to become the leading actress of the pre-war German cinema, and to be to the soldiers of the First World War, German and French alike, what Marlene Dietrich was to the soldiers of the Second. Her image sent the poet Apollinaire into ecstasies: 'She is all! She is the vision of the drinker and the dream of the lonely man.'[20] Kracauer has written: 'The German screen world would be incomplete without the characters Asta Nielsen created during the silent era.'[21] With the exception of this Danish actress the first two decades of the German cinema may be summarised in the words of the actor and director, Paul Wegener, speaking in 1920:

> It is quite understandable that the first people to descend on an as yet untried invention should be those who have failed in their own profession, those who in former times would have been sent to America to find an unknown fortune there. Adventurers of all sorts always head for new discoveries and inventions. So it was in the early days of the cinema. As a result this instrument, one of mankind's greatest discoveries, whose future possibilities have by no means yet been exploited, became at first a playground for people who did not know what to do with it. At first it was just a matter of running off a film, of running it off as cheaply as possible and selling it at the highest possible price. The idea that this instrument could be anything more than merchandise dawned only later.[22]

The First World War put the German cinema on its feet, although in the beginning it looked as if disaster threatened: the German market was cut off from its main source of films and equipment — France — by the war and it seemed to have neither the men, the resources, nor the experience to fill the gap. Demand was enormous and it grew rapidly: in addition to the needs of the existing network of cinemas, films were required to entertain the troops at the front. At first there was a flood of films with a patriotic theme, or at least a patriotic title, like *On the Field of Honour, The Call of the Fatherland* or *The Watch on the Rhine*, but once the victorious German advance had been halted and the exhilaration of the first months of war had begun to evaporate, audiences looked increasingly to the cinema for escape from the reality of their everyday lives, for entertainment pure and simple. The middle classes began to take the cinema seriously, although it remained primarily what it had been before, the opium of the working masses:

> Just as the sailor on the lonely ocean finds solace in the bottle, and
> the soldier in the trenches finds it in nicotine, so the factory, shop or
> office worker takes refuge in the cinema so frequently because as a
> rule it gives him what he is looking for: fantasy and sensation in
> contrast to monotony – and the illusion of being transported to a
> dream land of luxury and wealth, of the erotic and the exotic.[23]

The desire for escapist entertainment caused a boom in German film production: the number of production companies rose from 28 in 1913 to
245 by 1919.[24] The films made ranged from comedy to near pornography and included the first short comedies of Ernst Lubitsch and the
melodramatic adventures of Harry Piel, the German Douglas Fairbanks.
By contrast the industry also began to produce films that were to fore-
shadow the psychological and spiritual obsessions that were to pre-
occupy the German cinema during the 1920s and to give it the reputa-
tion of being the 'haunted screen'.[25] These films were *The Golem* (1915)
and *Homunculus* (1916). Both films dealt with figures who were
artificial creations. The Golem is a clay statue made by the Rabbi Loew
in the mediaeval Prague ghetto, a statue that can be brought to life by a
magic incantation. The statue is found by contemporary workmen
and taken to a dealer who discovers how to bring it to life. The live
statue falls in love with the dealer's daughter and becomes human; but
she rejects what is to her a monster and so he becomes one, rampaging
through the city until he falls to his death, his body shattered into clay
fragments. The sequel, *The Golem: How He Came into the World*, was
filmed in 1920. *Homunculus* was a man created in a test-tube, artificial
and without a soul. Discovering the secret of his genesis, he feels an
outcast, yearning for love. But he is constantly rejected when people
find out who he is: 'Homunculus, the man without a soul, the devil's
servant, a monster!' He seeks revenge by making himself dictator and
provoking the masses into a revolt so that he can crush them. He is
finally destroyed by a thunderbolt. Both Homunculus and the Golem
are characters who live abnormal lives and die abnormal deaths, both
search for love but remain unloved: their spirit however lived on to
haunt the German cinema with themes of psychological disturbance and
supernatural terror.

But how far was the cinema used for political purposes by the
German government during the First World War? Oskar Messter was, like
the Skobelev Committee in Russia, given the exclusive right to film at

the front and his firm provided German cinemas with a weekly newsreel
report from the battle-front.[26] These films from the front were subject
to censorship by the Supreme Command, and indeed all films shown in
Germany during the war were subjected to censorship by the military.
In July 1915 the government forbade the export of films to save
materials; in February 1916 it banned imports to save foreign currency
and to prevent the infiltration of enemy propaganda; finally, in January
1917 it introduced censorship of films for export to Allied and neutral
countries, so that it could control the image of Germany that was,
quite literally, being projected abroad.[27] It is clear then that the
German government was beginning to realise the potential of the
cinema for influencing morale and public opinion, and that, as the war
dragged on, it was becoming increasingly aware of the importance of
public opinion. German businessmen were also waking up to the
cinema's possibilities: before the outbreak of war they had already
detected the effects of what they took to be British propaganda on
their overseas markets, particularly in South America and in China, and
in November 1916 their concern led to the establishment of the German
Cinematographic Company (Deutsche Lichtbild-Gesellschaft) or
Deulig.[28] Deulig was backed by the industrialist Hugo Stinnes and by
Alfred Hugenberg, then chairman of Krupps and later press baron and
owner of Ufa, and was intended to organise the production and distribution of German films to counter British and French propaganda in
neutral countries.[29] Almost its first act was to establish a subsidiary
company to concentrate on films for the Balkans and the Orient,
although at this stage there was no intention of starting production
until the war was over. In January 1917 the Supreme Command set
up its own organisation, the Photographic and Film Office (Bild- und
Filmamt), or Bufa.[30] Whereas Deulig's purpose had been a commercial
and peace-time one, Bufa's was clearly political and closely allied to the
war effort: the first paragraph of its statute described it as a 'military
institution'.[31] The first attempts to co-ordinate its activities with those
of Deulig failed precisely because of this difference of purpose, but the
urgent need to counter enemy propaganda was becoming clearer month
by month On 4 July 1917 in a letter to the War Ministry, General
Ludendorff underlined the importance of the film as a propaganda
weapon:

> The War has demonstrated the overwhelming power of the image and
> the film as a medium for education and influence. Unfortunately
> our enemies have used the advantage they had over us in this field

so thoroughly that we have suffered considerable damage. For the
duration of the War the film will not lose its immense significance
as a political and military medium of influence. For this reason it is
absolutely essential, if the War is to be brought to a successful conclusion, to ensure that the film is used to maximum effect wherever
Germany can still exert its influence.[32]

Ludendorff regarded the centralisation of the German film industry as
'an urgent military necessity'.[33] At a time of virtual military dictatorship Ludendorff's ideas were to be treated as orders; hence, on 18
December 1917 a new umbrella organisation, financed jointly by
private industry and by the state, came into being. It was to be called
Universum-Film-Aktiengesellschaft, or Ufa for short.[34] From the point
of view of war-time propaganda, Ufa came too late, but it did exert a
fundamental influence on the subsequent development of the German
cinema in peace-time. Ludwig Klitzsch, one of the industrialists who had
helped to found Deulig, observed some years later: 'After the collapse
of 1918 Germany demonstrated its complete independence in the field
of film production to an astonished world. Ufa soon proved to be the
largest film enterprise in Europe.'[35] Four years after the end of the war,
Germany's film production was second only to that of the United
States.

The closing months of 1918 ushered in a period of prolonged social,
economic and political upheaval for Germany. The old order fell and
was replaced by a hesitant republic: political forms changed, but the
social and economic forces that underpinned those forms remained
largely unaffected. The revolution that had been anticipated did not
materialise. Deprived of the liberating purge of revolution and the
expected apocalypse, disappointed in their aspirations for the creation
of a new world, German artists, in all spheres of artistic activity, fragmented. Broadly, and very crudely, we can detect two conflicting
tendencies. Some artists endeavoured to harness their talents for what
they saw as the general good, exercising a social conscience and echoing
many of the experiments that were being conducted in Russia, which
for them was generally synonymous with an invigorating new world of
socialism. In a sense many of them were enjoying revolution at second
hand, and perhaps also at a safe distance. They tried to give art a definite social function and a clear political purpose. They also tried to
broaden its social base, to bring art to the people and the people to art.
In this group we may include men like Grosz, Heartfield, Piscator and
Brecht, and to some extent also the Bauhaus school. At the other end of

the spectrum were those whose art became introspective, rejecting the everyday in favour of the spiritual, the mystical or the downright abnormal. These artists would not upset the system because for the most part they had abandoned the political struggle, or considered it beneath them. They were conservative, if only by default, and their conservatism assured this artistic tendency of a greater role in that most commercial of all the arts – the cinema.

The best illustration of the problems facing the radical artist in the cinema during the Weimar Republic is provided by one of the first, and at the same time one of the most famous, films from the period, *The Cabinet of Dr Caligari*, made in 1919.[36] It is the classic example of revolutionary art tamed into reaction. The original script for the film was written by Hans Janowitz and Carl Mayer. A series of unsolved murders have been committed in a small north German town: suspicion falls on the somnambulist Cesare, who is dressed in a skin-tight black suit and kept in a coffin. Cesare is controlled by Dr Caligari. The hero, Francis, begins to suspect Caligari after Cesare has correctly predicted his friend's death. He spies on Caligari, but the doctor has substituted an effigy in Cesare's coffin and, while Francis watches this effigy, the real Cesare is abducting his girlfriend, Jane, and is chased by her father across the rooftops of the town. Cesare collapses with exhaustion, Jane is rescued and the truth about the effigy becomes apparent. Caligari escapes and Francis pursues him to a lunatic asylum where he has sought shelter. Francis is dumbfounded to discover that Caligari *is* in fact the director of the asylum, but he decides to confront him with the corpse of Cesare. The sight of the dead sleepwalker causes Caligari to lose his reason and he is put in a straitjacket. It was the scriptwriters' intention to portray Caligari as a symbol of the tyranny of unlimited authority, with Cesare, the common man, as his helpless and innocent victim. As Kracauer, who first brought the background of the film to light, has remarked: 'The revolutionary meaning of the story reveals itself unmistakably at the end, with the disclosure of the psychiatrist as Caligari: reason overpowers unreasonable power, insane authority is symbolically abolished.'[37]

The message of the script was clearly revolutionary: the message of the film was not. The director Robert Wiene, with the support of the producer Erich Pommer, placed the authors' story into a framework that negated its essential significance. Francis is a patient at the lunatic asylum; seeing Jane, a fellow patient, walk by, he begins to tell another inmate a clearly imaginary story of his relationship with her. That story is the one outlined in the original script; when it is completed

Francis and the other patients, who include Cesare, go indoors where the director of the asylum meets them. Francis attacks him, is restrained by the attendants and led into a sick-room, where the director comes to examine him. Donning his horn-rimmed spectacles, he *appears* to be Caligari; now the director understands Francis' illness he will, he says, be able to cure him. The revolutionary intentions of the original story are reversed and the film now appears to offer an anodyne reassurance that all is well, confirming reaction rather than convicting it. This change from script to film was facilitated by retaining the original distorted Expressionist sets and costumes for the original story, while filming the framework story against a more realistic and normal background. The central story is thus quite clearly placed in Francis' warped imagination and in a wider context authority is seen as sane while rebellion is equated with insanity.[38] Disinfected of its anti-authoritarian stance, revolutionary art was thus tamed into reaction.

Caligari set the tone for the Weimar cinema in more ways than one: in its general outlook, in its use of symbolism, and in its preoccupation with the grotesque, the tortured and the abnormal. It had, in Kracauer's words, shown 'the soul being faced with the seemingly unavoidable alternative of tyranny or chaos'.[39] This particular theme can be detected, either overtly or covertly, in a large number of films of the 1920s. The Weimar cinema is distinguished by an obsession with the nature and exercise of power; the Nazi film was concerned with the trappings of that power. If we take power as the central theme of the German film of this period we can include under the post-*Caligari* umbrella a large number of works that were not directly political, such as *Pandora's Box*, *Variety*, *The Blue Angel*, or even a mountain film like *The Blue Light*. There were however several films whose concern was either primarily or at least openly political: these include *Fridericus Rex* (which Kracauer describes as 'pure propaganda for a restoration of the monarchy'[40]), *The Joyless Street*, *Metropolis* and *The Testament of Dr Mabuse*.

Metropolis portrays a world of two extremes in which an upper class living above ground exploits a subterranean army of worker-slaves. This order of things is dislodged by the saint-like Maria who calls for the heart to mediate between the worlds of hand and brain, worker and ruler. In a desperate reaction the industrialist who controls Metropolis commissions the mad scientist Rotwang to build a robot Maria that incites the workers to a rebellion and unleashes an orgy of destruction and violence. The rebellion becomes self-destructive as the workers' city is inundated and at the end of the film the real Maria, the robot having been destroyed, seals a symbolic alliance between capital and labour: but this ensures only that the previous suppression of the worker-slaves will now give way to their submission. Goebbels was, needless to say, profoundly impressed by the film[41] and ironically it was *Metropolis* that almost bankrupted Ufa and placed it in the hands of Alfred Hugenberg.[42] The last film that Lang made in the Weimar period was *The Testament of Dr Mabuse*. He agreed to make the film only 'when I realised that there was a chance for a veiled comment on Nazism in the subject of an asylum director hypnotised by his patient'.[43] In a programme note for the film's American première he wrote:

> This film was made as an allegory to show Hitler's processes of terrorism. Slogans and doctrines of the Third Reich have been put into the mouths of criminals in the film. Thus I hoped to expose the masked Nazi theory of the necessity to deliberately destroy everything which is precious to a people ... Then, when everything collapsed and they were thrown into utter despair, they would try to find help in the 'new order'.[44]

Under the maxim that 'Mankind must be thrown into an abyss of terror' Mabuse exerts a hypnotic control over his psychiatrist, Baum, who like Dr Caligari leads a double life: on the one hand he is the respected head of a mental hospital while on the other he controls a vast underground organisation bent on crime and terror. The familiar alternatives of tyranny and chaos are once more paraded before us, but this time such an apparently bleak choice is portrayed as the figment of a madman's imagination. With the destruction of Mabuse and Baum the extremism of the National Socialists is also symbolically undermined. But the film was too late: it was ready for release in March 1933 and Hitler had come to power in January.

Power need not of course be exercised in a political context, although that does not necessarily deprive it of any political significance. We can find a large number of films from the Weimar period that deal with the exercise of power in other spheres, sometimes spiritual, sometimes psychological and sometimes a combination of the two. Films like *Nosferatu*, *Vanina*, *Waxworks* and *Dr Mabuse the Gambler* were concerned in the first instance with the exercise of supernatural tyrannical power. Others reflected resignation and even submission in the face of fate: *Destiny* and the two parts of Lang's *The Nibelungs* (*Siegfried* and *Kriemhild's Revenge*). Yet other films were concerned with the power of strange forces over the individual, and that power

was always destructive, especially if it was based on human emotions
like love: *Genuine, Warning Shadows, Phantom, Variety, Nju, Faust,
Pandora's Box, The Blue Angel* and *M*. Pabst's *Pandora's Box*, based on
plays by Frank Wedekind, portrays the destructiveness of sexual
passion. The principal character, Lulu, played by Louise Brooks, lures
men to their destruction but is herself destroyed in an uncontrollable
fit of passion by Jack the Ripper.[45] In *Variety* it is sexual jealousy that
causes murder,[46] as it does in *Warning Shadows*. In *The Blue Angel* an
upstanding pillar of society, played by Emil Jannings, is laid low by his
lust for the night-club dancer, Lola-Lola, played by Marlene Dietrich.[47]
Overwhelmed by the mysterious forces of sexual attraction, he sacrifices
first the respect of his pupils, then his career in exchange for a parody
of marriage that leaves him literally crowing like an impotent cockerel.
In *M* Peter Lorre, as the child murderer, succumbs helplessly to the
pathological impulses of his own twisted emotions:

> I can't help myself! I haven't any control over this evil thing that's
> inside me — the fire, the voices, the torment! . . .
>   I want to escape . . . to escape from myself! . . . But it's impossible.
> I can't. I can't escape.[48]

The murderer and the prostitute serve as symbols of the powerful forces
undermining the established order, forces that will destroy everything if
they are allowed to. We return therefore to the 'seemingly unavoidable
alternative of tyranny or chaos'. It has been said by many, and felt by
more, that Kracauer exaggerated, overinterpreted or oversimplified the
thematic coherence of the Weimar cinema.[49] It is said in part by those
who feel unable to accept the cinema as a serious art form and who
will therefore not apply to the film the criteria that they would apply
to a play, but it is also said by subsequent generations of film
enthusiasts. Kracauer himself points out that many of the films concerned, although highly regarded later, attracted only limited audiences
at the time. This was true of *Caligari*, which was 'too high-brow to
become popular in Germany',[50] and it was true of *Warning Shadows*,
of which the cameraman involved later wrote: 'It only found response
from the film aesthetes, making no impression on the general public.'[51]
It was however also true that the obsessions of the German cinema
mirrored important facets of the country's cultural life as a whole and
the film often found its inspiration from the outside cultural world:
The Blue Angel was based, for instance, on Heinrich Mann's novel,
Professor Unrath. But, even if the post-*Caligari* school had made

intellectual films for intellectual audiences, this need not detract from
the significance of the films they made, but may merely alter that
significance by placing it in a different context. Just as the Soviet films
of the 1920s are important in that relatively directed society, not for
the audiences they attracted but for what they tell us about the officially
encouraged image of that society, so the post-*Caligari* films of the
Weimar period are significant because they represent a cultural articu-
lation of a widely felt unease, what Eisner calls a 'subconscious world
full of anguish, unrest and a vague remorse, obsessed by the memory of
a glorious past'.[52] It was that unease, a sense of at least potential
helplessness, that became associated with the Weimar Republic and
assisted it into its grave.

Mass audiences did not however flock to see the *Caligari* type of
film, because they preferred a light form of escapism. *Caligari* and its
successors were intellectual films for intellectual audiences. The mass
audience looked for entertainment pure and simple. For this reason
German film companies, and particularly Ufa, made a large number of
so-called 'costume films' in the early 1920s. Eisner has remarked:

> The flood of historical films that swamped the German cinema
> from 1919 to 1923-24 — usually designated, rather significantly,
> by the term *Kostümfilme* — was an expression of the escapism of a
> poverty-stricken, disappointed nation which, moreover, had always
> been fond of the glitter of parades.[53]

One of the leading directors of these historical films was Ernst Lubitsch,
who shortly moved to Hollywood. He was responsible for *Medea, The
Pharaoh's Woman, Ann Boleyn* (described by Kracauer as 'an elaborate
depiction of Henry VIII's sex life'[54]) and *Madame Dubarry*, a film about
Louis XV's mistress that in Kracauer's eyes 'reduces the Revolution to
a derivative of private passions'.[55] Other directors imitated the style if
not the technique with films such as *Danton, Lucretia Borgia, Othello,
Carlos and Elizabeth* and *Peter the Great*, and even *Helen or the Fall of
Troy*. These films were intended mainly to satisfy home audiences but
they were also meant to emulate the worldwide success of the pre-war
Italian spectaculars like *Cabiria* and *Quo Vadis*. Even *Fridericus Rex*,
the pro-monarchist film mentioned earlier, was made 'not for Germany,
but for the whole world'.[56] But the demand for such films as inflation
gathered pace led Ufa to a rapid expansion that soon became an over-
expansion. With the financial difficulties that followed the stabilisation
of the mark in 1924-25 Ufa ran short of capital and had to accept

American assistance to save it from an untimely bankruptcy. Ufa had
hoped for arrangements that would have ensured it an outlet for its
own films in the US market, but it was in no position to insist. Instead
the largest film-producing company in Germany and Europe had to sign
agreements with Paramount, MGM and Universal that left those companies with an option on Ufa products but left Ufa with no similar right
to select the American films that would be shown through its European
distribution network.[57] In 1925 65 per cent of all films shown in
German cinemas had already emanated from the United States but the
new arrangements made the situation even worse the following year.

Table 10.1: Origin of Films Shown in German Cinemas, by % [58]

	1923		1926	
	German	American	German	American
Feature films	60.6	24.5	38.2	44.3
Short films	38.3	60.8	1.1	94.9

Ufa appealed unsuccessfully to the Reich government for assistance but
it was eventually a consortium of right-wing forces led by Alfred
Hugenberg that took control of the company in order, in his own
words, to 'preserve for the national outlook this German cultural
institution that has become so valuable'.[59] Ludwig Klitzsch, who with
Hugenberg and Stinnes had helped to found Deulig in 1916, became
the new chairman of Ufa: the wheel had turned almost full circle.
Klitzsch was also head of SPIO (Spitzenorganisation der Deutschen
Filmindustrie), the organisation of German film producers, and this
enabled Hugenberg, in addition to his considerable press empire, to
control the policy not merely of Ufa but of all the most important
sections of the German commercial cinema. One of the first decisions
taken by the new Ufa leadership involved a complete ban on further
showings of Soviet films in its cinemas:[60] *Battleship Potemkin* had been
too successful for their comfort.[61] Instead audiences were to be offered
an increasing number of films that conveyed the nationalist viewpoint
and in particular reiterated the values of the old Prussia: *The Flute
Concert of Sans Souci, Barberina, the Dancer of Sans Souci* and *The
Anthem of Leuthen* are obvious examples. At the same time the
tradition of escapist entertainment was continued by the 'mountain
film', a romantic *genre* that cast the same kind of spell over German
audiences as the South Seas have cast over the public for Hollywood

films. The most celebrated examples of this *genre* are *The White Hell of Pitz Palu* and *The Blue Light*, both of which starred Leni Riefenstahl, later director of *Triumph of the Will*.

In addition to the intellectual audience catered to by the post-*Caligari* school of film makers, and the mass commercial audience at whom the historical epics and costume and mountain films were directed, there was a third cinema audience in Weimar Germany: that for the so-called proletarian or workers' cinema. Just as Kracauer, with benefit of hindsight, may well have exaggerated the contemporary importance of the psychological preoccupations of the Weimar film because of an apparent continuity through to the Nazi period, so today's film historians in the GDR and elsewhere tend to exaggerate the contemporary significance of the proletarian cinema in the Weimar Republic for similar reasons of assumed historical continuity. One such historian has written recently:

> *Kuhle Wampe* was the last work of the proletarian-revolutionary film movement in Germany before the onset of fascism, which may well have interrupted a great development but could not destroy it. The tradition of socialist German film making established by this film and its predecessors was preserved by communist artists in exile and extended in collaboration with Soviet film artists. It was brought into the construction of a socialist film art in the German Democratic Republic.[62]

The proletarian cinema in Germany took its inspiration from, and was assisted by, the Soviet Union. It involved those artists already referred to who wished to give the art of the film a definite social function and a clear political purpose and to ensure that in Germany, as in the Soviet Union as they saw it, the cinema would become the art of the masses, by the masses and for the masses. To this end they were of course also concerned to provide a counterweight to what they regarded as the bourgeois cinema and its capitalist propaganda.

It would be misleading to assert, or to assume, that there was an unbridgeable gap between the proletarian and the commercial cinema in Weimar Germany: there are strong elements of social if not socialist realism in the sound films of Fritz Lang (*M* and *The Testament of Dr Mabuse*) and in the films of Georg Wilhelm Pabst, such as *The Joyless Street, The Love of Jeanne Ney, West Front 1918, Comradeship* and even *The Threepenny Opera*. The fact that Brecht's collaboration with Pabst in the filming of his stage success ended in the law courts, and that

Brecht lost his case, cannot obscure his willingness to collaborate in the first place. The assumption that realism and a social conscience were the exclusive prerogative of the proletarian revolutionary workers' cinema[63] was not held by Brecht when he agreed to write the screenplay for the film. In fact the script that he wrote for this commercial film was far sharper in its social criticism than the successful stage version had been. Admittedly it was for precisely this reason that Brecht was asked to revise the screenplay, and for the same reason that he failed to do so. But even the finished film, made without Brecht's participation and against his wishes, is just as trenchant and effective in its social criticism as was the play: indeed it brought the essence of Brecht's message to a far wider audience, and a commercial cinema audience at that.[64] Nevertheless, although the gap between them was not as great as might at first appear, the proletarian cinema did have a quite distinct identity from that of the commercial cinema, and a very different purpose and function.

We may trace the origins of an organised proletarian cinema in Germany back to the foundation in 1921 by Willi Münzenberg of the International Workers' Aid with the original intention of providing relief for the famine-struck population of Soviet Russia. Pursuing the maxim, 'We have to organise the intellectuals', Münzenberg proved himself to be a master propagandist. He virtually invented the front organisation and brilliantly exploited his discovery of the fellow traveller to create a large number of organisations, both in Germany and elsewhere, that involved even non-Communists in humanitarian and apparently non-partisan activities that effectively assisted the Soviet Union or the international Communist cause.[65] Since the Soviet Union was presented as the only bulwark against fascism in a troubled world while the ailing liberal democracies did nothing, it is hardly surprising that Münzenberg's activities were so successful. He established the Aufbau (Construction) organisation in Germany which acted as an umbrella for his various enterprises. Aufbau raised an international loan for the Soviet government in 1922, set up a publishing house (the Neue Deutsche Verlag), issued illustrated magazines like *Sowjet-Russland in Bildern (Soviet Russia in Pictures)* and later *Arbeiter Illustrierte (Workers' Illustrated)*, intended as a working-class antidote to the *Berliner Illustrierte*, the German equivalent of *Life* or *Picture Post*; by 1926 *Arbeiter Illustrierte* had a circulation of almost a million). Aufbau was also responsible for the bulk purchase in Germany of much-needed films, film stock and equipment on behalf of the beleaguered Soviet cinema organisations: in the years 1922-23 it supplied 80 per cent of the USSR's total imports

of these materials, and these figures included one million metres of
negative and five million metres of positive film stock.[66] In February
1926 International Workers' Aid, again acting through Aufbau, founded
Prometheus-Film GmbH to distribute and exhibit Soviet films in
Germany.[67] Thus it was that Berlin became the gateway for Soviet films
into the outside world and for films from the West into the Soviet
Union, and it was through the need to re-title Soviet films for a commercial audience in Germany that *October* became *Ten Days That Shook the
World* and *The Heir to Genghis Khan* became *Storm over Asia*.

However the most famous film imported from Soviet Russia was
Battleship Potemkin which achieved a *succès de scandale* after being
banned by the censor. Even when the ban was lifted, and the film
permitted for exhibition in a significantly cut version, members of the
German armed forces were still forbidden to go and see it.[68] The film
can only be described as a smash hit with German audiences: in the late
spring of 1926 it was showing at more cinemas in Berlin alone than in
the whole of the Soviet Union, and it was only the film's phenomenal
success in Germany that persuaded the Soviet film authorities to re-
release it in its country of origin.[69] But the difficulties experienced with
the German authorities over the exhibition and distribution of
Battleship Potemkin were symptomatic of the obstacles that Prometheus-
Film faced generally in trying to persuade commercial cinema networks
to show Soviet films.

In 1927 another organisation, Weltfilm, was set up to produce and
distribute proletarian films for proletarian audiences through workers'
organisations and clubs and trade union and Communist Party outlets.[70]
The films made and the organisation of distribution again followed the
Soviet example: many of the films made, almost all of them either
newsreels or documentaries, were designed to strengthen and develop
the workers' sense of class consciousness and common identity with
the cause. In this way KPD propaganda in the Weimar Republic may
be compared with that of the Bolsheviks in Russia before the October
Revolution.

In the meanwhile Prometheus embarked on a programme of co-
production with the Soviet firm Mezhrabpom (an acronym of the
Russian words for International Workers' Aid — Mezhdunarodnaya
Rabochaya Pomoshch'), which had been set up specifically for this
purpose. Their first co-production was *Superfluous People*, made in
1926 from a Chekhov short story. It was not a commercial success, as
it disappointed audiences who were expecting another *Potemkin*, and
it is chiefly remarkable for its cast which included Werner Krauss,

Heinrich George, Eugen Klöpfer and Fritz Rasp, all of whom went on to act in Nazi propaganda films. Other films co-produced in this fashion included *The Living Corpse*, from the play by Tolstoy and starring the Soviet director, Vsevolod Pudovkin, in the leading role, and *Salamander*, for which the Soviet People's Commissar for Enlightenment, Anatoli Lunacharsky, wrote the screenplay. None of these films however achieved the fame, or notoriety, of *Kuhle Wampe*.

Kuhle Wampe, subtitled *Whose World Is It?*, was written in part by Bertolt Brecht and directed by the young Bulgarian, Slatan Dudow. It took its main title from a colony of tents housing the unemployed on the outskirts of Berlin. The first two parts of the film depicted the gloom, misery and suffering that existed among the unemployed workers. The final part is set against the background of a workers' sports festival that offers a clear hope for a better future, if only the workers display an organised sense of solidarity. In March 1932 the film was banned by the censor on the grounds that: 'A film that so effectively undermines the audience's faith in the effectiveness and willingness of the state in the fight against poverty and misery rocks the foundations of the state which is based on a democratic republican constitution.'[71]

The censor's decision caused a storm of protest, and not only in the left-wing press. It was re-submitted and passed for exhibition, but only with major cuts, at the end of April.[72] The film's problem was that, for once, a proletarian revolutionary film really did have a revolutionary message. The closing song of the original film, excised by the censor, concluded with the verse:

Forwards, not forgetting
Our street and our field.
Forwards, not forgetting:
Whose street is the street,
Whose world is the world?[73]

This verse, like the scene of nude group bathing that preceded it, was too strong for the censor. The Republic already appeared to be tottering: messages like this could prove fatal. Visiting Berlin during the year the film critic Winifred Bryher observed:

After two or three days, the visitor wonders why revolution does not happen, not that there is any specific thing to provoke it apparent to the eyes, but outbreak against this odd insecure heaviness is to be

preferred than waiting for a storm that has sometimes got to burst
. . . The film that interests Berlin most at this moment is *Kuhle
Wampe.*[74]

It is perhaps curious and ironic that the cinema should apparently first
have been used on a large scale as a propaganda weapon by the left-
wing forces in Germany, for there is as yet no evidence that the
National Socialists had recourse to the cinema before they took power.
This use by the left is undoubtedly due to the Soviet example and to
Soviet assistance. But merely because we can clearly identify the KPD's
sponsorship of film for propaganda purposes, we must not fall into the
trap of assuming that this was a unique phenomenon. It cannot be denied
that the commercial cinema in Germany, as elsewhere, produced an
overwhelming majority of films that were either overtly or covertly
politically conservative: the reasons for this are obvious, because the
people who could afford to finance commercial film production had a
vested interest in the preservation of the existing economic order, even
if they were unhappy with some aspects of its politics. Furthermore, it
would be foolish to assume that Hugenberg, having built up a huge
press empire and acquired Ufa to 'preserve [it] for the national outlook',
was unaware of the political value of a largely narcotic cinema: he was,
after all, leader of the DNVP, the German Conservative Party. In a sense
therefore the Nazis did not have to worry about making their own film
propaganda at this stage, because Hugenberg was already determined
that Ufa would not rock the boat. If we are to find fault with the Weimar
cinema, it must be that it failed, with several notable exceptions, to
come to terms with contemporary social and political problems. This
is a valid criticism of the German cinema before the Nazi takeover and
in that sense Kracauer's 'From Caligari to Hitler' thesis, though perhaps
exaggerated and oversimplified, is justified. It is however a criticism
that can justifiably be levelled with the benefit of hindsight at most
cinemas in most places at most times[75] and it is certainly a valid
criticism of the cinema anywhere in the 1920s — even of the Soviet
cinema.[76] Complaining about the ban on *Kuhle Wampe* in 1932 a
German critic wrote that the issues at stake were: 'Should Germany
be photographed or not? That is the first question. The second question
is: how should it be photographed?'[77] Within a year the Nazis were to
provide their own answer to this question, and for twelve years there
would be no more questions, only answers.

Notes

1. G. Lukács, 'Gedanken zu einer Aesthetik des Kino', reprinted in: K. Witte (ed.), *Theorie des Kinos. Ideologiekritik der Traumfabrik* (Frankfurt-am-Main, 1972), p. 142.

2. Letter from General Ludendorff, Chief of the German Army General Staff, to the Imperial War Ministry in Berlin, dated 4 July 1917 and reprinted in: W. von Bredow and R. Zurek (eds), *Film und Gesellschaft in Deutschland. Dokumente und Materialien* (Hamburg, 1975), p. 102.

3. O. Kalbus, *Vom Werden deutscher Filmkunst* (Altona-Bahrenfeld, 1935), vol. 1, p. 1.

4. S. Kracauer, *From Caligari to Hitler. A Psychological History of the German Film* (Princeton, 1947), p. 18.

5. H. Duenschmann. 'Kinematograph und Psychologie der Volksmenge. Eine sozialpolitische Studie', *Konservative Monatsschrift für Politik, Literatur und Kunst*, 1912, no. 9, 920.

6. Ibid., 921.

7. Ibid., 924-5.

8. Ibid., 925.

9. Ibid., 924.

10. Ibid., 925.

11. Ibid., 930.

12. Kracauer, *From Caligari to Hitler*, p. 16.

13. In 1902 the average film had been 60 metres long; in 1906, 150–300m; 1910, 400–700m; 1910-14, 700–1,000m; 1915-18, 1,000–2,000m. Figures cited in: Bredow and Zurek, *Film und Gesellschaft in Deutschland*, p. 18.

14. K. Zimmereimer, *Die Filmzensur* (Breslau-Neukirch, 1934), pp. 27-8.

15. A. Kallmann, 'Die Konzernierung in der Filmindustrie, erläutert an den Filmindustrien Deutschlands und Amerikas' (Unpublished doctoral thesis, Jena, 1932), p. 5, quoted in: P. Bächlin, *Der Film als Ware* (Basle, 1945), p. 214, note 23.

16. K. Demeter, 'Die soziologischen Grundlagen des Kinowesens', *Deutsche Rundschau*, 1926, no. 10, 57 (hereafter: 'Grundlagen'.)

17. K. Demeter, 'Die Entwicklung des deutschen Films zu einem Faktor der Weltpolitik und Weltwirtschaft', *Archiv für Politik und Geschichte*, 1925, no. 2, 607 (hereafter: 'Entwicklung'.)

18. Demeter, 'Grundlagen', 59.

19. E. Altenloh, *Zur Soziologie des Kino* (Jena, 1914), p. 10.

20. Quoted in: P. Diaz, *Asta Nielsen. Eine Biographie unserer populären Künstlerin* (Berlin, n.d.), p. 7.

21. Kracauer, *From Caligari to Hitler*, p. 27.

22. *Der Spiegel*, 15 February 1920, quoted in: Demeter, 'Entwicklung', 609.

23. K. Demeter, 'Die Filmpropaganda der Entente im Weltkriege', *Archiv für Politik und Geschichte*, 1925, no. 8, 216.

24. A. Jason, 'Zahlen sehen uns an . . .', in: *25 Jahre Kinematograph* (Berlin, n.d.), 67.

25. L. Eisner, *The Haunted Screen* (London, 1969), translated from the revised French edition, *L'écran démoniaque* (Paris, 1965).

26. O. Messter, *Mein Weg mit dem Film* (Berlin, 1936), pp. 28-30.

27. Demeter, 'Entwicklung', 621-3.

28. Ibid., 629.

29. Bredow and Zurek, *Film und Gesellschaft in Deutschland*, p. 20.

30. H. Traub, *Die Ufa* (Berlin, 1943), p. 21.

31. Ibid., p. 137.

32. Bredow and Zurek, *Film und Gesellschaft in Deutschland*, p. 102.

33. Ibid., p. 104.

34. Demeter, 'Entwicklung', 632.

35. Quoted in: Bredow and Zurek, *Film und Gesellschaft in Deutschland*, p. 28.

36. *Caligari* is discussed at length in both Kracauer, Chapter 5, pp. 61-76, and Eisner, pp. 17-27. The origins of the script and the changes made in the finished film are also dealt with in: R. Hempel, *Carl Mayer. Ein Autor schreibt mit der Kamera* (Berlin, GDR, 1968), Chapter 2, pp. 25-63.

37. Kracauer, *From Caligari to Hitler*, p. 65.

38. The screenplay is available in: *The Cabinet of Dr Caligari* (London, 1972).

39. Kracauer, *From Caligari to Hitler*, p. 77.

40. Ibid., p. 115.

41. *New York World Telegram*, 11 June 1941, quoted in ibid., p. 164.

42. P. Jensen, *The Cinema of Fritz Lang* (London, 1969), p. 58. The screenplay is available in: *Metropolis* (London, 1973) and the film is discussed in: Jensen, pp. 58-69; Kracauer, *From Caligari to Hitler*, pp. 162-4; Eisner, *Haunted Screen*, pp. 223-36; and *Fritz Lang* (London, 1976), pp. 82-94.

43. F. Lang, 'La nuit viennoise', *Cahiers du cinéma*, August 1965, pp. 42-60.

44. Quoted in : Kracauer, *From Caligari to Hitler*, p. 248.

45. The screenplay for this film is also available in the Lorrimer series: *Pandora's Box* (London, 1971).

46. H. Luft, *E.A. Dupont* (Paris, 1970), pp. 173-81; Kracauer, *From Caligari to Hitler*, pp. 125-7; Eisner, *Haunted Screen*, pp. 278-84.

47. *The Blue Angel* (London, 1968); H. Weinberg, *Josef von Sternberg. A Critical Study* (New York, 1967), pp. 48-55; Kracauer, *From Caligari to Hitler*, pp. 215-18.

48. *M* (London, 1968), pp. 103-4.

49. R. Manvell and H. Fraenkel, *The German Cinema* (London, 1971), p. 15; Eisner, *Haunted Screen*, p. 326, despite the views she expressed in 'The German films of Fritz Lang', *Penguin Film Review*, no. 6 (1948), pp. 53-61.

50. Kracauer, *From Caligari to Hitler*, p. 77.

51. F. Wagner, 'I believe in the sound film', *Film Art*, 1936, no. 8, p. 11.

52. Eisner, *Penguin Film Review*, p. 54.

53. Eisner, *The Haunted Screen*, p. 75.

54. Kracauer, *From Caligari to Hitler*, p. 49.

55. Loc. cit.

56. Kalbus, *Vom Werden deutscher Filmkunst*, vol. 1, p. 55.

57. Traub, *Die Ufa*, pp. 63-4.

58. Ibid., p. 60.

59. Quoted in ibid., p. 65.

60. Ibid., p. 74.

61. G. Kühn, K. Tümmler and W. Wimmer (eds), *Film und revolutionäre Arbeiterbewegung in Deutschland 1918-1932* (Berlin, GDR, 1975), vol. 1, pp. 323-69; Kracauer, *From Caligari to Hitler*, p. 173; L. Furhammar and F. Isaksson, *Politics and Film* (London, 1971), p. 32; N.I. Kleiman and K.B. Levina (eds), *Bronenosets Potëmkin* (Moscow, 1968), pp. 224-48.

62. Kühn *et al.*, *Film und revolutionäre Arbeiterbewegung*, vol. 2, p. 19.

63. The term was first used by *Die rote Fahne*, 1 February 1930. Some of the articles on the cinema published by the KPD organ are reprinted in: K. Brauneck (ed.), *Die rote Fahne* (Munich, 1973).

64. Brecht's version of this affair, and the lessons that he drew from it, may be found in: B. Brecht, 'Der Dreigroschenprozess. Ein soziologisches Experiment', *Versuche*, vol. 3 (Frankfurt-am-Main, 1959), pp. 243-300. See also: W. Gersch, *Film bei Brecht* (Berlin, GDR, 1975), pp. 39-97; F. Ewen, *Bertolt Brecht. His*

Art and His Times (London, 1970), pp. 279-81; M. Esslin, *Brecht. A Choice of Evils* (London, 1959), pp. 37-40; Kracauer, *From Caligari to Hitler*, pp. 236-9; Eisner, *The Haunted Screen*, pp. 316-19 and 343-5.

65. Münzenberg's role is discussed in: R. Fischer, *Stalin and German Communism* (Cambridge, Mass., 1948), pp. 610-15; cf. G. Nollau, *International Communism and World Revolution* (London, 1961), and: W. Münzenberg, *Die dritte Front* (Berlin, 1930).

66. Yu. Fridman, 'Dvizhenie pomoshchi mezhdunarodnogo proletariata Sovetskoi Rossii v 1921-1922 godakh', *Voprosy istorii*, 1958, no. 1, 100.

67. Kühn *et al.*, *Film und revolutionäre Arbeiterbewegung*, vol. 2, p. 9.

68. Ibid., vol. 1, pp. 323-32.

69. R. Taylor, 'From October to *October*: the Soviet political system in the 1920s and its films', in: M. Clark (ed.), *Politics in Camera* (Oxford, 1979).

70. Kühn *et al.*, *Film und revolutionäre Arbeiterbewegung*, vol. 2, p. 10.

71. Quoted in ibid., vol. 2, p. 137, and W. Gersch and W. Hecht (eds), *Bertolt Brecht. 'Kuhle Wampe'. Protokoll des Films und Materialien* (Frankfurt-am-Main, 1969), pp. 112-13.

72. Kühn *et al.*, *Film und revolutionäre Arbeiterbewegung*, pp. 128-83; Gersch and Hecht, *Bertolt Brecht*, pp. 101-79; Gersch, *Film bei Brecht*, pp. 101-39; Kracauer, *From Caligari to Hitler*, pp. 243-7; Y. Aubry, *Slatan Dudow* (Paris, 1970), pp. 392-406.

73. Gersch and Hecht, *Bertolt Brecht*, p. 77.

74. Bryher, 'Notes on some films', *Close Up*, September 1932.

75. It has, for instance, recently been levelled at the British cinema newsreels of the 1930s in: J. Lewis, 'Before hindsight', *Sight and Sound*, vol. 46, no. 2 (Spring 1977), 68-73.

76. R. Taylor, *The Politics of the Soviet Cinema, 1917-1929* (Cambridge, 1979), *passim*.

77. B. von Brentano, 'Der verbotene Film *Kuhle Wampe*', *Die literarische Welt*, 22 April 1932, quoted in: Gersch and Hecht, *Bertolt Brecht*, pp. 162-4.

11 GERMANY: THE NEEDS OF REVOLUTION

> May the bright flame of our enthusiasm never be extinguished.
> It alone gives light and warmth to the creative art of a modern
> political propaganda ... It may be a good thing to possess
> power that rests on arms. But it is better and more lasting to
> win the heart of a people and to keep it.
>
> Joseph Goebbels, September 1934[1]

When the Nazis came to power in January 1933 the German film
industry was probably already the most powerful in Europe. Whereas
by this time the Soviet cinema had become largely isolated culturally,
politically and economically, the German cinema was second only to
Hollywood in the considerable thematic and stylistic influence that it
exerted over the commercial cinema of Europe as a whole. This was
largely a consequence of Germany's sheer size and her central geo-
graphical position, but it also resulted from the way in which a significant German-speaking population was scattered across Central and
Eastern Europe in the areas that had formerly been part of the German
and Austrian empires. This cultural and ethnic legacy can be traced
back to the way in which Bismarck had unified Germany in the 1860s
and the way in which the victorious Allies had dismembered it in 1919.
The presence of large numbers of ethnic Germans (*Volksdeutsche*)
beyond the frontiers of the Reich had enabled the German cinema to
achieve a high degree of international penetration even after the advent
of sound (with its obvious linguistically based limitations) had confined
most national film industries within their own national state frontiers.

There were of course many other differences between the Germany
of 1933 and the Russia of 1917. The Nazis inherited a cinema with
strong and distinctive national tradition at a time when the film was
already accepted as a respectable and effective medium for the transmission of ideas. They also inherited an efficient and loyal state
machine and a passive and orderly population. They did not have to
fight a civil war with broken weapons. Their ideology was not class-based:
it did not therefore create an internal class enemy to disrupt the
existing order of society. Their ideology was based on race: it therefore
created an 'external' racial enemy — the Jew — who comprised only
0.8 per cent of the total population in 1933[2] and against whom the

156

rest of the population could safely unite, first to deprive him of his rights and later to destroy him altogether.

Propaganda was of immense significance to the Nazis, as it had been to the Bolsheviks before them, and for somewhat similar reasons. Both started as small minority groups and both wanted to gain a broader basis of support. Both relied on a combination of propaganda of the word reinforced by propaganda of the deed, in accordance perhaps with the old adage that 'actions speak louder than words'. In the Bolshevik case this propaganda of the deed consisted largely of the encouragement and organisation of strikes and demonstrations; in the Nazi case the threat of coercion was cruder and more overt: street-fighting and brawling were commonplace in the dying days of the Weimar Republic and were blamed by the Nazis on their arch-enemy, the Communists.

There was some difference of opinion between Goebbels and Hitler as to the exact role of propaganda after the takeover of power. Hitler, as he expressed himself in *Mein Kampf*, felt that propaganda and organisation to some extent counterbalanced one another:

> If propaganda has imbued a whole people with an idea, the organisa-
> tion can draw the consequences with a handful of men. Propaganda
> and organisation, in other words, supporters and members, thus stand
> in a certain mutual relationship. The better the propaganda has
> worked, the smaller the organisation can be, and the larger the
> number of supporters, the more modest the number of members can
> be, and vice versa: the poorer the propaganda is, the larger the
> organisation must be, and the smaller the host of followers of a
> movement remains, the more extensive the number of its members
> must be, if it still hopes to count on any success at all.[3]

Thus, in the initial stages of the movement, when the organised member-ship was small, propaganda would be tremendously important. But its significance would wane as the organised membership of the movement increased; once the Party controlled the levers of state power, propaganda would fade into relative insignificance and organisation would take pride of place. Goebbels, however, who had masterminded the Party's activi-ties in Berlin before the takeover, felt that propaganda should continue to play an important role even after the Nazis had come to power. Propaganda would be necessary to mobilise the masses in support of the new state and its ideological foundations.

The principal purpose of the apparatus of Nazi propaganda was to convert the passive acceptance of the new régime into a more active participation in the construction of the new order. In April 1933 Goebbels said: 'We are not satisfied with having 52% of the nation and terrorising the other 48%. We want the people as the people, not only passively but actively.'[4] But, because they already had the passive acquiescence of the majority of the population, the Nazis could afford to be less aggressive in their propaganda than the Bolsheviks had been. There were, of course, ideological reasons for their reluctance to centralise and nationalise the cinema industry in the early days of their rule. This reluctance was increased by the Party's dependence in practice on big business for its finances, and more especially by the fact that the largest film-producing firm of Weimar Germany, Ufa, was already in the hands of Alfred Hugenberg, press baron and leader of the nationalist conservative party, DNVP, with whom Hitler was still co-operating. With friends like Hugenberg, Hitler had no need to create enemies.

The changes that the Nazis intended to make in the German film industry were first indicated in a speech that Goebbels made on 28 March 1933, just over a fortnight after his appointment as Reich Minister for Popular Enlightenment and Propaganda on 13 March. Speaking to film workers, he claimed that he 'had for many years realised to what heights the German film could be led by the power and ingenuity of the German spirit'.[5] He further argued that the German cinema was in a state of spiritual crisis which 'will last as long as we do not have the courage to reform the German film from the roots up'. Goebbels analysed the cause of this crisis as the uncertainty that had prevailed in the industry and assured his listeners, 'Now *we* are there. And even the most doubting Thomas will be convinced that we shall be in power for at least four years. What is, remains: we shall not go away!' He thus dispelled any suspicions that the Nazis might be just a passing phenomenon. No German film producer was going to bury his stock of films until the storm had blown over! Goebbels went on to tell the industry what was expected of it in the Third Reich and began by mentioning four films that had left a deep impression on him: *Anna Karenina*, starring Greta Garbo, for its 'intrinsically cinematic art', Fritz Lang's *The Nibelungs*, because of its contemporary relevance, Luis Trenker's *The Rebel*, which could 'overwhelm even a non-National Socialist', and, above all, Sergei Eisenstein's *Battleship Potemkin*. Of this, the most famous of all Russian revolutionary films, Goebbels remarked:

It is a fantastically well-made film and displays considerable cine-matic artistry. The decisive factor is its orientation. Someone with no firm ideological convictions could be turned into a Bolshevik by this film. This proves that a political outlook can be very well contained in a work of art and that even the worst outlook can be conveyed if this is done through the medium of an outstanding work of art.[6]

By contrast the German cinema had produced films that were 'washed out and shapeless' and it had ignored the fact that the German people had been 'living through the greatest drama of suffering in history'. The Weimar cinema had been dominated by liberalism, which Goebbels described as 'anarchy of the spirit', by a search for objectivity, which he denounced as dangerous, and by the Jews. In other words, the cinema had reflected all the weaknesses that the Nazis perceived in the republican system itself. But Goebbels was astute enough to realise that a monolithic cinema would be counterproductive. Art must be in close touch with the people. 'Dangerous experiments', he argued, 'are all too often the excesses of a sick mind.' How Stalin would have agreed with him. The Minister envisaged a kind of umbrella role for the state: 'Art is free, and art should remain free, but it must get used to certain norms.' Those norms would of course be laid down shortly by the Party, but Goebbels attempted to offset this veiled threat in his closing remarks, designed to convey his appreciation of the German cinema, and the fact that this appreciation was shared by Hitler: 'On many evenings in the past, after the exhausting struggles of the day, I have myself sat in a cinema with the Reich Chancellor and found relaxation. Do not think that we do not remember this with gratitude.'

None the less the first measures to control, or at least to guide, the German cinema were not long delayed. The Propaganda Ministry was already well established when on 14 July 1933 a provisional Reich Film Chamber (*Reichsfilmkammer*) was established.[7] It was to embrace everyone working in the film industry, whether in production, distribution or exhibition, and it was made permanent by the legislation of 22 September 1933 which created similar organisations for the press, theatre, music and fine arts, all of which were further subsumed into the Reich Chamber of Culture (*Reichskulturkammer*).[8] It became compulsory for all those active in the German cinema to join the Film Chamber,[9] but those of non-Aryan stock were automatically excluded. Goebbels was given the power to issue exemptions to this condition (*Sondergenehmigungen*).[10] One of the most notable of these exemptions was granted to Otto Wernicke, who would normally have been excluded from the industry on the grounds that his wife was Jewish. Instead, having starred in *SA Man Brand*, he went on to appear in films like

Operation Michael in 1937, *D III 88* in 1939 and *The Great King* in 1942.

The creation of the Reich Film Chamber dealt with the personnel in the industry; the films themselves were to be regulated in accordance with the new Cinema Law (*Lichtspielgesetz*) of 16 February 1934.[11] This replaced the Law of 12 May 1920, which had regulated films during the Weimar Republic, and altered it in several important respects. According to the 1920 Law the censorship body (*Reichsfilmprüfstelle*) was empowered to ban a film that threatened 'to endanger public order or security, to harm religious sensibilities, to brutalise or deprave, or to endanger German prestige or Germany's relationships with foreign states'. This had already been modified by an emergency decree of 6 October 1931 to include a film that might 'endanger the essential interests of the state'.[12] The 1934 Law retained the wording of the modified legislation but added 'National Socialist, moral and artistic' to the 'religious' sensibilities hitherto protected. In future all screenplays and films were to be subjected to prior censorship by the *Reichsfilmdramaturg*. It was said in favour of this prior censorship that it would save the producer of a film money because it insured him against producing a film that was likely to be banned.[13] History was to show that this was wishful thinking. Under the 1934 Law, completed films were still to be submitted to the *Reichsfilmprüfstelle*, but with two differences. First, the censorship office in Munich was closed down and decisions centralised in Berlin; second, the chairman of each censorship committee, who was an official of the Propaganda Ministry, was to have the casting vote in any disputed decisions.[14] The Ministry's hand was further strengthened by an order of 28 June 1935 which gave Goebbels himself the right to overrule decisions of the censorship office.[15] Finally the Minister could also exercise control through the *Reichsfilmintendant* who, as head of the Film Section of the Propaganda Ministry, was directly subordinate to Goebbels.[16] This post was held by Dr Fritz Hippler, later director of *The Wandering Jew*.

In addition to direct censorship the German film industry relied on a system of negative taxation: films that had been awarded a 'predicate' (*Prädikat*) received a subsidy when shown in German cinemas. The Nazis expanded this system to subsidise the exhibition not merely of films that had artistic value, but also of those that were considered to be politically valuable as well. Thus an exhibitor would have a financial incentive to show a film that had the *imprimatur* of the authorities, in addition to the other pressures that could be put on him to conform. In this way too the production of political films would be encouraged.

It has been argued that only a very small number of the films produced during the Third Reich can be construed as political. Albrecht has demonstrated that, of the 1,094 films given their première between 1932 and 1945, only 153 (or 14 per cent) can be described as overtly political and propagandistic in their content and presentation.[17] But this does not of course mean that the so-called non-political film was in fact apolitical. Goebbels knew, as Lenin had known before him, that entertainment was an essential part of a complete propaganda organisation, if only because it lulled audiences into a sense of security and kept them coming to the cinema. In February 1941 he remarked, 'Even entertainment can from time to time perform the function of equipping a nation for its struggle for existence.'[18] Again like Lenin, Goebbels felt that the principal short-term propaganda effort should be directed towards the newsreel, especially during war-time. In February 1942 he observed that, 'Millions of people today get their best information on the war, its causes and effects, from the newsreel.'[19] Three months later he tellingly remarked that, 'In war, news policy is a military resource. It is used to wage war, not to convey information.'[20] Truth was not seen by Goebbels as a worthwhile end in itself, only as a means to that end. During the war he felt that realism, the illusion of truth rather than truth itself, was of supreme importance. This may explain why he had the invasion of Britain filmed in Antwerp harbour so that the newsreel could be distributed and shown at the same time as the planned invasion was taking place. In May 1942, before the tide of war turned against the Reich, the Minister said, 'The more realistically the German people regard the war situation, the sooner they will deal with the problems that still lie before us.'[21] In April 1943 the German newsreel film of the victims of the Katyń massacre was widely shown to bring home to the population the reality of the Bolshevik threat.[22] But realism and reality could be overdone. Seven months later Goebbels was complaining about the film material of the results of Allied bombing raids on Berlin:

> The newsreel pictures of Berlin that have been shown to me are beneath all criticism. They show only images of terrible suffering and nothing can be seen of the relief measures. But I intend to make of the battle of Berlin a heroic song. The Berliners deserve it too.[23]

Realism then was not synonymous with reality; it was to be something better, inspiring the German people and uplifting them to greater efforts, greater victories. It was to be National Socialist realism — not what was, but what ought to be.

Direct film propaganda during the Third Reich was largely confined to the newsreel, and the newsreel was the first part of the German film industry to be brought under complete and effective control. When the Nazis came to power the film newsreel scene in Germany was dominated by the Ufa-Tonwoche, and the Deulig-Woche newsreel which was released through Ufa cinemas.[24] And Ufa was controlled by Hugenberg. It was therefore politically easier, as well as more desirable, to gain control of the newsreel companies first: the newsreel, for the Nazis as for the Bolsheviks, was to be the vanguard of the revolution. By 1937 the Ufa and Deulig newsreels were being shown in two-thirds of the cinemas in Germany,[25] the rest being served mainly by the Bavaria-Tonwoche, which in 1938 became the Tobis-Wochenschau.[26] But we now know that from 1937 onwards the German government was in fact surreptitiously buying shares in German film companies through an intermediary trust company called Cautio-Treuhand GmbH.[27] Overt nationalisation was initially avoided because it was felt that state control would reduce the effectiveness of the newsreel; it was also politically useful to keep the American Fox newsreel in distribution, especially if only on an insignificant scale. With the outbreak of war the situation radically altered. The newsreel companies were openly centralised and nationalised on 21 November 1940 and formed into the unified Deutsche Wochenschau GmbH.[28] The new umbrella organisation for the rest of the cinema, Ufa-Film GmbH (called Ufi to distinguish it from its predecessor), was not established until 10 January 1942,[29] and with this Goebbel's weaponry was complete. As he himself observed:

> Film production is flourishing almost unbelievably despite the War. What a good idea of mine it was to take possession of the films on behalf of the Reich several years ago! It would be terrible if the high profits now being earned by the motion-picture industry were to flow into private hands.[30]

The Deutsche Wochenschau became the main vehicle for direct propaganda on a regular basis, although there remained of course films in documentary format like *Baptism of Fire, Victory in the West* and *The Wandering Jew*. But this does not mean that the feature or entertainment film, even the comedy or the musical, were devoid of political or propagandistic content. I have already mentioned the value of entertainment in lulling the audience into a sense of submission, in catching them, as it were, with their trousers down. Goebbels went as far as to say that, 'Even entertainment is nowadays politically important, if not even decisive for the outcome of the war.'[31] Art was the servant of the state and so-called 'non-political' films had the same aim as the 'political': they were merely more skilfully disguised. Here Goebbels differed again from Hitler. The Führer preferred a complete separation of propaganda from art. (This separation was to serve Leni Riefenstahl well in the early post-war years, because she felt able to claim that *Triumph of the Will* was 'art' rather than 'propaganda'.) In conversation with the actress Tony van Eyck, Hitler said:

> Certainly, on the one hand I want to use the film fully and completely as a medium of propaganda, but in such a way that every viewer knows that today he's going to a political film. Just as in the Sportpalast he doesn't expect to hear politics mixed with art. It makes me sick when people make politics under the guise of art. Either art or politics.[32]

But films like *Triumph of the Will* were the very films that Goebbels disliked because he feared that they would cause a hostile audience reaction. Speaking on 9 October 1933 he attacked the tendency to make films like *Hans Westmar* and *SA Man Brand*:

> We National Socialists do not place any particular value on our SA marching across the stage or screen. Their domain is the street . . . The National Socialist government has never asked that SA films should be made. On the contrary — it sees danger in a surplus of them.[33]

The danger was that same danger that was to delay nationalisation of the newsreel companies: people would expect propaganda from such films and their resistance would then be raised.

Goebbels had arranged in October 1938 for the newsreel to be shown as the first item in every film programme. There were increasing complaints that audiences were coming in late during these newsreels, thus destroying their effect. In March 1941, therefore, a five-minute interval was instituted between the newsreel and the feature. Any cinema ignoring this new regulation could be fined a maximum of RM 10,000. But it was not long before audiences, instead of just coming in late, quite deliberately mingled in the foyer until the interval, thus avoiding the newsreel and the overt propaganda altogether. Then

Goebbels was forced to order that German cinemas should be locked once the newsreel had begun and no one else be admitted. The literally captive audiences were thus effectively prevented from voting with their feet and there is evidence to suggest that instead they voted with their voices, at least in the closing stages of the war, by laughing and jeering at the newsreels they had once applauded.

The German newsreel was not merely nationalised in the organisational sense: it was also given a distinctive and unified image. The length of each newsreel was standardised to 15-20 minutes, which according to research findings was the optimum length of time for audience concentration. Every newsreel was introduced by a martial fanfare and a shot of the German eagle, as designed by Albert Speer. Thus the new centralised Deutsche Wochenschau acquired a distinctive and national identity. There were still different editions for different parts of Germany, but the number was reduced from 15 to 8. The structure of a German war-time newsreel differed considerably from that of the newsreels produced by the Western Allies.[34] On the one hand, there was a far greater dependence on the visual image as opposed to the spoken word, and consequently a greater appeal to the emotions rather than to man's reason. On the other, and strengthening the appeal to the irrational, one scene faded into another, through the juxtaposition of the visual imagery, although the logical connection between the two might not be, and indeed in the circumstances did not need to be, apparent. British and American newsreel items were clearly compartmentalised, and each compartment clearly labelled.

Goebbels, then, preferred indirect propaganda. He was particularly partial to the historical parallel and in March 1942 he stated that 'We must remember the great Prussian prototypes in the way we carry out this war. For us they are an example and a stimulus at the same time. If we base ourselves on them, then nothing serious can happen to us.'[35] Of *The Great King* in particular Goebbels wrote, 'With this film we can make politics as well. It is a great help in the struggle for the soul of our people and in the process of a lasting hardening in the German power to resist, which we need to survive this war.'[36] As well as *The Great King*, the German film industry provided other examples of the Prussian spirit in *Fridericus* and *Kolberg*, and of its continuation in the Bismarck films, *Bismarck* and *The Dismissal*. The propagandist message in these films, with the possible exception of *Kolberg*, was relatively muted, but their heroes appeared, as intended, as examples for the contemporary German to emulate, as did the heroes of films like *Carl Peters*, *Paracelsus*, *Friedrich Schiller: The Triumph of a Genius* and

Friedemann Bach. The same can be said of what on the surface appear to be much lighter films, such as *Request Concert*, which centred on a popular record request programme on the radio, the German equivalent of *Forces' Choice*. The programme was used as a framework within which the united war-time effort of the German people could be demonstrated, the common struggle of the forces and the home front. The film had a distinguished cast, including Ilse Werner, Carl Raddatz and Joachim Brennecke and briefly featuring a variety of celebrities from Eugen Jochum and the Berlin Philharmonic Orchestra to the lively singer Marika Rökk, at the other end of the musical spectrum. It is the Olympic Fanfare from the 1936 Berlin Olympics that finally brings the hero and heroine together, evoking one of the more glorious moments from the short history of Nazi Germany and allowing a brief shot of the Führer. The underlying message of the film is made clear by the closing song, 'Denn wir fahren gegen Engelland!' (For we're marching against England!). Box office receipts show that *Request Concert* was one of the most popular films to be made during the war.[37]

A similar use of entertainment features for indirect propaganda purposes can be seen in the musical version of the life of Mary, Queen of Scots, *The Heart of a Queen*, starring the Swedish actress, Zarah Leander, who in some ways filled the gap in the German film industry that had been left by Marlene Dietrich's departure for Hollywood. The English maltreatment of the Scots is symbolised by Elizabeth's maltreatment of Mary and her ultimate betrayal. Although Mary is eventually executed, her bravery in the face of death and her anti-English stance give her the ultimate moral victory. Dressed to meet death as a nun, she remarks, 'Kings conquer in life, hearts in eternity', and the picture fades on a carving of Christ.

Suffering and self-sacrifice were also among the main themes of Veit Harlan's *The Sacrifice*, which starred his Swedish wife, Kristina Söderbaum, as the vivacious mistress of Carl Raddatz. The sacrifice of the title is that of Raddatz's wife, played by Irene von Meyendorff, who sublimates her own feelings to preserve her marriage to the man who is, in effect, her Führer. His mistress dies, after an obviously difficult life, of typhoid. The consummation of her sacrifice is reached in a quite remarkable sequence in which she imagines that she is saying farewell to her beloved. In this scene Harlan makes full use of the techniques of the cinema: superimposition of the lovers' faces, choral soundtrack, scudding clouds and the sea, all at once. This powerful scene alone belies the assertion that there was no talent to be found in

National Socialist art. But even this film reinforces the political precepts of the regime: in the novel by Rudolf Binder on which the film is based, it is the husband who dies. But Goebbels saw this as a vindication of adultery and insisted that in the film at least it should be the mistress who died, thus emphasising the sanctity of marriage. It is perhaps a lesson that Goebbels himself would have done well to learn.

Some feature films were of course more overt in their propaganda content. *U-Boats to the West!* and *Stukas* were obvious glorifications of the German navy and air force respectively. Other films portrayed an obvious enemy, such as the Jew, in *Jew Süss, The Rothschilds* and *Linen from Ireland*; the British, in *Uncle Kruger, Carl Peters, The Fox of Glenarvon* and *My Life for Ireland*; or the Bolsheviks, in *GPU* and *Frisians in Peril*. These films, with their stereotyped heroes and villains, quite clearly told the German people what the National Socialists wanted the German cinema to tell them. Many films were altered at the behest of either the Party or the Ministry. Indeed the director of *Titanic*, Herbert Selpin, was murdered when he lost patience with the delays caused by interference in his work schedule.[38] This particular film, made in 1943, is also loaded with anti-British propaganda. The Titanic has acquired a German First Officer who spends most of the voyage arguing with the president of the shipping line, a British knight, that the headlong dash across the Atlantic to regain the Blue Riband for Britain can only be suicidal. He is eventually proved right, of course, but succeeds in ensuring that his adversary is brought to trial, only to see him acquitted by the corrupt British courts. In this sense, the film is a perfect piece of anti-British propaganda but unfortunately, and in the circumstances somewhat ironically, Goebbels eventually decided that the scenes of the sinking of the Titanic were too realistic and horrifying to be shown in war-time Germany. Perhaps they were too reminiscent of the newsreel scenes of the bombing of Berlin that he had also criticised, but he no doubt also realised that the Titanic itself could be interpreted as a metaphor for the sinking of a German ship of state. The film therefore received its première in occupied Paris and was not shown in Germany until after the war, and then only briefly, because of complaints from the British occupation authorities!

The Nazis thus created a whole series of methods by which they could control the German cinema. They controlled the composition of its membership through the Reich Film Chamber. They controlled the content of its films by censorship and prior censorship. Gradually they controlled the industry itself, by first covert and then overt nationalisation. In May 1935 Goebbels said, 'The essence of any propaganda is to win people over to an idea in such a profound and vital way that they become addicted to it and can never escape from it.'[39] In February 1934 he made the cinema's position in this process clear: 'The film is one of the most modern and far-reaching media that there is for influencing the masses.'[40]

Notes

1. *Der Kongress zu Nürnberg vom 5. bis 10. September 1934. Offizieller Bericht* (Munich, 1934), pp. 140-1. The speech also features in Leni Riefenstahl's official film of the 1934 Party Congress, *Triumph of the Will*, but on the sound track the word 'lasting' *(dauerhaft)* is replaced by 'fortunate' *(glücklich)*. Different versions of speeches by Nazi leaders are unfortunately not uncommon.
2. According to the official census figures for 16 June 1933 there were then 499,682 Jews living in Germany.
3. A. Hitler, *Mein Kampf* (Munich, 1933), pp. 653-4. This translation is based on that by Ralph Manheim (London, 1969), p. 530.
4. J. Goebbels, 'Der Sinn der sozialen Revolution', stenographic record of a speech given on 24 April 1933, quoted in: H. Herma, 'Goebbels' conception of propaganda', *Social Research*, vol. 10, no. 2, May 1943, 202, note 7 and subsequently.
5. The full text of this speech is printed in: C. Belling, *Der Film in Staat und Partei* (Berlin, 1936), pp. 27-31.
6. Ibid., p. 27.
7. K. Wolf, *Entwicklung und Neugestaltung der deutschen Filmwirtschaft seit 1933* (Heidelberg, 1938), p. 12.
8. Ibid., p. 14.
9. Belling, *Der Film in Staat und Partei*, p. 40.
10. G. Albrecht, *Nationalsozialistische Filmpolitik* (Stuttgart, 1969), pp. 208-9.
11. A. Funk, *Film und Jugend* (Munich, 1934), pp. 35-6.
12. Ibid., p. 34.
13. Ibid., p. 35.
14. Albrecht, *Nationalsozialistische Filmpolitik*, p. 32.
15. D. Hollstein, *Antisemitische Filmpropaganda. Die Darstellung des Juden im nationalsozialistischen Spielfilm* (Berlin, 1971), p. 19.
16. Albrecht, *Nationalsozialistische Filmpolitik*, p. 32.
17. Ibid., p. 107.
18. Speech to the Film Chamber, 15 February 1941, quoted in: E. Leiser, *Deutschland, erwache! Propaganda im Film des Dritten Reiches* (Reinbek bei Hamburg, 1968), p. 53.
19. 2 February 1942; quoted in Albrecht, *Nationalsozialistische Filmpolitik*, p. 94.
20. 10 May 1942; quoted in ibid., p. 95.
21. 14 May 1942; ibid., p. 58.
22. Ibid., p. 59.
23. Loc. cit.
24. K.W. Wippermann, *Die Entwicklung der Wochenschau in Deutschland: Ufa Tonwoche Nr 410/1938* (Göttingen, 1970), p. 16.
25. H. Traub, *Die Ufa. Ein Beitrag zur Entwicklungsgeschichte des deutschen Filmschaffens* (Berlin, 1943), p. 161.

26. Wippermann, *Die Entwicklung der Wochenschau in Deutschland*, p. 17.

27. K.N. Scheffler, 'Die Verstaatlichung der deutschen Filmwirtschaft 1937 bis 1942 und die Bildung der "Ufa-Film GmbH." ("Ufi")', *Deutsche Filmkunst* (Berlin, GDR), vol. 9, no. 1 (1961), 20-3.

28. Wippermann, *Die Entwicklung der Wochenschau in Deutschland*, p. 17.

29. Scheffler, 'Die Verstaatlichung', 20.

30. L.P. Lochner (ed.), *The Goebbels Diaries* (London, 1948), p. 5.

31. 8 February 1942; quoted in: Albrecht, *Nationalsozialistische Filmpolitik*, p. 90.

32. H. Traub, *Der Film als politisches Machtmittel* (Munich, 1933), p. 27.

33. O. Kalbus, *Vom Werden deutscher Filmkunst* (Altona-Bahrenfeld, (1935), vol. 2, p. 119.

34. S. Kracauer, 'The conquest of Europe on the screen: the Nazi newsreel 1939-40', *Social Research*, vol. 10, no. 3, September 1943, 337-57.

35. 20 March 1942: Albrecht, *Nationalsozialistische Filmpolitik*, p. 81.

36. 19 February 1942; ibid., p. 82.

37. Leiser, *Deutschland, erwache!*, p. 53.

38. D.S. Hull, *Film in the Third Reich* (Berkeley, Cal., 1969), pp. 228-9; J. Richards, 'Two Titanics', *Focus on Film*, no. 28, October 1977, 43-6.

39. 8 May 1933; quoted in Leiser, *Deutschland, erwache!*, p. 40.

40. 9 February 1934; ibid., pp. 40-1.

12 GERMANY: THEMES AND VARIATIONS

All art is tendentious. Art has a purpose, a goal, a direction.

Goebbels, 1937[1]

The differences between the stereotypes of Bolshevik and Nazi propaganda reflect and illuminate the differences between the respective ideologies. Soviet socialism, under the slogan 'All power to the Soviets!', proclaimed the dictatorship of the proletariat and with it a faith founded on a class-based analysis of the development of human society. German National Socialism centred on a faith in the virtues of organic nationhood under the slogan 'One people! One Reich! One Führer!' The apotheosis of that faith can be seen most clearly in the fusion between blood and soil expressed in Paula Wessely's speech at the end of *The Homecoming*. The German population of Poland have been imprisoned and while they wait for the Luftwaffe and the Panzer divisions to liberate them, she comforts them with the following words:

Just think what it will be like, my friends, just think what it will be like when there are just Germans around us, and when you go into a shop it won't be Yiddish or Polish that you hear, but German! And it's not just the whole village that will be German, but everything all around us will be German. And we'll be in the middle of it, in the heart of Germany. Just think, my friends, what it will be like! And why shouldn't it be like that? We'll be living on the good old warm soil of Germany. In our own country and at home. And at night, in our beds, when we wake from our sleep, our hearts will quicken suddenly in the sweet knowledge that we are sleeping in the middle of Germany, in our own country and at home, surrounded by the comforting night and millions of German hearts that beat softly and as one. You are at home, my friend, at home with your own people. There will be a wonderful feeling in our hearts when we know that the soil in the field and our little bit of life, the rock, the waving grass, the swaying branches of the hazelnut and the trees, that all this is German. Just like us, belonging to us, because it has all grown from the millions of German hearts that have been buried in the earth and have become German earth. Because we don't just live a German life, we also die a German death. Even when we're dead, we're still German, we're still a real part of Germany. A handful of soil for our grandchildren to grow corn in. And from our hearts the vines will grow high up into the sun that doesn't scorch them but gives them light and gives the grapes their sweetness too. And all around us the birds sing, and everything is German.

To be German was to have reached the pinnacle of human achievement, to have something to live up to and something to die for. Time and again the characters in Nazi films return to this point. The heroine of *GPU*, hounded by the Soviet secret police, says, 'One must have something to die for — I cannot live.' In *Refugees* the leader figure voices similar sentiments: 'To be able to die for something is the best thing. I should like a death like that.' It is Germany that gives these people a cause to fight and die for. In *The Hallgarten Patrol* the hero has 'died so that our people can live'. He dies, but his name lives on in the annals of martyrdom alongside the names of *Hitler Youth Quex* and Horst Wessel (in *Hans Westmar*, which, significantly, was subtitled *One of Many*). The sacrifice of those who died in the 1923 Munich Beerhall Putsch is commemorated in the blood flag sequence of *Triumph of the Will*, while the epic quality of the frequent images of fluttering banners superimposed on columns of men marching into the future emphasise that death has been metamorphosed into eternal life and that in the National Socialist movement the spirit of the nation will last forever.

What then were the component parts of the national ideal that justified the individual's ultimate sacrifice? They combined, like the movement itself, elements of the traditional German virtues with those of the aggressive new master race that Hitler was trying to perfect. Perhaps this was the implication of Hess's extraordinary statement, recorded in *Triumph of the Will*, that 'The Party is Hitler, but Hitler is Germany, just as Germany is Hitler!' National Socialism played upon the social instincts of mankind. Like Christianity, like Soviet socialism, it told the individual that he belonged to a larger grouping, a community towards which he had certain duties and responsibilities, and from which he would in return draw certain benefits and comforts. For the Nazis this idea was encapsulated in another slogan: 'The community before the individual' (*Gemeinnutz geht vor Eigennutz*). Because, through Christianity, this ideal was already part of the German cultural tradition, it was accepted without demur by the population at large. There was no room for doubt in the New Order. Resistance was confined to intellectuals who fell into the category of well-known left-wing trouble-makers anyway: as a character in *Sky Dogs* remarks:

'We've no time for the swines who always put themselves first and question the reasons for an order, instead of simply carrying it out.' He is echoing Hitler's demand that the German people must 'learn to be so fanatical in their faith in ultimate victory that, even if we suffer an occasional reverse, the nation will interpret it on what I should like to call a higher plane: this will pass, and in the end victory will be ours!' He went on: 'In other words, it is essential, without in any way discounting or even discussing the possibility of error, that as a basic principle the rightness of the leadership should be emphasised again and again. That is the crux of the matter.'[2] In *Kolberg* the mayor questions an order but, before his question is answered, he has to be taught that 'Orders are orders'. There must therefore be a clearly defined hierarchy in society, with a mass that obeys orders and a leader who gives them: 'Führer, command – we follow!'

The leader figure (*Führergestalt*) epitomised the best characteristics of his people: strength and determination, piety and simplicity, humanity and generosity. The only film that was constructed around Hitler himself was *Triumph of the Will* and it is difficult to see how another film maker could have elaborated on the myth that Riefenstahl depicts. As Leiser says, 'He had been shown once and for all the way he wanted to be seen. No actor was ever asked to portray him.'[3] But the depiction of Hitler in the Party rally film offered a model for other film makers to emulate in their portrayals of the leader stereotype. As in the Soviet cinema, history was to become a useful weapon.[4] The two examples most frequently plucked from German history were those of Frederick the Great and Bismarck, both of whom had already figured prominently as representatives of 'that old Prussian spirit' in the nostalgic propaganda of right-wing nationalist circles in the Weimar period. Once again the Nazis were building on the foundations laid by others, and their audiences did not really need the constant reminders of the contemporary significance of historical events. As Bismarck observes in *The Dismissal*: 'Abstract concepts are eternal. It is men who come and go.' At the end of the film he emphasises the point by saying, as he stands against a background painting of the coronation of Kaiser Wilhelm I: 'My work is done. It was only a beginning. Who will complete it?' The answer was of course obvious. Bismarck is clearly presented as a man of destiny ('Every man has his character, and his character is his destiny'), a born leader who, because of his unusual gift, must be granted the 'unlimited plenary powers' that he asks for. He is reviled by worthless journalists (but in *Bismarck*, made two years earlier, he remarks that, 'The newspapers are not the nation') and contrasted with the bickering and impotent politicians (an allusion also to the Weimar period). He is a man of great strength, but also of great wisdom. When his advice is ignored, he is ultimately proved to have been right. When his advice is followed, the fatherland is strengthened. He is a true leader of his people, and a true servant of his king and in the earlier film the latter comments that, 'Faithful servants deserve faithful masters'. An almost mystical link is thus established between the leader and the led, a mutual faith and trust, and when an assassin attempts to destroy that link, he has of course to be an English Jew. The film was, after all, made in 1940.

In *The Great King* the sacrifices that a leader makes for his people are depicted. Frederick punishes an officer for using his own initiative, for 'There must be discipline', but he makes the same stringent demands on himself. As his son lies dying, Frederick is unable to go to his bedside: duty calls. He is a lonely figure, unable to trust his generals, able in fact to trust only his own judgement. He is a lonely figure, but determined. As an Austrian general remarks, he is a 'born king': 'We dance, while he marches.' When his Commander-in-Chief suggests an accommodation with France, Frederick will brook no compromises: 'I shall not give them a single village . . . The French will always be the enemies of Prussia . . . There's no place for traitors in my state, not even high-born traitors.' Again the message was clear, and SS reports show that that message got across to German audiences: 'Throughout the film audiences have seen a "mirror image of our own time". Many people have compared the King with the Führer and have recalled seeing, while the film was running, a newsreel clip showing the Führer alone at headquarters.'[5] The King's close bond with his native soil is underlined by the framework within which the film is set. It begins with the Prussian defeat at the Battle of Kunersdorf, the destruction of the village and the mill: in Frederick's words, 'Germany is in a terrible crisis. How many enemies I have, but I have faith in my cause.' The image of the burning mill haunts him throughout the film: 'I shall not survive the ruin of my fatherland.' It is only after the resounding Prussian victory at the battle of Schneidnitz that Frederick feels able to return to Kunersdorf. He has redeemed himself, the mill has been rebuilt and the sails are turning once more, but he has paid the price that all great leaders have to pay, for the price of greatness is loneliness: 'You see, I stand alone.'

Although Bismarck and Frederick the Great were perhaps the two most important leader figures in the Nazi cinema, they were by no means the only ones. Some characters were taken from the history, or

alleged history, of the movement itself: the most obvious examples are
Hans Westmar (or Horst Wessel in disguise), *Hitler Youth Quex* and
SA Man Brand. In the first of these films Westmar's sacrifice wins over
the workers to the cause of National Socialism: as the SA march past in
a torchlight procession at the end of the film, the raised clenched fists
of the Communist salute gradually give way to the Nazi version. In
Hitler Youth Quex there is a key scene in which the SA group leader
argues with Quex's father, who is a Communist: their differing allegiances to class or nation are exposed, but it is the Nazi view that triumphs,
and Quex sacrifices himself for it. Other leader figures are taken from
German history, like *Carl Peters*, the explorer, or *Friedrich Schiller:
The Triumph of a Genius*. In this film the hero puts forward the
ultimate justification for the privileged position of the leader: 'Genius
is simply a term ordinary people use to describe an extraordinary man:
it is a yardstick that the world has created for him . . . The genius can
find his own way to fulfilment. He does not need imperfect institutions.' Nevertheless a leader, although by that very fact alone and apart,
must retain contact with his people, like *The Great King*, Nettelbeck in
Kolberg, *Uncle Kruger* or the squadron leader in *Stukas*. The leader
usually displays the characteristics of simplicity and piety: this applies
as much to *Uncle Kruger* as to the village elder in *Frisians in Peril*, or
the head of the family in *The Degenhardts*, the story of a middle-class
Lübeck family and their fortunes under the Third Reich. The connection between blood and soil that can be seen in *The Homecoming, The
Eternal Forest* and other films set in the countryside, can also be
detected in this film. When the RAF have bombed the city, Degenhardt,
standing in the ruins of its principal church, recalls the famous German
composers who have played there. They include Bach. This was another
method of emphasising the continuity between the Third Reich and
previous German history, and presenting the former as the apotheosis
of the latter. The Berlin Philharmonic, under Wilhelm Furtwängler,
make an appearance in *Request Concert* and Furtwängler himself was
invited to the première of *Hans Westmar* in October 1933, while the
first movement of Bruckner's Fourth Symphony was played at the first
night of *Hitler Youth Quex* a month earlier. All this also served to set
the Third Reich apart from, and indeed above, the decadence of the
Weimar Republic.

The depiction of the leader figure also reveals something of the
assumptions that the Nazis made about the respective roles of men
and women in the family. The father, like the Führer, was evidently
the protector of women, children and, where appropriate, natives too.

He ventured into the outside world and assured his family of their place in it. The mother, an emotive figure in Nazi as in Soviet films, played her traditional role in the German family, bounded by the three Ks – *Kinder, Küche, Kirche* (children, kitchen, church). There were exceptions, of course, like Olga Feodorovna in *GPU*, but they merely served to prove the rule that a woman would only find fulfilment in her traditional role in the bosom of her family. This role was so sacrosanct that the breach of it could be used as a potent propaganda weapon against the enemy held responsible: the British in *Uncle Kruger* and the Bolsheviks in *GPU* and *Frisians in Peril*. The family, the community, the nation, the leader – all were points on a single continuum, and somewhere on that continuum every German was supposed to be able to find a place, be he worker or peasant, soldier or civilian: all were merged into the people's community, the marching columns of the mass.

Like the Soviet cinema, the Nazi film had to create a contrasting negative stereotype, a scapegoat to explain away the ills of the world. There were three principal external enemies upon whom the blame for many misfortunes was heaped: the Jews, the Anglo-Saxons (and specifically the English) and the Slavs, be they Poles or Russians, Liberals or Bolsheviks. All three categories of villain displayed the same broad characteristics and on occasions they were deliberately confused: the Jews and Anglo-Saxons (a name that implies miscegenation anyway!) were mixed in *The Rothschilds, Uncle Kruger* (the reporter) and *Bismarck* (the assassin). Bolsheviks and Socialists were often of dubious racial origin, frequently having distinctly oriental features. This applies to the part played by a suspiciously Lenin-like Paul Wegener in *Hans Westmar* and to the part of the Bolshevik Commissar in *Frisians in Peril*. This latter role was in fact played by the same Mongol actor who had taken the part of the heir to Genghis Khan in Pudovkin's *Storm over Asia*: Valery Inkizhinov thus has the unique distinction of having participated in both Soviet and Nazi propaganda films. Sometimes the villain's racial characteristics are not so obvious and have to be unmasked: he may have wormed his evil way into civilised society, like the Jew in *Jew Süss, The Wandering Jew* or *Linen from Ireland* or the Bolshevik in *GPU* who hides behind a façade of disarmament groups and friendship societies, presumably because he does not have the guts to be himself. The enemy is always sly, unreliable and hypocritical, able and willing to play on the weaknesses and doubts of the intellectual, to corrupt him, as the British do to Jan Kruger in *Uncle Kruger* and the French do to Claus in *Kolberg*. The Bolsheviks, being cruder, usually have to make do with force or blackmail, as in *GPU*.

The depiction of life in foreign countries is designed to bolster the image of the villain and to confirm for the viewer that life is much better in the Reich. Curiously, many of the criticisms made of foreign countries could equally well be applied to Nazi Germany, indeed in some cases they could be applied with greater justification. The English are accused of inventing concentration camps, of uprooting whole families, when the policies of the Nazis were disrupting the lives of millions throughout Europe. The Bolsheviks are accused of espionage, arson, murder and terrorism, all of which were familiar Nazi weapons in Eastern Europe. The English plutocrats and royalty operate behind closed doors, holding the mass in complete contempt; the only distinction between them and their Nazi counterparts is that the latter have the ideological justification that they are 'geniuses' who 'can find their own way'. The Jews are portrayed in the squalid ghetto that National Socialism forced them into. The Bolsheviks are philistines, slaves to their ideology by which 'the authorities' decide everything, even the abolition of God. The Bolshevik enemy is perhaps the worst, if only because he represents such an enormous threat, both externally and internally. The Jew was being dealt with, and a lingering respect remained for the English *Gentlemen*, objects of caricature as much as hatred. But the Bolshevik was both an ideological threat and a racial threat: even if not Oriental, he was at best a Slav, and they were considered to be sub-humans (*Untermenschen*). In *Frisians in Peril* the commissar displays his utter cynicism: 'I have never met anyone who loved me or whom I loved. Until now I've lived without bothering about either my conscience or my heart.' The ruthless agent in *GPU*, wreaking a trail of human havoc, would doubtless have voiced the same sentiments. Nowhere else does the viewer find the sense of community, of pride in belonging, that he will find in the Germany around him. We are back to blood and soil.

The enemy is also degenerate, and here the external enemy merges into the internal, for many of the sequences depicting degeneracy abroad also constitute an attack on the degeneracy of the Weimar period, which makes the Third Reich seem by contrast to be a haven of health and hygiene. The Parisian cabaret in which the Prince of Wales has immersed himself while his mother lies dying (*Ungle Kruger*) looks like a paler version of the night club in *The Blue Angel*. Such moral weakness is the fundamental characteristic of decadence and therefore provides further evidence that the enemy's days are numbered, while the future belongs to National Socialism. In the words of the marching song:

> Today Germany is ours.
> Tomorrow the world.

This, and similar music, was usually accompanied by an image of a column of uniformed men, Hitler Youth, Labour Corps, Army, marching with firm step into the future, a future assured by the symbol of the swastika superimposed on the screen. The audience could be certain that here, in this emblem of Germany's rebirth and new-found strength, they had found a symbol before which the Star of David, the Hammer and Sickle and the Union Jack would tremble. One of the many films that ended in this way was *Hitler Youth Quex*. He dies with the words of the Hitler Youth's marching song on his lips:

> Our flag flutters before us.
> We march into the future as one man.
> We are marching for Hitler through night and through need
> With the flag of youth for freedom and bread.
> Our flag flutters before us; Our flag is the new age.
> And the flag leads us to eternity!
> Yes, the flag means more than death!

This was National Socialist realism.

Notes

1. From a speech delivered to the first annual meeting of the Reich Film Chamber on 5 March 1937 in the Kroll Opera House and reprinted in: G. Albrecht, *Nationalsozialistische Filmpolitik* (Stuttgart, 1969), p. 457.

2. Speech of 10 November 1938, reprinted in: E. Leiser, *Deutschland, erwache!* (Reinbek bei Hamburg, 1968), p. 40. This is my own translation, but Leiser's book is available in English as *Nazi Cinema* (London, 1974) and this extract appears on p. 46.

3. Leiser, *Deutschland, erwache!* (Reinbek), p. 24; *Nazi Cinema* (London), p. 29.

4. See the quotations at the head of Chapters 15 and 16.

5. Quoted in Leiser, *Deutschland, erwache!* (Reinbek), p. 142; *Nazi Cinema* (London), p. 162.

13 TRIUMPH OF THE WILL

> The Führer above all!
> Above the tremendous symphony of crowds, marching
> columns, meetings, commemorations, marches and congresses
> — his words on the present — for the future.
>
> Leni Riefenstahl, 1935[1]

The film of the 1934 Party rally in Nuremberg is not a typical Nazi propaganda film. We have seen that Goebbels preferred indirect propaganda for the feature-length film, concentrating *direct* propaganda in the newsreel. Nevertheless, it would be impossible to discuss the Nazi cinema without discussing *Triumph of the Will*; it is the Nazi film that everyone has heard of. At the same time it is a superb example of documentary cinema art — and a masterpiece of film propaganda. Despite Goebbels' reservations, and despite the fact that the film was apparently not widely shown in ordinary cinemas during the Third Reich, Riefenstahl's work is clearly worthy of closer examination.

In 1935 Leni Riefenstahl published a booklet entitled 'Behind the Scenes of the Reich Party Rally Film', in which she set out her purpose and her technique in making the film. It is from this booklet that our opening quotation is taken. According to the titles for the film, *Triumph of the Will* was made 'by order of the Führer' and 'fashioned' by the director. In her booklet Riefenstahl is effusive in her praise of Hitler and in a sense the film can be seen as a paean of gratitude:

> The Führer has recognised the importance of film. Where else in the world has the opportunity for developing the film in its abundance of expression into the interpreter of an event been so perspicaciously recognised?
>
> Once again Adolf Hitler has given an unprecedented example . . .
>
> In the world we have seen documentary films; governments have had them made and parties have ordered campaign films. *The belief that a real and strong experience of a nation can find new experience in the film was born in Germany*.
>
> In this way the Führer has given the contemporary film both its sense and mission.[2]

In the section of her booklet entitled 'The Final Form' Riefenstahl expounds her method and purpose in 'fashioning' *Triumph of the Will*. For this reason the section is worth quoting in full:

> An observer standing behind me with the original programme for the Party Rally would probably judge my method to be 'self-willed'. I compose the Party Rally from the abundance of effective motifs as they jump out at me from the screen.
>
> It does not matter that everything should appear on the screen in the right chronological order. The creative line demands that one should, instinctively and conscious of the real experience of Nuremberg, find a coherent way to fashion the film so that it seizes and carries the listener and viewer from act to act, from impression to impression, in an ever more overwhelming crescendo.
>
> I search for the inner dramatic force of such a re-creation. It is there. It will be transmitted to the people as soon as the film material of Nuremberg has been fashioned, as soon as speech and sentence, mass image and head, march and music intensify in such a way that they are true to the sense of Nuremberg. The Führer himself coined the title of the film *Triumph of the Will*. In so doing he indicated the sense that this film reveals.
>
> In this way there rises above the basic motif of this victorious title a film from the German present – a triumphal procession of the knowledge, courage and strength to fight and to win for our German people.
>
> A heroic film of fact – in the will of the Führer his people triumph.[3]

Leni Riefenstahl did not merely reorganise the events of the rally for dramatic effect; according to the memoirs of Albert Speer, she actually re-created and re-filmed some of the speeches.[4] In this documentary the important thing was not so much realism as a *sense of realism* and it is for this reason that the film was subtitled 'The Document of the Reich Party Rally 1934'.

As Barsam has rightly pointed out, 'something of a legend has grown up around the film'.[5] Tales of vast expenditure and resources appear to have been exaggerated. Riefenstahl herself now claims that she was given only two weeks to plan the film and lived in constant hope that the task would be given to someone else; according to her the film cost only 280,000 Reichsmarks to produce and the total crew numbered 172, including 16 cameramen using 30 cameras. They were backed up by 29 newsreel cameramen and all were dressed in SA uniform so that they were not noticeable.[6] Riefenstahl has also claimed that Goebbels was responsible for the obstructive attitude of Nazi officials towards the making of the film; the finished article does not however suffer from these obstructions. Almost 61 hours of film were shot and it took the director five months to edit them into the final version. *Triumph of the Will* had its première in the largest cinema in Berlin, the Ufa-Palast-am-Zoo, on 28 March 1935 before an audience that included Hitler. The film was reasonably successful in the larger cities but not with a wider public and for this reason it was not used generally for propaganda purposes. Goebbels' strictures had been justified; nevertheless he praised the film and awarded it the National Film Prize on 1 May 1935. It is now illegal to exhibit the film publicly in either German state.

Like the Wagnerian operas echoed in its music, *Triumph of the Will* begins with an overture, a prologue without vision. Thus the audience in the cinema, sitting in the dark, alone and yet of the mass, is lulled into submission by the music. The opening titles are followed by four titles which set the rally in its historical context and breed a sense of expectancy in the viewer:

> On 5th September 1934, 20 years after the outbreak of the War, 16 years after the beginning of German suffering, 19 months after the beginning of Germany's rebirth.[7]

The scene is thus set, the tension created (in the same way that Eisenstein created tension before Lenin's arrival at the Finland Station in *October*) – and Hitler appears as saviour, descending quite literally from the clouds. The next title reads: 'Adolf Hitler flew again to Nuremberg to review the columns of his faithful followers.'

We then see two sequences intercut with one another: on the one hand the Führer's aircraft flying through the clouds, casting its shadow on the city streets below; on the other the marching columns of the faithful come to welcome him. The aircraft lands and the two sequences of the leader and the led merge, but their relationship with one another has already been firmly established. The cheering crowds and marching troops as Hitler drives from the airfield to his hotel emphasise his position as the focal point of the film and the Rally. These mass images are counterbalanced by two brief and more intimate episodes: one in which a small girl presents Hitler with a bunch of flowers, and another in which a cat stops washing its paws to glance at the motorcade. The city of Nuremberg is at one with its Führer. This part of the film concludes with Hitler's arrival at his hotel. He is greeted rapturously by his followers, protected and supported by his troops. The camera lingers on their uniforms, insignia and boots — images of strength to which the film later returns.

The next part of the film is calmer, more reflective; it represents an interval between the excitement of the saviour's arrival and the opening session of the rally itself. It opens with a brass band concert held by torchlight in front of the hotel. The torchlight evokes the procession through Berlin of 30 January 1933 while the bonfire recalls older, more mystical celebrations of Walpurgis Night. Hitler listens to the music, as do his stormtroopers, while images of eagles, swastikas and an illuminated 'Heil Hitler!' sign predominate. There is relaxation, but also anticipation. That anticipation is accentuated the following morning. We are shown Nuremberg at dawn and the spirit of German history as reflected in its architecture. A window opens on the awakening city to show swastika flags in the flowerpots. The music is the hymn, 'Awake! The dawn of day draws near', from Act 3 of Wagner's *The Master Singers of Nuremberg*. Chimneys start to smoke; the city awakens to the new day, the new era. The camera then turns its attention to the camps where the faithful are sleeping. Sounds of reveille reverberate on the sound track. The faithful emerge from their tents and the period of reflection is over.

We see the camaraderie of the camp: men stripped to the waist, shaving, washing and combing one another's hair. The emphasis again is on the mass: mass accommodation, mass ablutions, mass feeding. There is a great deal of horseplay and boyish fun and games. The emphasis on youth underlines the importance of the coming generation. Next we see the followers on their way to the day's activities. They are dressed in different regional costumes, demonstrating the unity of Germany in its diversity. Fruit and flowers emphasise that the Nazi era is an era of plenty, and of plenty for all, a real people's community (*Volksgemeinschaft*). The crowd greet Hitler who inspects the assembled troops before departing to the accompaniment of Wagnerian music and a chorus of 'Sieg Heil!'

With the next scene of the film the rally itself opens in a vast hall decorated with eagles, swastikas, flags and a large sign at the far end proclaiming, 'Alles für Deutschland!' (Everything for Germany). The opening speech is made by Rudolf Hess, the Deputy Führer. He begins by paying tribute to the memory of President Hindenburg, recently deceased: 'We remember the Field Marshal as the first soldier of the great war and thus also remember our dead comrades.' And so we return to the first title of the film ('20 years after the outbreak of the World War') and to the period of Germany's weakness and suffering. By contrast Hess then welcomes the foreign representatives to whom Germany under National Socialism can display her regained strength and unity. He then continues, 'and the Party, in sincere friendship, welcomes in particular the representatives of the military forces, now under the leadership of our Führer'. The rally is taking place only two months after the Röhm purge, in which the SA were brought to heel, and a month after Hindenburg's death, the abolition of the Presidency, Hitler's emergence as Führer, rather than mere Chancellor, and the new personal oath of allegiance to the Führer that the armed forces were now obliged to swear. Hess is thus presenting an image of unity after recent difficulties and this is another theme reiterated later in the film. The concluding section of Hess's speech confirms the supreme position of the Führer:

> My Führer, around you are gathered the flags and banners of this National Socialism. Only when their cloth has worn thin will people, looking back, be able to understand fully the greatness of our time and conceive what you, my Führer, mean for Germany.
>
> You are Germany. When you act, the nation acts. When you judge, the people judge. Our gratitude is our pledge to stand by you for better or for worse, come what may! Thanks to your leadership, Germany will achieve her goal of being a homeland, a homeland for all the Germans in the world. You were our guarantee of victory; you are now our guarantee of peace. Heil Hitler! Sieg Heil! Sieg Heil! Sieg Heil!

Hess touches upon most of the themes that are central to the message of *Triumph of the Will*: leadership, loyalty, unity, strength and Germanness.

Hess's speech is followed by a series of short extracts from other speeches which fade into one another. Wagner, the Gauleiter of Bavaria, reads the Führer's proclamation denouncing revolution – a further sign that the socialist elements in the National Socialist movement, as typified by the SA, are now dead and buried. Apart from the importance of the actual message transmitted by the words, this part of the film has a deliberate propagandist purpose in familiarising the German people with their leaders in the pre-television age. The other speakers are Alfred Rosenberg, the ideologist; Otto Dietrich, the head of the Reich Press Chamber; Fritz Todt, in charge of Autobahn construction;

Fritz Reinhardt, head of the Party school for speakers; Walter Darré, Minister of Agriculture; Julius Streicher, Gauleiter of Franconia and publisher of the notoriously vitriolic periodical *Der Stürmer*; Robert Ley, head of the German Labour Front DAF; Hans Frank, Minister of Justice; Joseph Goebbels and finally Konstantin Hierl, leader of the Labour Service. Each speaker makes brief remarks about his particular area of responsibility to demonstrate the way in which Nazism has put Germany on the move once more. The last speaker, Hierl, provides a link between this scene and the one that follows: 'The German people are today mentally and spiritually prepared for the introduction of general and equal labour service conscription. We await the order of the Führer.' The image dissolves into a close-up of the German Labour Front flag and we find ourselves in the next scene, at a huge outdoor rally of the Front's members.

The German Labour Front represented an attempt by the Party to organise the work-force along military lines. The membership wore uniforms on parade and carried spades instead of rifles. Hierl calls on the workers to 'Present spades', which they do like a massed army. The military aspect of the Front is emphasised again by the declaration of loyalty which follows, from all parts of the Reich (and from the Saar, which was to return to Germany the following year). Then, emphasising their unity, the leader and workers alternate the following phrases:

One people, one Führer, one Reich – Germany! Now we are all working together. In the bogs. In the quarries. In the sandpits. We are diking the North Sea. Greetings, German man. We are planting trees. Rustling forests. We are building roads. From village to village, from town to town. We provide the farmer with new acreage. Fields and forests, acres and bread – for Germany!

There follows a ceremony of remembrance for those who fell in the World War. Flags are dipped and Hierl proclaims, repeating the military imagery: 'We did not stand in the trenches, nor did we stand under the drumfire of the grenades; nonetheless we are soldiers.' Another flag is dipped as each battlefield is mentioned and then the Nazis killed during the Weimar Republic by 'Red Front and reaction' are commemorated and assured, 'You are not dead, you are alive – in Germany!' Hitler, the saviour, offers the dead of the past in effect resurrection in his new thousand-year Reich. He then speaks, emphasising the ideal of labour and of service to the community, be it the Labour Front or the nation itself:

You represent a great idea, and we know that for millions of our comrades labour is no longer a divisive concept, but a unifying one, and that in particular there will no longer be anyone in Germany who will value manual labour less than any other form of labour. The whole nation will pass through your school. The time will come when no German will be able to enter the community of this nation, without first having passed through your community. And we know that not merely are the hundreds of thousands at Nuremberg looking at you, but the whole of Germany is seeing you for the first time. You are Germany and I know that, just as you are serving Germany in loyal devotion, Germany sees today, in proud joy, its sons marching in your ranks.

As Hitler finishes speaking the image dissolves into a column of singing workers, marching towards the camera.

There follows another nocturnal respite. This time we are at an SA rally. There is a bonfire and firework displays, stormtroopers appear in silhouette, men carry flaming torches. The atmosphere is one of mystery and blood brotherhood. The effect is however somewhat spoiled by the appearance on the rostrum of the new SA leader, Viktor Lutze, who reaffirms, in an unusually high-pitched voice, the absolute loyalty of the Stormtroops to the Führer.

From the SA by night the film passes to the Hitler Youth by day. The scene opens with a blast on the trumpet and a roll of the drums. We see the fresh faces of the youth movement, individually and *en masse,* as they welcome Hitler to the Youth Stadium. The leader of the Hitler Youth, Baldur von Schirach, introduces the leader to the led, underscoring yet again the value of loyalty:

At your order, my Führer, a young people is standing here, a young people that knows neither class nor caste. The young generation of our people models itself on you. Because you represent the greatest selflessness in this nation, young people want to be selfless too. Because you embody fidelity for us, we want to be faithful too.

Hitler's position as leader is thus once again made clear before he speaks, heightening the effect of what he has to say. He tells 'My German youth!' that they are but a small portion of the youth of Germany as a whole; they are in Nuremberg as representatives of the others. The Hitler Youth constitute the future generation of Germans and to them will fall some of the major tasks in the construction of the new classless society, bound together by blood and spirit:

> We want to be a united nation and you, my youth, are to become
> this nation. We do not want to see any more classes and strata and
> you must not allow them to develop among you. One day we want
> to see *one* nation and you must educate yourselves for it. We wish
> this people to be obedient and you must practise obedience. We
> wish this people to be peace-loving but also brave, and it must be
> prepared for war. You must therefore be prepared for war, and at
> the same time courageous. We do not wish this nation to become
> soft but want it to be hard and you will have to steel yourselves for
> this while you are still young. You must learn to accept deprivations
> without breaking down. Whatever we create and do today, we shall
> pass away, but in you Germany will live on. And when nothing is
> left of us, you will have to hold high the banner that we once lifted
> out of nothing. And I know it cannot be otherwise, because you are
> flesh of our flesh, blood of our blood, and in your young minds
> there burns the same spirit that rules us. You cannot but be united
> with us. And when the great columns of our movement march
> victoriously through Germany today, I know that you will join these
> columns. And we know that Germany lives before us, Germany
> marches with us, and Germany follows behind us.

The speech is punctuated by shots of the crowd and their expressions
of support. At one point we see the word 'Saar' spelt out by the
clothing of the spectators. In 1934 the Saar had not yet been returned
to Germany, although Germany, by this and other means, was already
laying claim to it. The boys of the Hitler Youth demonstrate their
enthusiasm by interspersing Hitler's speech with cheers and applause; at
the end they begin to sing the Horst Wessel song, as if inspired by his
words.

The next scene is a very brief one depicting military manoeuvres by
the cavalry and armoured divisions of the Wehrmacht. In the finished
version of the film this scene must be regarded as an interlude.

There follows an outdoor rally held in the early evening. 180,000
Party members are assembled, with 250,000 spectators. Hitler is placed
apart and photographed from below to emphasise that only he is an
individual, the identity of the other participants is merged into the mass.
There is a sea of Nazi flags. As darkness falls, torches and floodlights
become more prominent and a huge illuminated eagle looms on the
horizon. Hitler speaks; images of him, in close-up and in long-shot, are

intercut with the faces of the crowd and with the marching columns. The military grandeur of the occasion is reflected in the imagery of Hitler's words:

> It is not the state that commands us, but we that command the state. It is not the state that has created us, but we who are creating the state for ourselves. No, this movement is alive and it rests in rock-solid foundations, and as long as a single one of us can breathe he will devote his strengths to this movement and intercede for it as in years gone by. Then drum will join drum, banner will join banner, group will join group, region will join region and then at last the formerly divided people will follow this mighty column of the united nation.

He concludes by calling on the assembled multitude to swear an oath and consummate the ideal of national unity: 'Let us therefore take a vow this evening: namely, at every hour of every day to think only of Germany, of the people, the Reich and of our German nation. To our German people – Sieg Heil! Sieg Heil! Sieg Heil!'

With this crescendo, the apotheosis of Hitler's divinity is almost complete. He has become, in his own words, the 'lord who created our nation', the saviour who will ensure Germany's resurrection. He is the leader, alone and above the crowd, but at one with it in spirit and will. His relationship with the mass is quite unique. This scene ends with a torchlight procession, originally shot in colour – Hitler's 'mighty column of the united nation'.

Once more *Triumph of the Will* moves from night to day, from the evocation of the national spirit to the commemoration of the past. The next scene begins with the outdoor memorial service in the Luitpold Arena. We are shown a vast assembly of massed ranks, the ultimate submergence of the individual in the crowd. Three figures make their way up the middle of the huge arena: Hitler, Himmler (head of the SS) and Lutze (head of the SA). Their appearance together on such an occasion emphasises once again that the Party is united, its recent troubles are over; this theme is underlined in the next speeches. The three figures walk to the accompaniment of funereal music to a memorial amid an avenue of flaming torches. The scene is essentially static and restrained: the only movement is provided by the three figures laying the wreath, by the fluttering of flags and banners and by the slow movement of the camera sited in a lift on one of the flag-posts. (This camera can be seen moving in a subsequent shot.) The tranquillity

of the wreath-laying sequence is broken by a trumpet call which leads
into a massive march-past of banners and over 100,000 men. Members
of both SA and SS march towards the rostrum on which Hitler is
standing and peel off to both sides: the music is a stirring military
march. We are shown a sea of flags and Lutze introduces Hitler. Both he
and Hitler reiterate that the movement's troubles are now over. Hitler
goes even further and suggests not only that there have been no real
divisions in the movement, but also that neither he nor the SS were
responsible for the purge of the SA:

> Men of the SA and SS, a few months ago a black shadow arose over
> the movement. And the SA has as little to do with this shadow as
> any other institution of the Party. They deceive themselves who
> think that even a single crack has appeared in the edifice of our
> united movement. It stands firm just like this formation here —
> unbroken. And if anyone sins against the spirit of my SA this will
> break not the SA but only those who dare to sin against them. Only
> a madman or a deliberate liar could think that I, or anyone, would
> ever intend to dissolve what we have ourselves built up over many
> long years. No, comrades, we stand firmly by our Germany and we
> must stand firmly by this Germany. Now I hand over the new flags
> to you, in the conviction that I am handing them over to the most
> faithful hands in Germany. In times past you have proved your
> loyalty to me a thousand times, and it cannot and will not be
> different in times to come. [The crowd interrupts with: Heil!
> Heil! Heil!] And so I greet you as my old, faithful men of the SA
> and SS. Sieg Heil! Sieg Heil! Sieg Heil!

Hitler goes out of his way to reassure his followers in the SA that they
are not held personally responsible for the misdemeanours of their
former leaders, and that their position in the movement is unimpaired.
In fact, the SA had been placed under Hitler's personal command after
the Röhm Purge to ensure that it did not become a law unto itself.
   Hitler's speech is followed by the solemn consecration of the battle
flags seen earlier. Each one is 'blessed' by the Führer with his own
personal banner, the 'blood flag', supposedly stained with the blood of
the martyrs during the abortive Munich beer-hall putsch of November
1923. By this gesture the continuity of the movement is underscored,
the sacrifice of those commemorated at the beginning of the scene is
given meaning and purpose and Hitler's Christ-like image is reinforced,
because in a sense he is now raising the dead. Close-up shots of the

consecration are intercut with long-shots of the gun salute, to heighten
the dramatic effect, while on the sound track we hear the strains of the
Party marching song, the Horst Wessel Song: the past and the present
are mystically united in the movement and in Hitler's person.

The next scene is the longest in the film, lasting slightly over 18
minutes. It is also the most tedious — the military march-past. It begins
with a brief prelude showing the mediaeval architecture of Nuremberg,
while the music offers us more themes from Wagner's *The Master
Singers of Nuremberg*. Against this setting we see the Nazi banners
which adorn the city. Hitler drives through the streets to take up his
position on the podium. The parade is long, almost endless, and
involves all sectors of the armed and labour services from all parts of
Germany. As each contingent marches past, Hitler shakes hands with its
leader. Most give the Nazi salute, but the army still gives its traditional
salute. The inclusion of the Labour Front reiterates for the last time its
quasi-military role as it marches off into the distance, as if it were
heading for the trenches of a war. The camera is everywhere, portraying
the marching columns from every angle, and setting them against the
background of the city. As column follows column the overwhelming
impression is one of immense physical strength; this complements the
spiritual strength of the commemoration and we are ready for the final
episode, the closing session of the rally and the closing sequence of the
film.

The setting is the Luitpold Hall: at one end the platform, decorated
with flowers, banners and swastikas, is dominated by a vast eagle; at the
other end is the large slogan 'Alles für Deutschland!' (Everything for
Germany!). Hitler arrives in the hall; his favourite march is played. The
standard-bearers enter, approach the platform and peel off to either
side. The outside rally is brought indoors, the rhythm reaches its
climax. Hitler speaks. He reminds his audience that the movement
began as an embattled minority determined to take power. Now that it
has power the Party will remain the political élite of the nation for
ever: the 'constant changes have finally been replaced by a stabilising
force', by the best elements of the German nation:

> The Party will for all time to come be the élite of the political
> leadership of the German people. It will be immutable in its teaching,
> as hard as steel in its organisation, supple and adaptable in its tactics:
> but overall it will be like a religious order. However it must be our
> aim that all respectable Germans will become National Socialists.
> Only the best National Socialists are Party members . . . It is our

wish and will that this state and Reich shall endure in the millenia to come . . . Only when we in the Party, with everyone's co-operation, make it the highest embodiment of National Socialist thought and being will the Party be an eternal and indestructible pillar of the German people and Reich. One day the magnificent, glorious army – those old, proud warriors of our people – will be joined by the political leadership of the Party, even more deeply rooted in tradition, and then these two institutions will together educate and strengthen German man, and carry on their shoulders the German state, the German Reich . . . people will come and go, will be moved, pleased and inspired anew, because the idea and the movement are a living expression of our people and thus a symbol of the eternal. Long live the National Socialist movement! Long live Germany!

There is little concrete content in this culminating speech, but it has a powerful impact, albeit the impact of empty rhetoric. The camerawork differs from that in previous speeches: this time Riefenstahl has concentrated on the close-up for, having placed Hitler in his context, having shown us Hitler the deity, she now feels able to unleash on us Hitler the man. This scene, and the whole film, culminate in Hess's extraordinary remark: 'The Party is Hitler. But Hitler is Germany, just as Germany is Hitler.' Hitler's apotheosis is complete. The film ends with a column of men marching towards the screen, superimposed upon a fluttering swastika banner, to the accompaniment of the Horst Wessel Song. Germany's future is assured, guaranteed by the man who has given it the ideology, the organisation, the strength, and by the saviour who has brought it faith and resurrection.

In May 1935, in awarding *Triumph of the Will* the National Film Prize, Goebbels commented:

This film marks a very great achievement amongst the total film production for the year. It is topical in that it shows the present: it conveys in monumental and hitherto unseen images the overpowering events of our political life. It is the great cinematic vision of the Führer, seen here for the first time with a forcefulness that has not been revealed before. This film has successfully avoided the pitfall of being merely a politically slanted film. It has translated the powerful rhythm of this great epoch into something outstandingly artistic; it is monumental, imbued with the tempo of marching formations, steel-like in its conviction and fired by a passionate artistry.[8]

Thirty years later Leni Riefenstahl claimed in an interview that 'Everything is real. And there is no tendentious commentary for the simple reason that the film has no commentary at all. It is history. A purely historical film.'[9]

Notes

1. L. Riefenstahl, *Hinter den Kulissen des Reichsparteitag-Films* (Munich, 1935), p. 11.

2. Ibid., p. 15.

3. Ibid., p. 28.

4. A. Speer, *Inside the Third Reich* (London, 1970), p. 62. Speer refers to the filming of the 1935 rally, but this is clearly an error.

5. R.M. Barsam, *Filmguide to 'Triumph of the Will'* (Bloomington, Indiana, 1975), p. 22.

6. Ibid., p. 23. In an interview in 1965 Riefenstahl stated that she used only two cameras: M. Delahaye, 'Leni et le loup: entretien avec Leni Riefenstahl', *Cahiers du Cinéma*, September 1965, 46.

7. I have taken my quotations from the 16mm copy of the film available from the Imperial War Museum, London. The translations are my own. In many cases the sound track of the film differs from the official stenographic report of the Party Congress in: *Der Kongress zu Nürnberg vom 5. bis 10. September 1934. Offizieller Bericht* (Munich, 1934), and from the translated extracts in Barsam.

8. 'Die Verkündung der Buch-Filmpreise 1934/35', *Der Neue Weg*, 15 May 1935, 255.

9. Delahaye, 'Leni et le loup', 49.

14 THE WANDERING JEW

> In the cinema, more than in the theatre, the spectator must
> know whom he should hate and whom he should love.
>
> Fritz Hippler, 1942[1]

Fritz Hippler's *The Wandering Jew*, produced in 1940, ranks as one of
the most virulent propaganda films ever made. Despite the moral
reservations the contemporary spectator may have about the film (and
the present writer hopes that such reservations will be considerable),
he cannot deny that it is also one of the most powerfully effective. *The
Wandering Jew* builds to a climax that can make even a Jew feel anti-
Semitic, and it is for this reason that its circulation has been so firmly
restricted.

A major part of the film's strength lies in its pretence of documentary
objectivity. In this it contrasts with that other famous example of anti-
Semitic cinema, Veit Harlan's *Jew Süss*, which was released a matter of
months beforehand. Harlan's film was a period costume feature,
although its propagandist message was nevertheless crystal clear.
Hippler's film, however, purports to tell its audiences the truth about
the Jews: it is a 'documentary film about world Jewry',[2] just as *Triumph
of the Will* was the 'document' of the 1934 Party rally. A contemporary
critic wrote after the première on 28 November 1940:

> *The Wandering Jew* is not a fiction film, but a documentary film
> about world Jewry. It portrays, it reports, coolly and objectively, it
> operates in the style of film reportage which aims to exert its effect
> only through the incorruptible image. But its effect on the viewer
> lies precisely in this cool objectivity.[3]

That critic's description of the film is not perhaps the one that would
spring immediately to the mind of the viewer today. None the less it is
the film's façade of 'cool objectivity' that makes it such an effective
piece of propaganda even today. The director himself observed at the
time of the film's release:

> If you just allow the images in the film to take effect on you you
> will have to admit that even the most vicious caricatures and

portrayals are far less powerful in their negative effect than what reality shows us. Everyone who has had the opportunity of seeing these images says the same thing: a symphony of disgust and horror.[4]

Full disgust and horror are only released in the closing sequence of the film when a kosher ritual slaughter is depicted. This, the climax of the film, allegedly shows the Jews as they really are, rather than as they pretend to be. It is the basic tenet of *The Wandering Jew*, and of most of the anti-Semitic propaganda of Nazi Germany, that the oriental barbarian has insinuated himself cleverly into civilised European society, which he now exploits parasitically. The opening lines of the commentary make this point:

The civilised Jews that we know in Germany give us only a incomplete picture of their racial character. This film shows genuine shots of the Polish ghettoes. It shows us the Jews as they really are, before they conceal themselves behind the mask of the civilised European.

It is only Germany's actions in 1939-40 that have forced the Jews to reveal themselves in their true colours:

The war in Poland has given us the opportunity to get to know Jewry at its heart. Nearly four million Jews live here in Poland, although you would seek them in vain among the rural population. Nor have they suffered from the chaos of the war, as has the native population. They squatted indifferently, as non-participants, in the dark street of the Polish ghetto — and within an hour of the German occupation they had resumed their money dealings.

Although it is undoubtedly true that the Jewish population of Poland, as of other European countries, was overwhelmingly urban, it could hardly be claimed, even in late 1940, that they had remained unaffected by the chaos of the war. The German authorities had already begun to round up the Jews and concentrate them in the already overcrowded ghettoes of Warsaw, Łódź, Kraków and Lublin and since November 1939 Polish Jews had had to wear the yellow star. The overcrowding of the ghetto and the dirty and unhygienic conditions that the accompanying images of the film portray are thus the direct result of the German invasion and the prophecy is therefore self-fulfilling, the objectivity deliberately deceptive:

We recognise that here there lies a plague spot that threatens the
health of the Aryan people. Richard Wagner once said: 'The Jew
is the evil force behind the decay of man'. And these pictures
confirm the accuracy of his statement.

The home life of the Jews shows a marked lack of creative
ability. To put it plainly, the Jewish houses are dirty and neglected.

To emphasise to the audience that the Jews are an alien force the musical
accompaniment becomes distinctly oriental in tone at points where we
are supposed to be disgusted. The Jews, we are told, 'rarely engage in
useful work'. The German authorities have tried to use them in salvage
work, but, 'You can easily see that they aren't used to hard work and
they don't like it either.' This part of the commentary accompanies
scenes of the Jews who have been put to work. They handle their tools
awkwardly, as if unfamiliar with them, but their awkwardness is partly
due to a lack of strength caused by near starvation. Here again the
film's objectivity is misleading, purporting to prove that the Jews have
a genetic predisposition towards barter and haggling: 'They rush into
trade because it accords with their character and inclination.' They
pass this tendency on to their children, perpetuating it through their
religious teachings:

These children see no ideals before them like our own. The egoism
of the individual is not used in the service of higher common goals.
On the contrary, the Jewish racial morality proclaims, in contrast to
the Aryan morality, that the unrestrained egoism of each Jew is a
divine law. His religion in fact makes a duty out of treachery and
usury.

The Aryan attaches a sense of value to everything he does whereas,
'For the Jew there is only one object of value – money. How he earns
it is a matter of complete indifference to him.' The Aryan, according to
the commentary then, creates responsibly for the common good: the
Jew, however, trades unscrupulously for his own ends, accumulating
wealth and influence so that he can move out of street trading and the
ghetto and into the world of big business, high finance and grand
houses and stylish living, while still always living off the honest toil of
others:

They need other people because they need the goods with which to
carry on business. The things that are valued by the creative Aryan

peoples have been reduced by the Jew to the level of a mere piece of merchandise, which he buys and sells but cannot produce himself. He leaves production to the labourers and peasants of the people upon whom he has imposed his presence.

The Jews are a race without farmers and without manual labourers, a race of parasites.

By showing the way in which Jews allegedly insinuate themselves from small-scale to large-scale operations by preying on others, the film returns to its original image of the Jew concealing himself 'behind the mask of the civilised European'. The Jews may not appear to present an immediate or major threat but this is a dangerous illusion, a sign of undue complacency. According to the film, the Jew presents an insidious, because concealed, threat, and one that is growing and must be brought under control. The message of this part of the commentary is that Jews will always be Jews, that the 'civilised European' Jew is only a guise for new and more dangerous forms of parasitic exploitation:

> Whenever a sore shows itself on the body of a people, they settle themselves firmly and feed on the decaying organism. They find their business among the diseases of the people, and for this reason they do their utmost to increase and perpetuate every form of sickness.

Jewish history is a history of wandering from place to place, wherever there is business to be done:

> Their homelessness is of their own choosing and is in accordance with their whole history.
>
> Four thousand years ago their Hebrew forefathers were already on their travels. They left the Land of Two Rivers (Mesopotamia), wandering down the coast towards Egypt where, for a while, they carried on a flourishing trade in grain. When the local farming population showed resistance towards the foreign usurpers and speculators, they emigrated once more and set out on their looting raid into the Holy Land, where they settled and pillaged pitilessly its lawful and culturally more advanced inhabitants. Here, in the course of the centuries, there developed the final mongrelised Jew from the oriental Near Eastern race with negroid admixture — differing from us Europeans, coming as we do from quite different racial elements, in body and above all in soul.

The film never explains how a backward race could have outwitted its more advanced neighbours, nor does it justify its assertions about differing cultural levels. It is significant that the Jews should have been accused of despoiling the Holy Land: the holiest of Christian holies has been defiled by the advent of that lowest of the low in Nazi eyes, the 'mongrelised Jew from the oriental near Eastern race with negroid admixture'. The influx of Jews from the Middle East into Europe is blamed on the 'cosmopolitan Empire of Alexander the Great' and the 'limitless Empire of the Romans'. Wherever the Jews settled they were allegedly unpopular: 'The people of Spain and France rose against them in the 13th and 14th centuries and they travelled on further. Mainly to Germany.' From then on the Jews lived like parasites off the Germans, following them wherever they went. In contrast to the 'cosmopolitan Empire of Alexander the Great' the commentary now refers to the 'culture-bringing, creative waves of German colonisation of the east'. Clearly a double standard applies! This whole sequence depicting the spread of the Jews outward from Mesopotamia until 'vague ideas of human equality and freedom' in the nineteenth century caused them to 'spread like an irresistible tide, flooding the towns and nations of Europe, indeed the whole world' is illustrated by black, tentacle-like lines on a map of the world. The threat is now made clear.

The Jewish threat is not however the only one to come from the east. There is a history in German literature and thought of a fear of oriental despotism and barbarism. In the cinema this fear found expression in a film like *Nosferatu*: like the Jews, Nosferatu comes from the east to upset the stability of the German way of life. He brings with him a plague of rats and this brings us to the next section of the film, where the comparison is made explicit:

> Comparable with the Jewish wanderings throughout history are the mass migrations of an equally restless animal, the rat . . . Wherever rats appear they bring ruin, they ravage human property and food-stuffs. In this way they spread disease: plague, leprosy, typhoid, cholera, dysentery, etc. They are cunning, cowardly and cruel and are found mostly in large packs. In the animal world they represent the element of craftiness and underground destruction – no different from the Jews among mankind.

By associating the Jews with rats the film will have us believe that they are literally less than human: by associating them with disease-bearing parasites the distinction is compounded. It is further emphasised by the assertion that, 'This Jewish race of parasites perpetrates a large part of international crime'. From the powerful and emotive scenes of rats running through the sewers in disgustingly unsavoury conditions, we return to the 'cool objectivity' of statistics: these are produced to demonstrate that Jews figure prominently in the world of crime, out of all proportion to their total number in the population: the climax of the statistics is that for crimes connected with prostitution, underlining the earlier statement that 'Wherever a sore shows itself on the body of a people, they settle themselves firmly and feed on the decaying organism':

> In 1932 the part played by the Jews, who represent only a small percentage of the world population, in the entire drug trade of the world was 34 %, in robberies it was 47%, in card-sharping and crimes involving games of chance it was 47%, in international crime organisations it was 82%, and in prostitution 98%.

No source is given for these figures. It is further alleged that the terminology of international crime derives from the Hebrew and Yiddish languages: this is supposed to serve as further proof of the close connection between the Jews and crime, although no examples are given.

We now come to the part of the film which purports finally to strip the 'mask of the civilised European' from the Jew. The close-ups of Jewish faces allegedly 'refute impressively the liberalistic theories of the equality of all who bear a human face'. These are the Jews as they really are, and as most Germans have never seen them: we are shown a number of shots of men with long hair, beards, skull-caps and caftan, and each shot fades into one of the same man dressed in conventional European clothing. The Jews, by changing their appearance in this manner, represent an almost invisible threat to the health of the Aryan race:

> Of course they change their outward appearance when they leave their Polish nests to go out into the rich world. Hair and beard, skull cap and caftan are the distinguishing characteristics of the Eastern Jew for everyone. If he appears without them, then it is only the more keen-eyed among us who recognise his racial origins. It is an intrinsic characteristic of the Jew that he always strives to hide his parentage when he is among non-Jews.

We are now shown the Jewish peril *en masse*: first, 'A mass of Polish
Jews, now still wearing caftans and now ready to steal into Western
civilisation.' These Jews look awkward in their ill-fitting suits, rather
like monkeys at a zoo, dressed for a tea party: the implication is quite
clearly that Jews, being less than human, were never intended to wear
the clothes of the civilised European. Nevertheless, over the generations
they become accustomed to their new garb: we are shown sophisticated
Berlin Jews of the Weimar period:

> It is true that their fathers and grandfathers still lived in ghettos, but
> there is no trace left now in their external appearance. Here in the
> second and third generation, the Aryanisation has reached its zenith.
> In all superficialities they attempt to imitate their hosts. And people
> lacking in intuition allow themselves to be deceived by this
> mimicry and regard them as being in truth their equals. Therein lies
> the dreadful danger. For even these 'civilised' Jews remain foreign
> bodies in the organism of their hosts, no matter how much their
> outward appearance may correspond to that of their hosts.

The continuing alienness of the Jew applies, according to the commentary, even to Jews who have assumed the manners of the aristocrat:
the Rothschilds are quoted as the supreme example and to support
the argument, an extract from the Hollywood film, *The House of
Rothschild*, is shown. Taken out of context, the element of humour
in the original film is lost. Instead, the Jews appear in a very bad light,
as tax evaders, schemers and parasites. The extract comprises the scene
where Papa Rothschild sends his sons to different parts of Europe to
establish branches of what is to become the banking House of
Rothschild. He says to them:

> Union is strength. You must always stick together. None of the
> brothers must suffer failure while another is successful. Our five
> banking houses will rule Europe. One firm, one family – the
> Rothschilds. That will be your strength. When this power comes,
> think of the ghetto.

The pathos of the original has also been lost: 'Think of the ghetto' now
appears like a sinister threat. The intended effect of the American film
has been reversed, and this reversal is underlined by the ensuing
commentary:

So Nathan goes to London and becomes an Englishman, Jacob goes to Paris and becomes a Frenchman, Salomon goes to Vienna and becomes an Austrian, Carl goes to Naples and becomes an Italian, but Amschel stays in Frankfurt and remains a German. And yet, of course, they all remain Jews. So that when, during the period of the French Revolution, the Jews were recognised as rightfully enfranchised citizens of their respective countries, they suddenly belonged to two nations simultaneously.

The map of the Rothschild penetration of Europe is of course similar to that of the expansion of the Jewish race generally and of the spread of plague-carrying vermin. To the film propagandist there is no difference.

The Jews then have successfully established themselves in positions of world power. The commentary goes on to tell us that, 'They are an international power. Although only a small percentage of the world's population, with the help of their capital they terrorise the world's stock exchanges, world opinion, and world politics.' Clearly the Jews pose a problem that must be dealt with before it is too late. Our attention is directed towards the latest examples of this alleged Jewish threat:

Today New York is the centre of Jewish power, and the New York stock exchange, the financial centre of the world, is ruled by the Jewish banking-houses – Kahn, Loew, Warburg, Hanauer, Wertheim, Lewisohn, Seligmann, Guggenheim, Wolf, Schiff, Kraus, Stern, etc. These kings of finance love to keep themselves in the background and let their power dramas take place behind the scenes.

In appearance they have adapted themselves to their host nation. They look almost like genuine Americans.

The film pursues this point by providing illustrated examples of prominent Jews in public life: Bernard Baruch ('the Jewish financial adviser and friend of the American president, in the mask of a smart American citizen'), Otto Kahn ('Jewish Wall Street banker, flatters himself in the pose of an Anglo-Saxon Lord'), Léon Blum, former French Prime Minister and leader of the Popular Front government, ('he holds himself', says the commentator in a particularly backhanded compliment, 'like a true Frenchman. Millions of French workers honoured him once as their party head') and finally, Hore-Belisha, the former Secretary of State for War, whose role enables this sequence to end with a shot of 'English soldiers saluting their Jewish commanding officer'. It is not

surprising that Jewish 'contamination' of the English and French blood
stock should be depicted in this film: *The Eternal Forest*, made in
1936, had already depicted the French as heavily threatened by an
influx of African blood, and Goebbels had already described the English
as 'the Jews among the Aryans', by way of extending Napoleon's
alleged assertion that they were nothing but 'a nation of shopkeepers'.
It is however of great interest to see the USA denounced in this way, a
year before Pearl Harbor, and this denunciation suggests that German
propagandists had already abandoned any real hope of attracting
American support: indeed, in view of the allegations about Jewish
power contained in the film, it would have seemed logical to expect the
film itself to encourage American support for Britain and France.

Having demonstrated, to its own satisfaction at least, that Jewish
influence is still rife amongst the Allies or potential Allies, the film then
reasserts that 'the Jew remains a rootless parasite, even when he is in
power. His power does not come from his own strength, it only lasts as
long as misled people are prepared to carry them on their backs.' This
assertion carries us back to the Jewish threat in Germany itself, and to
the Weimar Republic. Here *The Wandering Jew* recalls the opening
sequence of *Triumph of the Will* and the slogan carried on Nazi Party
banners: 'Germany, awake!':

> Let us remember those vile days, when Germans lay stretched
> defenceless on the ground.
> It was then that the Jews seized their chance. They came to the
> forefront as if, like faithful citizens, deeply disturbed about the fate
> of the German people.
> And so they hurried into the so-called National Assembly in
> Weimar, where Germany's future was to be decided.

This part of the film is intended to reiterate the view that the Weimar
Republic was essentially an alien constitutional structure foisted by a
foreign conspiracy upon a weakened and prostrate country, whose
morale, as well as physical power to resist, had been completely sapped.
We are shown pictures of those responsible:

> The Jewish representative Landsberger, on his left: Scheidemann.
> The Jew Hirsche, Prime Minister of Prussia. The Jew Theodor Wolf,
> chief editor of the *Berliner Tageblatt*. The Jew Georg Bernhard, head
> of the Ullstein publishing-house. The Jew, Hugo Preuss, creator of
> the German republican constitution. The Jew Walther Rathenau,

Foreign Minister of the German Republic. The Jew Hilfferding, German Minister of Finance. The Jew Bernhard Isidor Weiss, assistant chief of police in Berlin.

The last named of these 'guilty men' was a favourite target of the Nazis, and Goebbels had collaborated in the production of a vicious work entitled 'The Book of Isidor' in 1928.[5] Despite the allegation that the Jews more or less ran the Weimar Republic for their own ends, the commentator goes on to assert that they were also responsible for undermining law and order:

Masquerading as selfless public benefactors, they promised great things, and incited the masses to break the bonds of civil order. Unchecked personal freedom and enjoyment of life to the full for the individual, rejection of all obligations to an ideal and denial of all higher values. Recognition of the lowest material form of pleasure, unrestrained criticism of the most sacred things, revolt, in fact, against everything that had existed, incitement of youth, stirring people up to class war and terror acts. It is no accident that this false doctrine, which disrupts whole nations, sprang from the brain of a Jew.
Karl Marx, son of the rabbi and lawyer Margochei in Trèves.

The connection made in this way between the Jews and the dark forces of disorder allows the propagandist to play on the memory of Nazi assertions of a Jewish-Bolshevik world conspiracy, which itself harks back to the imagery of things like the Protocols of the Elders of Zion. Again we return to the Jew hiding behind the mask of a civilised European: 'The founder and first organiser of the German Social Democratic Party was the Jew Ferdinand Lassalle-Wolfson. The Jewess Rosa Luxemburg, whose real name was Emma Goldmann, one of the most notorious communist agitators.' Names like these are trundled in the mud, mentioned only to be belittled and smeared, to be fitted into the stereotype that has already been created. No attempt is made to understand, let alone sympathise with, the historical origins of the Jewish dilemma, nor does the propagandist allow his audience pause for thought on these matters.

To strengthen the case made in *The Wandering Jew* the commentator then brings us some statistics from the Weimar Republic that demonstrate the disproportionate preponderance of Jews in the upper echelons of society, and their disproportionate absence from the more

menial tasks and strata. They have achieved this status, 'Not by honour-
able work, but by usury, swindles and fraud', for Jews have also been
prominent in the world of crime. The nadir of the Jewish role thus
established, the film goes on to survey the part played by Jews in
influencing or corrupting the artistic life of the nation:

> Jews are, however, most dangerous when they are allowed to meddle
> in the people's holy of holies, in its culture, in its religion and art,
> and to give their presumptuous judgements on it. The Northerner's
> concept of beauty is by nature completely incomprehensible to the
> Jew and will always remain so.
> The rootless Jew has no feeling for the purity and neatness of the
> German idea of art.
> What he calls art must titillate his degenerate nerves. A smell of
> fungus and disease must pervade it, it must be unnaturally grotesque,
> perverted or pathological.

The viewer is then shown a series of paintings exhibited at the 'Degenerate Art' exhibition held in the Haus der Kunst in Munich in 1937.
This exhibition took place at the same time as the first anti-Semitic
exhibition under the title 'The Wandering Jew', which was also held in
Munich. The film now lambasts the Jews for unleashing a torrent of
'vulgarisation and bastardisation', pornography and sexual perversion:
'Under the cloak of ingenious or even learned discussion they tried to
turn the healthy urges of mankind on to degenerate paths.' Here the
propagandist is on fairly safe ground, playing on the familiar popular
prejudices about the artist, and about modern art in particular. His
technique in *The Wandering Jew* is several steps further down the road
from accusations made against Eisenstein for making films that were
'incomprehensible to the millions'. The Jews, it is alleged, turned all
the Teutonic virtues into vices: 'Tucholsky, one of the sickest porno
graphers, coined these words: that treason is an honour, and that the
heroic ideal is the most stupid of all ideals.' Examples from the film
world follow, and in particular excerpts from *Dimitri Karamazov –
Murderer* and from Fritz Lang's film *M*. Both these films delve inside
the mind of a murderer and try to convey to the audience some understanding of the motives that drove him to commit his crime. But to the
Nazis the murderer is just a criminal, unless of course he happens to be
a Nazi. In the concluding section of this sequence other Jews
denounced as such are Richard Tauber the singer, Ernst Lubitsch the
film director, Emil Ludwig (or Ludwig-Cohn, as the film would have it)

the writer, and 'the Jew Chaplin'. Chaplin's popularity is particularly difficult to explain away, and the only way in which this can be done effectively is by maintaining that the German people were fooled into accepting his art at its face value:

> The Jew Chaplin was welcomed by an enraptured mob when he visited Berlin. It cannot be denied that at that time a portion of the German public applauded unsuspectingly the foreign Jew, the deathly enemy of their race. How was that possible? A mendacious dogma of human equality had dimmed the healthy instinct of the people.

This assertion acts both as a conclusion to the sequence of the film dealing with the Jewish role in art and simultaneously serves as an introduction to the final part of the film which allegedly exposes the Jewish religion in its true colours.

Christianity, according to *The Wandering Jew*, has propagated the delusion that Jews and Christians were brothers, and Christian art had, perhaps unwittingly, perpetuated this view:

> High-minded German painters and poets had projected their conceptions of the ideal into the biblical figures of the Hebrew tribal history. Abraham, Isaac and Jacob are considered as pillars of a particularly high standard of morality and ideals of noblest humanity.

Man has, however, since become aware that his ideas of the Jewish ancients were idealised conceptions, bearing but a tenuous relationship to reality. The celebration of the Purim festival is taken as an example, and we are shown film of it: 'We must correct our historical picture. This is what genuine Hebrews look like.' The festival, we are told, may be dismissed by 'the German educated class, with its prudent and objective spirit of tolerance' as an example of 'original folklore and strange customs'. But its true significance can only be understood against the background of Jewish religious observance and teaching, for 'The Jew is brought up in the law of his race'. The guardians of the religious tradition, the rabbis, are denigrated as 'masters of the art of hypocrisy', 'not peaceful theologians but political distorters'. In other words the propagandist is once again hammering away at the theme that everything is not quite as it seems, and that the Jew, regardless of appearances, represents an insidious threat. The commentator remarks

that, 'The politics of a race of parasites must be made in secret!' The
'threat' is illustrated with a few carefully chosen extracts from the
Talmud, for example: 'Five things did Canaan recommend to his sons:
love each other, love pillage, love excess, hate your master, and never
speak the truth.' Having exposed the Talmud, the film attempts to
belittle the ritual of a synagogue service, making its symbolism appear
both cheap and sinister: 'they count on the fact that people do not
understand their language and thus the secret ambiguity of their
symbols. Therefore they agree to appear before the cameramen even
while at worship.' The practice of the synagogue is ridiculed and the
teachings of the Torah extracted out of context to confirm the closing
assertion of this sequence: 'That is no religion and no religious service,
that is a conspiracy against all non-Jews, of a cunning, unhealthy,
contaminated race, against the health of the Aryan peoples and against
their moral laws.'

By now the viewer has experienced almost the whole gamut of anti-
Semitic propaganda. He has been shown how the European Jew is only
a façade behind which the 'real' Oriental Jew still lurks, how the Jews
have spread rat-like from the Middle East, infiltrating and infecting the
body politic, financial and cultural. The apparently pernicious influence
of the Jews in the Weimar Republic and in the film world has been
particularly emphasised, and finally the Jewish religion has been
exposed as a façade behind which the Jewish race plots a further
expansion of its power and influence. Battered by rhetoric, blinded by
a profusion of images, his resistance undermined by the film's pseudo-
scientific documentary approach, the viewer is now to be dealt the
coup de grâce while he is at his lowest ebb: the slaughterhouse
sequence, which is alleged to have been the rationale for the whole film.

This final sequence is introduced not by the commentator but by
titles rolling across the screen, thus conveying the impression that this is
a 'document':

One of the most instructive customs of the Jewish so-called religion
is the slaughter of animals. The following pictures are genuine. They
are among the most horrifying that a camera has ever taken. We are
showing them in spite of this, without regard for objections on the
grounds of taste. Because, more important than all objections is the
fact that our people should know the truth about Judaism.

When the film was released in Germany it was shown in two versions.
At the opening season at the Ufa-Palast am Zoo the film was shown

twice daily: once at 4 p.m. in a shortened version, and once at 6.30 p.m. in the complete version. Contemporary advertisements announced:

> Since additional original material of Jewish animal slaughters will be shown at the 6.30 performance those of a sensitive disposition are recommended to see the 4 o'clock performance.
> Likewise women will only be admitted to the 4 o'clock performance.[6]

According to Veit Harlan, the director of the anti-Semitic costume feature film *Jew Süss*, Goebbels had originally intended the scenes from the Warsaw ghetto abattoir to be included in that film; Harlan had been able to dissuade him on the grounds that, 'The public would be nauseated'. Harlan claimed that the sequence was so powerful that he had had to drink a whole bottle of cognac in order to sit through it, and even then, 'Most of the time I shut my eyes'. Goebbels also accepted Harlan's view that the effect of these shots would diminish the effectiveness of the rest of the film: 'Goebbels saw that straight away and I was rid of the scene.'[7] But Goebbels was unwilling to drop the shots altogether, and so the idea for *The Wandering Jew* as a prelude to these scenes, and as a means of making them more effective, arose and the project was handed over to Fritz Hippler, the *Reichsfilmintendant*.

It is impossible to recapture the effect of a powerful set of images in words and I shall therefore only attempt a cursory description of the contents of this notorious sequence. The commentator asserts that, 'Seemingly their so-called religion prevents the Jews from eating meat that has been butchered in the ordinary way. Therefore they let the animals bleed to death.' We see the first shots of an animal being tethered. The commentary contrasts Jewish callousness with 'Germanic respect and love for animals' and portrays the National Socialists as the apostles of the Germanic tradition. But, we are told, the Jewish-dominated press portrayed all moves to protect animals as anti-Semitic, and a series of newspaper cuttings is shown in quick succession to support this allegation: the cuttings rise to a climax with a shot of a headline in the Social Democratic Party paper *Vorwärts* proclaiming 'Assault on the constitution repulsed' and one from the Communist Party paper *Die rote Fahne* announcing that the Nazi motion to outlaw kosher ritual slaughter has failed. Thus, once more, the left-wing parties are tainted with the Jewish brush and the inability of the Weimar Republic to take action to protect Germanic standards is underlined. The commentator then asserts that the 'Jewish press' could only get away with this because so few Germans had witnessed a ritual

slaughter, and this assertion provides the justification for showing the
following scenes: 'These pictures are unequivocal evidence of the
cruelty of this form of slaughter. At the same time they reveal the
character of a race that conceals its crude brutality under the cloak of
pious religious practices.' We are now shown the horrifying sequence
of an animal, its legs tied, having its throat slit open, writhing in agony,
moaning and groaning, while a grinning Jewish butcher pulls out its
entrails. Whatever the effect of the previous scenes of the film, the
impact of this scene is overwhelming: it leaves the audience battered
into submission.

The film concludes, in contrast, with a series of decrees and laws
passed by the National Socialist government outlawing Jewish ritual
slaughter techniques. Then we see decrees dealing with the problem
of the Jews themselves: 'Just as it dealt with this cruel slaughter, so
the Germany of National Socialism will deal with the whole race of
Jewry.' The Jews are deprived of the right to German citizenship, of
the right to marry non-Jews, and are gradually excluded from the life
of the new Reich. The film ends with Hitler's speech to the Reichstag
of 30 January 1939, and the threats contained in this speech make it
clear that the ritual slaughter sequence we have just seen is but an
allegory for the fate that is awaiting the Jews who are, in the Nazi
view, no better than the animals that they themselves have been killing:

> If international finance Jewry inside and outside Europe were to
> succeed in pushing people into another world war, then the result
> would be, not the bolshevisation of the earth and the consequent
> victory of Judaism, but the destruction of the Jewish race in Europe.
>   The eternal law of nature, keeping the race pure, is the legacy
> that the National Socialist movement bequeaths to the German
> people in perpetuity. It is in this spirit that the German people
> marches into the future.

We see Hitler as the saviour of the Aryan race, depicted by young blonde
Germans photographed against the sky: columns of SA and SS men
march through Nuremberg, and this image dissolves into one of flags
and banners. We are back at the final scene of *Triumph of the Will* and
the German people's tryst with destiny.

The Wandering Jew was shown at 66 cinemas in Berlin alone[8] but
Security Service reports on its reception suggest that audiences, after
Jew Süss, were already tiring of anti-Semitic propaganda: 'Statements
like "We've seen *Jew Süss* and we've had enough of Jewish filth" have

been heard.'[9] Nevertheless in August 1941 the German authorities in the occupied Netherlands decreed that every Dutch cinema should include *The Wandering Jew* in its programme during the following six-month period. And so the film became at the same time a prelude to the holocaust, a propagandist's excuse for it, and a perverted documentary-format record of its early stages.

From the National Socialist point of view the film ends on a note of hope and optimism. The contemporary critic already quoted observed, presumably out of conviction rather than pure cynicism: 'When the film concludes by showing German people and scenes of German life, then the viewer breathes again. From the lowest depths he comes once more to the light.'[10] In January 1941 *The Wandering Jew* was shown in Łódź (then called Litzmannstadt), where much of the ghetto material had been filmed. The magazine *Film-Kurier* reported:

The film camera wandered through the ghetto of Litzmannstadt before the orderly hand of German authority had intervened and cleaned out this Augean stable so that it could get a realistic and unvarnished picture of the stinking pit from which world Jewry acquires its steadily increasing numbers.

The figures and faces shown in the film once moved through the streets of this city, trading and sponging. Here they felt safe under the protection of the Polish authorities, who let them do as they wished and considerably furthered their interests. Here, because of the astonishingly high population, they held almost all economic and cultural life in their hands — in so far as one can talk of a cultural life under Polish hegemony.

The film created a very strong impression.[11]

Notes

1. F. Hippler, *Betrachtungen zum Filmschaffen* (Berlin, 1942), p. 100.
2. From the titles of the film. An English translation of the commentary is provided with the copies of the film that are available from the Imperial War Museum, London, and I have largely followed this.
3. A. Brodbeck, 'Der ewige Jude — Uraufführung des grossen Dokumentarfilms', *Deutsche Allgemeine Zeitung*, 29 November 1940, reprinted in J. Wulf, *Theater und Film im Dritten Reich. Eine Dokumentation* (Reinbek bei Hamburg, 1966), p. 457.
4. *Der Film*, 30 November 1940.
5. Cf. E.K. Bramsted, *Goebbels and National Socialist Propaganda 1925-1945* (London, 1965), pp. 36-7; 471.
6. Wulf, *Theater und Film im Dritten Reich*, p. 456; see also D. Hollstein, *Antisemitische Filmpropaganda. Die Darstellung des Juden im nationalsozialistischen Spielfilm* (Munich, 1971), p. 114.

7. V. Harlan, *Im Schatten meiner Filme. Selbstbiographie* (Gütersloh, 1966), p. 112.

8. Brodbeck, 'Der ewige Jude'.

9. Report dated 20 January 1941, quoted in E. Leiser, *Nazi Cinema* (London, 1974).

10. Brodbeck, 'Der ewige Jude'.

11. *Film-Kurier*, 20 January 1941 quoted in Wulf, *Theater und film im Dritten Reich*, p. 458.

15 UNCLE KRUGER

> The historical film is not a museum. Only the names are
> historical. The ideas are contemporary . . . The Boers' fight
> against England has its parallel in today's great struggle.
> Germany would have shared these people's fate if the Führer
> had not recognised the danger . . . The historical film is the
> child of our century. It is the mirror of the past, the bulwark
> of the present, a guide for the future.
>
> Ewald von Demandowsky, 1941[1]

In their propaganda campaign against the British (or, more accurately,
the English[2]), the Nazis not surprisingly selected four of the murkier
episodes in the history of Britain's relationships with other peoples:
Palestine, India, Ireland and Africa.[3] Palestine and India did not
become the subject of feature films: in Palestine there was a double
enemy, the British and the Jews, and, although they could easily be
depicted as conniving to suppress the Arabs, this would have complicated the simplicity of the propagandist's message. In India the problem
would have been slightly different: although there was ample genetic
evidence that the Indians had Aryan connections, it would have been
difficult for the Nazis to portray coloured people as superior, even to
the British, whom Goebbels once described as the 'Jews among the
Aryans'.[4]

The subject of Ireland produced two powerful films: *The Fox of
Glenarvon* in 1940 and *My Life for Ireland* in 1941. These films, like
Uncle Kruger, were intended to prepare German audiences for Operation
Sealion, the invasion of the British Isles. They constitute a powerful
indictment of the crimes committed by the British against their nearest
neighbours, and they would make far more effective propaganda for
the IRA than the slaughter of innocent civilians. But it was in Africa,
and in the long envied process of imperial expansion and colonisation,
that the Nazis found the most fertile ground for their propaganda.

The first anti-British film produced under the Nazis was *The Riders
of German East Africa*, made by Herbert Selpin in 1934. But in this
film, and in *A Man Wants to Go to Germany*, made in the same year,
the British, although clearly identified as the enemy, are portrayed as
individuals with some sympathy. In the first film the British soldier is

secretly relieved when the German friends he is supposed to be guarding escape, while in the second the British prison-camp commandant regards his job as unfitting for an officer. But in 1934 Britain, while still a potential enemy, was also a potential ally to be wooed. By 1941 the situation was of course quite different: in Selpin's *Carl Peters* the British Empire is castigated as a threat to Germany's legitimate interest in acquiring colonies and a 'place in the sun'. The Germans are depicted as paternal protectors of the natives while the British abuse and exploit them: the moral superiority of the Germans clearly makes them more fitted for the responsibilities of imperialism and colonisation. The same message comes across in *Germanin*, made in 1943, in which the German doctor brings to Africa a cure for sleeping sickness and the British role is confined to putting obstacles in his way. A similar contrast in attitudes may be discerned in the most famous anti-British film of all, Hans Steinhoff's *Uncle Kruger*, released in 1941 and set in the Boer War.

The original idea for the film came from the man who was to play the leading role, Emil Jannings.[5] The Boer War already had a place in the collective German memory as an example of the way in which a weak power can be pushed around by a strong one: what happened to the Transvaal in the Boer War had also happened to Germany in the Treaty of Versailles, and would undoubtedly happen again if she relaxed her vigilance. The programme that was issued for the film's première drew comfort from the parallel. Referring to the events in southern Africa as 'one of those mediaeval raids', the programme continued:

> The Boers' desperate struggle against England is the first signal of a new era[6] which pits the tradesmen's methods of the Empire against the combined strength of a united people. In this sense Bismarck's words as an old man gain a prophetic significance: 'South Africa will one day be the grave of England as a world power. England will bleed to death there.'[7]

This is the same kind of wishful thinking that was to manifest itself in *Kolberg* and it is perhaps significant that Goebbels took the same close and detailed interest in *Uncle Kruger* that he was to take in Veit Harlan's epic.[8]

The film opens in a hotel room in Switzerland where Kruger (President of the Transvaal from 1883 to 1900) is living out his last days in exile. The hotel is besieged by reporters eager to record his reaction to the British victory in South Africa. One of them offers the manager 300 francs as a bribe to gain admittance to Kruger's suite. The reporter is Jewish but the manager is Swiss: he takes the money and says that he will give it to the Red Cross. Right and wrong are thus clearly established. But the reporter succeeds in bribing a page. Upstairs in a darkened room Kruger is being examined by a doctor who warns him that for the sake of his health, he must stop taking such an interest in the events of the outside world. We see Kruger from behind: he is old and frail. At this point the reporter bursts into the room. He fires questions at the old man and takes photographs. The popping of his flash-bulb emphasises the shock of the intrusion: Kruger faces the camera and we see from his dark glasses that he is now completely blind. Delighted with his scoop, the reporter leaves. He has brutally shattered the calm of Kruger's retirement and his action has predisposed the audience to sympathise with the old man. Left alone with the nurse, Kruger asks her to read the newspaper to him. She picks up *The Times* and reads (from the front page!) the headline: 'The Boers have become British citizens'. To this Kruger retorts, in Goebbels' very own words: 'The world forgets quickly and, if you go on repeating a lie for long enough, people will believe it in the end.'[9] He then begins to recount the history of the Boer settlement of southern Africa and the bulk of the film's action takes place within the framework of a flashback: in this sense too *Uncle Kruger* has affinities with *Kolberg*, for the flashback provides an opportunity for the film maker to underline the significance of past events for the present and the immediate future. In an interview Emil Jannings characterised Kruger as 'the first conscious pioneer against England' and his work as 'an example above all for us Germans who are now bringing the struggle against England's imperialism to an end'.[10]

We see the Boer pioneers, the *Voortrekker*, moving across the screen: 'Thus was the Transvaal born'. The film cuts to a conversation between Cecil Rhodes (played by Ferdinand Marian, who specialised in oily villains, playing *The Fox of Glenarvon* and *Jew Süss*) and Dr Jameson, who are scheming and gloating over a map of Africa. Rhodes has designs on Boer territory to secure the mineral deposits there: he is prepared to go to war to get it. He is then like the Wandering Jew: he manipulates other people and speculates at their expense, while the hard toil, the productive labour, is left to others, in this case, the Boer *Voortrekker*. Rhodes orders Jameson to create border disturbances to give Britain an excuse for war, and at the same time he despatches an emissary to London to enlist the support of the Secretary of State for the Colonies, Joseph Chamberlain. Until Chamberlain's support is guaranteed Rhodes contents himself with the thought that he has the support of the missionaries. In the next scene we see three missionaries singing 'God Save the Queen': one of them is distributing Bibles to a line of natives, while another distributes the guns with which the Africans are to stir up trouble. The altar is covered with the Union Jack: the missionaries are thus seen as tools of the British government, and Britain is seen as a cynical exploiter of the native population for its own selfish purposes.

The following scene offers a complete contrast to the scheming and degenerate British. It is set in Kruger's office. Jameson has been arrested for gun-running and for irresponsibly distributing arms to the natives. He is heatedly denying the charges when Kruger enters. After an argument in which Kruger reasserts the Boers' right to live in peace, Jameson is released, because he is not the principal enemy, only his agent. As Kruger says, 'If you want to kill a tortoise you must wait until it sticks its head out from under its shell.' The President then holds his audience hour: the simplicity of his surroundings and his accessibility to his own people contrast favourably with the aura that surrounds the British authorities: Kruger is a man of the people, Rhodes is clearly not. This is underlined by the encounter with an elderly warrior who has come to complain to the President that he is being replaced by younger men. When Kruger suggests the possibility that the old man may now be too old to fight, he is challenged to a finger-pulling contest which the warrior wins. He is allowed to resume his duties to his intense delight: thus are the problems of the Transvaal solved. The next visitors are a couple who want to sell their farm to the British, who want to mine the land underneath it for gold. Kruger is angry and tells them that 'You don't abandon the land you inherited from your forefather!' Again we can see similarities with the attitude of the Kolbergers here. The incident results in a new piece of legislation forbidding Boers to sell their land to a foreigner.

The next scene shows us Kruger the family man. His son Jan returns with his family from England, where he has been studying at university. The son is inclined to admire the British way of life and give them the benefit of the doubt, but the father distrusts them completely. He turns to his son when a messenger brings news of a native uprising, pinning the responsibility on 'Your friends, the English'. When Jan protests, Kruger repeatedly mutters, 'England is our enemy'. The scene that follows has been excised from some versions of the film. It depicts a native encampment where a war dance is being performed. The chief, putting the last touches to his war paint, is dressed in a British uniform and a portrait of Queen Victoria hangs on the wall. None the less he refuses to tell Kruger who supplied the arms, but gives in when threatened. Both he and Kruger, speaking in the local dialect, calm the natives down. To the natives Kruger behaves like a father to his children, and in the film all the inhabitants of the Transvaal are seen as members of one great family. The British, on the other hand, exploit the native population, using them for their own commercial and political ends: it is therefore the duty of the Boers to protect the natives against the British.

From the simplicity of the native village the film takes us to the splendours of Buckingham Palace. Queen Victoria, attended by a John Brown complete with kilt, has a fit of coughing and asks for her 'medicine'. This turns out to be a bottle of whisky. The Queen has granted an audience to Chamberlain, who brings news of border troubles. She is unwilling to take action, although he urges the annexation of the Transvaal. 'Providence', he tells her, 'has called upon England to educate small and backward nations. It is our duty to take over the Boer lands.' Victoria reminds him that the Boers have friends all over Europe, but especially in Holland and Germany: England, on the other hand, is friendless. Chamberlain is driven to reveal the discovery of gold: 'We British are the only ones capable of carrying the burdens of wealth without becoming ungodly.' Victoria relents: 'If there's gold, then of course it's our country.' But, rather than go to war, she decides to invite Kruger, who is referred to as 'the old fool', to London on a state visit. After all, 'treaties are cheaper than wars'. Kruger is obviously suspicious of the invitation, but accepts it to his son's evident delight. He is received with great pomp and ceremony. In private conversation Victoria and Kruger discuss their rheumatism: affairs of state no longer interest her and she is portrayed as the innocent and senile dupe of evil schemers like Chamberlain and Rhodes. She also, unlike them, has a touch of humanity. While the treaty of friendship is being signed, Rhodes and Jameson have started the mining, albeit unauthorised, that will precipitate the war. The British are thus unscrupulous and hypocritical, and the film mocks Chamberlain's claims about godliness. Kruger is attacked in the Boer parliament and prepares his resignation: he is a man of principle. Then he is visited by Rhodes, who is quite clearly devoid of any principles at all. He offers Kruger a blank cheque to sell out his people. Kruger refuses, throws him out, and decides to stay on to lead the struggle.

The Transvaal mobilises for war. The Boers, who are defending their own land, assemble in Pretoria with arms and banners denouncing England. Jan Kruger argues with his father that war will mean 'the end of our liberty', but the President throws him out too and goes out on to the balcony to address his people. The war begins with a spectacular battle that results in victory for the Boers. Kruger arrives and asks his troops to kneel and pray to their God in thanksgiving. Jeffrey Richards has written of this scene: 'The sequence, shot over his shoulder as he stands on top of a hill to bless his kneeling followers grouped at the bottom, looks like nothing less than the Sermon on the Mount.'[11] In contrast to this Christ-like apparition the British are represented in the next scene by their new commander-in-chief, Lord Kitchener, who declares total war: in 1941 total war is thus seen as a British invention and therefore to be abhorred, but two years later very similar sentiments were being publicly expressed by Goebbels. Kitchener declares: 'No more humanitarian day-dreams! That means we must hit the Boers where it hurts. Their farms must be burnt, the women and children separated from the men and put in concentration camps. From now on all Boers without exception are outlaws. No distinction will be made between soldiers and civilians.' Thus the concentration camps are also a British invention. Kitchener's general threat is particularised in the next scene at Jan Kruger's farm. A drunken British soldier enters and attempts to rape Jan's wife while he is out of the room. Jan at last identifies with the Boer cause: he shoots the soldier dead and enlists in his own army. This action, and his subsequent sacrifice, compensate for his earlier ambivalence: in the end he comes out on the right side. The war resumes and Pretoria is bombarded by the British, who use women and children as shields: the news of this atrocity sends Kruger blind with horror. Jan persuades him to visit Europe to mobilise support for the Boer cause. There are touching scenes of family farewell as Kruger leaves his beloved land and people for the last time.

In London Queen Victoria lies dying. Attempts to find her son, the dissolute Prince of Wales, lead to a seedy night club in Paris. The British are decadent as well as unscrupulous. On her deathbed Victoria reveals the true British credo: 'On the day when nations cease to hate one another, Britain is lost.' She predicts that at some time in the future Britain will be punished for her crimes: clearly the task has fallen to Germany in 1941. This is the message of *Uncle Kruger* to its embattled audience: Emil Jannings himself said: 'One must have something to say to the world, if it is to listen.'[12] While Victoria dies repentant, thus confirming her essential goodness, her troops in South Africa are committing the most bestial atrocities, the kind of thing that the German armies were committing on the Eastern front on civilian

and military victims alike. Jan Kruger's farm is burnt down and his
wife is told, 'Don't worry. We are taking you to a concentration camp.'
We see the farm in flames, the horses fleeing in panic, and corpses
being interred in a mass grave. Then, as a climax to this sequence, we
are taken inside a British concentration camp.

The scenes in the concentration camp owe much to Eisenstein and
they are the nearest that the Nazi cinema ever got to fulfilling Goebbels'
demand that it should produce a German *Battleship Potemkin*. It was
typical of the cynicism of the Nazi propaganda machine that it should
have accused the enemy of, and condemned it for, using the very method
of dealing with troublesome elements that the Nazis were themselves
using. The tactic embraces a curious mixture of moral opprobrium and
uneasy self-justification. The camp consists of tents lining a hillside,
rather like the encampment of the Teutonic Knights in *Alexander
Nevsky*. The women, including Kruger's captured wife, gather and
complain about the food. They are abused and beaten. The camp
commandant is a large, fat man with facial features that are clearly
intended to suggest Winston Churchill. He breakfasts lavishly, tossing
large lumps of meat to his bulldog, while the Boer women and children
starve. Typhoid is rampant, the prisoners' situation desperate. Outside,
one of the Boer women waves a tin of meat that has gone bad (echoes
of *Potemkin*) and the medical orderly is summoned to pass judgement.
He is tempted to agree with the women's complaint but is cowed by the
commandant into pronouncing the food good. The women are outraged, but silenced by the two shots with which the commandant kills
the woman who first complained. Boer lives are cheap in a British
concentration camp.

Meanwhile Kruger is given sympathy but no active assistance on his
tour of the courts of Europe. Back in the Transvaal Jan returns to find
his farm razed to the ground and abandoned. He makes his way to the
concentration camp at night and eventually manages to communicate
with his wife. But they cannot hold hands through the barbed wire: in
their ruthless pursuit of gold the British divide even man and wife
from one another. Worse is yet to come: Jan learns that his children
have all been killed. A patrol appears and he is shot and captured. The
following morning Jan is hanged from a tree stump at the top of the
hill, hanged in front of his wife and mother and the other Boer women
and children. The scene on the gaunt and arid hillside reminds the
viewer of Christ's agony on Golgotha and Jan's sacrifice for his people
echoes Christ's sacrifice for mankind in the imagery of the film. Jan's
dying words are: 'Our faith is greater than death. England be damned!'

The commandant shoots Jan's wife dead and this sparks a rebellion. The inmates rush up the hill towards the scaffold, just as the crowd in *Potemkin* rushes up the Odessa Steps. Like that crowd too the Boer women and children are mown down by the descending troops. The scene dissolves into a landscape of crosses, orphaned children crying on the sound track. The British stand condemned.

In the closing scene of the film we return to Kruger's hotel room in Switzerland. To a crescendo of music Kruger proclaims:

> That was the end. That is how England subjugated our small nation by the cruellest means. But one day the time for vengeance will come. I do not know when, but so much blood cannot have been shed in vain, so many tears cannot have been shed for nothing. We were only a small, weak nation. Great and powerful nations will rise against the English tyranny. They will crush England and then the way will be open to a better world.

The message for the 1941 audience is crystal clear, and SS reports demonstrated that it had got across: 'For wide circles of the population the film had undoubtedly fulfilled its propagandistic purpose. The belligerent attitude towards England has been significantly strengthened and deepened.'[13] The film was released on 4 April 1941 in Berlin. Shortly afterwards it became the first film to be honoured with the new designation 'Film of the Nation'. Emil Jannings was presented with something called the 'Ring of Honour of the German Cinema' and, at the Venice film festival, *Uncle Kruger* won the Mussolini Prize for the best foreign film. For obvious reasons there was much support for the idea, voiced by Kruger in the film, that 'One can never come to an understanding with the English'.

Notes

1. E. von Demandowsky, 'Le film historique et nous', in *Ohm Krueger. Un film d'Emil Jannings de la Tobis* (Paris, 1941), no page nos.

2. The Germans, like most foreigners, were generally confused about the distinction between the English and the British. This did not however prevent them from establishing two short-lived radio stations aimed at fomenting nationalism in Wales and Scotland. Nor did it prevent them from making the two Irish films mentioned or from using the life of Mary Stuart as an allegory for English exploitation of Scotland. This last film, *The Heart of a Queen*, starred Zarah Leander as a musical Queen of Scots and portrayed the English as foppish and effeminate schemers.

3. See, for instance: W. Ziegler (ed.), *Über die englische Humanität. Ein Dokumentenwerk* (Berlin, 1941?).

4. E. Leiser, *Nazi Cinema* (London, 1974), p. 105.
5. Interview with Hans Steinhoff in *Völkischer Beobachter*, 5 March 1941.
6. This was also the title of a collection of Goebbels' speeches published in 1934.
7. *Zur festlichen Aufführung des Emil Jannings Films der Tobis 'Ohm Krüger'* (Berlin, 1941), no page nos.
8. F. Hippler, *Betrachtungen zum Filmschaffen* (Berlin, 1943), p. 110; C. Riess, *Das gab's nur einmal* (Hamburg, 1956), p. 639.
9. This analysis of *Uncle Kruger* is based on the 16mm copy available for hire from the Imperial War Museum, London.
10. *Filmwelt*, 13 December 1940.
11. J. Richards, *Visions of Yesterday* (London, 1973), p. 351.
12. From the text of a radio talk reprinted as: E. Jannings, 'Über den Film. Aus einer Rundfunk-Rede zu seinem Film *Ohm Krüger*', *Nationalsozialistische Monatshefte*, June 1942, 342-3. ¿
13. Quoted in: D. Hollstein, *Antisemitische Filmpropaganda. Die Darstellung des Juden im nationalsozialistischen Spielfilm* (Munich, 1971), p. 135.

16 KOLBERG

> The people should find the strength to be equal to their fore-
> fathers. Then this film will really be both a monument to
> Gneisenau and Nettelbeck and a monument to the citizens
> of Kolberg, but above all it should be a monument to how the
> Germans are today.
>
> Veit Harlan, 1943[1]

Kolberg may aptly be characterised as the swansong of the Nazi
cinema. The project had first been mooted in 1940-41 but it was not
until June 1943, after the Red Army's victory at Stalingrad, after the
Allies had adopted their demand for Germany's unconditional surrender,
and after Goebbels' declaration of total war, that the Propaganda
Minister informed Veit Harlan that he was to be responsible for the
film: 'The film is to demonstrate, through the example of the town
that gives it its title, that a people united at home and at the front will
overcome any enemy.'[2] Harlan's wife, the actress Kristina Söderbaum,
who had just renewed her Swedish citizenship for self-protection but
who was none the less to play the leading female role in the new film,
wrote in her diary, 'Horror of horrors. We have just been informed that
Veit must finally make *Kolberg. Hic incipit tragoedia*. What can we do?'[3]

Goebbels made clear in his diary that *Kolberg* was to have a peculiar
significance: 'I expect an extraordinary amount from this Harlan film.
It fits exactly the military and political landscape that we shall probably
have to record by the time this film is shown.'[4] In his autobiography
Harlan expands on the practical effects of Goebbels' expectations:

> The film would cost what it had to cost. And it cost about 8½
> million marks. That was about eight times what a good film normally
> cost at that time . . . I could have whatever materials I wanted, and
> that included taking as many soldiers as I wanted away from their
> posts and from their training. Goebbels wanted to see powerful battle
> scenes. He wanted to make the 'greatest film of all time' that would
> put the American epics in the shade.[5]

Apart from being allowed to borrow the crown, orb and sceptre of the
Holy Roman emperors in an attempt to lend the film the appearance of

greater authenticity, Harlan employed 6,000 horses and 187,000
soldiers, including crack horsemen from Vlasov's Cossack Army, in the
battle scenes. This was more men than had taken part in the original
battle, and it continued while the Red Army crossed the frontiers of
the Reich and entered East Prussia. In an ironic reflection of *Alexander
Nevsky* tons of salt were imported on to the set to give the illusion of
snow. In other words, no expense was spared. Why? Harlan provides at
least a partial answer:

> During the shooting I constantly discussed with the officers the
> sacrifice that the film involved for the military. Most of them were
> glad, and none was keen to get back to the front as soon as possible.
> But nobody understood why a film should be so important.
>   It was the year 1944. Stalingrad had long fallen and the danger of
> a war that had been completely lost moved ever more uncomfortably
> close to us . . . [Hitler as well as Goebbels must have been convinced
> that the distribution of a film like this would be more useful than a
> military victory. They must have been hoping for a miracle. And
> what better to perform a miracle than this 'dream factory' that is the
> cinema?] [6]

As in *The Wandering Jew* it was the appearance of authenticity, rather
than authenticity itself, that was to make the propaganda message of
the film so powerful. *Kolberg* is set in the Napoleonic wars, specifically
in 1806-7, when France overran the fragmented German states and
forced upon them the humiliating Peace of Tilsit. City after city fell,
but Kolberg resisted by forming a civilian militia to fight a last-ditch
resistance, and it is here that we find the key to the film's political
purpose, the meaning of Goebbels' assertion that 'a people united at
home and at the front will overcome any enemy'. The need to put this
message across at all costs overrides any real considerations of authenticity. Where the truth conflicts with the message, the truth is abandoned:
the film's prologue announces that it is 'based on historical facts', but
some (like the fact that the British assisted the beleaguered citizens of
Kolberg) are understandably suppressed, while others (like the fact that
Lucadou was still commandant when the fighting started) are distorted.
It is a method not unknown to some historians. In December 1943,
when production was just beginning, Veit Harlan and Wolfgang
Liebeneiner, who had both recently been awarded the title of
'professor',[7] gave a joint press conference at which the problem of
historical authenticity was discussed. It was resolved, according to a

contemporary press report, in the following manner:

> At the outset Professor Liebeneiner had asked whether films in
> historical costume were ever justified, i.e. films that are set in a
> period when there were as yet no films. Only later did we appreciate
> that one of the principal tasks of the film is its capacity to transmit
> to posterity a true picture of the past and, seen in this light, all the
> films that we are making today will one day be truly 'historical'.
> Should a historical film therefore attempt to remain true in all
> respects to the history that has been handed down to us? – In a
> certain sense, yes, for the film should not falsify history. But art,
> and film art in particular, consists to a great extent of omission. And
> so a historical film can only ever show a part, a small chapter of
> history that should nevertheless remind us of the great events.[8]

Kolberg was a 'symbol of the heroism of German man'.[9]

The first scene of the film is set in Breslau in 1813 as the Napoleonic
wars (known in German as the 'Great Patriotic War of Liberation') draw
to an end. The opening and closing scenes of the film thus serve as a
framework within which the heroic tale of the city of Kolberg can be
told in the context of the victories of 1813, thus avoiding the need for
any embarrassing mentions of the town's surrender and the humiliating
conditions of the Peace of Tilsit. Gneisenau seeks an audience with the
King of Prussia, Frederick William II, to ask him to address an appeal to
his people. In the background, and sometimes also in the foreground, a
choir intones the lines of Theodor Körner's patriotic poem written in
1813: 'The people arise, The storm breaks'. Significantly, it was this
poem that had been used by Goebbels in the speech launching the total
war effort that he gave in the Berlin Sportpalast on 18 February 1943.[10]
It became the slogan for the whole campaign and gave rise to the name
Volkssturm (People's Storm) for the armed civilian militia raised by the
Nazis to defend the Reich in its dying days and recruited from the aged,
the infirm, the adolescent and all those who had for one reason or
another been ineligible for conventional military service. The *Volkssturm*
represented the realisation of Goebbels' ideal, expressed in the film
through the words of Gneisenau in this scene:

> In Kolberg at that time an idea came to me, the idea of a popular army.
> What I then perceived obscurely, Scharnhorst has achieved. Now
> universal conscription is in force. Now the people are turning to their
> weapons. In Kolberg then I lived through the hour of birth of German
> freedom, when princes and kings had abandoned their people.[11]

The king, who maintains that war is a matter for the military alone and describes Gneisenau as a 'German dreamer' questions his view of Germany's rulers. This enables Gneisenau to reiterate the *Führerprinzip*, or leadership principle: 'A king must lead his people, that is his natural and divinely ordained task, and, if he cannot do that, then he must resign.' There is something of a contradiction in the propaganda here for, although Gneisenau is voicing Goebbels' sentiments, it is clear that, in Hitler's view at least, it was the German people rather than their leaders, who should 'resign' if they were not up to the task that confronted them. None the less the opening scene of the film makes it clear that it is Gneisenau's task to convince his king, through the example furnished by the inhabitants of Kolberg, of the necessity for popular involvement in the fight against the enemy, for a policy of total war.

The scene changes to Kolberg in 1806. Nettelbeck the mayor is discussing with his fellow councillors how they should react to the onward march of Napoleon and his forces. Some are for capitulation, but Nettelbeck retorts, 'Against cannons you can only use cannons, not sentimental feelings.' To capitulate would mean, 'We'd be vassals where we could be lords, masters in our own house.' The discussion is interrupted by the arrival of a group of battle-weary Prussian soldiers seeking quarters. They are led by the wounded Lieutenant Schill. Werner, Nettelbeck's close friend in whose farmhouse the scene is set, tells the soldiers to make themselves at home. He at least is prepared to realise the alliance between civilian and military that alone can save Prussia's honour.

The next scene is an interlude from the immediate problems of Kolberg, although its central figure is their principal architect, Napoleon. Having encircled Berlin, he comes to pay tribute at the tomb of Frederick the Great in Potsdam. It is interesting to note that the scene is played in French to lend it the appearance of greater authenticity – a technique not adopted by Hollywood until many years later. It is a short scene and Napoleon says only, 'Frederick the Great. Friedrich der Grosse . . . Would I be here if you were still alive?' In other words, it is great leaders who make history, not history that makes great leaders. The relevance of that message to Kolberg, and to the Germany of 1945, is obvious.

In the following scene Nettelbeck argues with Lucadou, the commandant of the city, about the distribution of provisions. The citizens are starving while the military warehouses are bursting at the seams. Their argument reflects and develops that between Gneisenau and Frederick William II. Lucadou believes in the distinction between

citizen and soldier, Nettelbeck does not and this conflict is encapsulated
in the following exchange:

Lucadou: Is that a matter for civilians?
Nettlebeck: It's a matter for every rational man.

Although the actual content of their exchange is important from the
point of view of the film's political message, it is not in itself decisive.
Propaganda does not usually persuade by the strength of rational
argument and the viewer is already prejudiced in favour of Nettelbeck,
partly by the framework and context of the film and partly also by the
actors who play the principal characters. Gneisenau is played by
Horst Caspar, the hero of *Friedrich Schiller: The Triumph of a Genius*.
Nettelbeck is Heinrich George, who had taken the role of a benevolent
patrician figure in the same film and in *Jew Süss* and *The Degenhardts*.
His opponent, Lucadou, is played by Paul Wegener, who specialised in
villainy in such films as *Hans Westmar, My Life for Ireland* or *The Great
King*. Before a word of dialogue has been spoken the audience is sub-
consciously aware of the representatives of the forces of good and evil,
and predisposed of course towards what the film makers regard as the
forces of good.

Lucadou's villainy, or at least his incompetence, is underlined in the
next scene when Schill inspects the city's defences and discovers that
the cannons are rusted and useless. Schill remarks, 'Children, children,
you're making it so easy for Napoleon!' Werner's daughter, Maria,
whose relationship with Schill will provide the love interest that
Goebbels demanded in the film, comments that these are Nettelbeck's
sentiments. The manner in which she makes this comment emphasises
Nettelbeck's importance as a leader of his own people:

Maria: That's what Uncle Nettelbeck is always saying. Stay with us,
lieutenant, with us in Kolberg. I don't understand much about it,
but my godfather, Nettelbeck, is always saying that we have been
betrayed and cheated with our commandant, Lucadou. Everybody's
talking about our poor cannons and the poor food supplies. The
fortress, as it now stands, is not ready for an attack.
Schill: So.
Maria: Says Nettelbeck.

Nettelbeck is a *Führer* prototype: of his people, for his people, with his
people. To an innocent helpless young girl like Maria (a part in which

Kristina Söderbaum appears to have specialised) the mayor is 'uncle'
and actual godfather. He protects his people, looking after their
interests in ways that they could not manage without his leadership.
Maria's words also speak volumes about the role of women in the Nazi
image of the world, a world that for her will be lived within the traditional
limits of 'Kinder, Küche, Kirche' (children, kitchen, church).

The scene changes to the Werner household. Claus is demonstrating
his other-worldliness by playing the violin in an upstairs room while the
wounded Schill rests below. This leads into the first tentative love scene
between his sister, Maria, and the lieutenant. He treats her like a child:
it is, after all, a man's world in Kolberg. The next scene develops the
confrontation between the Lucadou view, that war is a matter for
soldiers, and the Schill/Nettelbeck view, that in war all men must
become soldiers. Lucadou dismisses Schill's volunteer formation as
'Sunday soldiers' who will only spread confusion. He asks Schill what
they are up to and Schill's reply would serve as a justification for the
Nazi *Volkssturm*:

> They want to make the whole people fit for military service. They
> want to become a people of soldiers, and we need that, colonel.
> The salvation of the fatherland lies with its citizens. It depends on
> their courage and on their steadfastness. If a fortress is besieged
> there is no longer any difference between citizens and soldiers.

Lucadou maintains that war is 'a craft that must be learnt', to which
Schill retorts: 'Learnt, yes, but a craft, colonel? It's not a craft but an
affair of the heart, and the Kolbergers have heart.' Schill has become
an honorary Kolberger, an accolade that will never be accorded to the
commandant. To him, as to Napoleon, Kolberg is 'a few little houses'
that are no cause for concern. The following image contrasts sharply
with this assessment, as Maria sings a rustic love song.

In the next scene Nettelbeck reads to his fellow councillors an
ultimatum from the French and the ensuring discussion provides an
opportunity for a further rehearsal of the arguments for resistance or
capitulation. One councillor, Reeder, confesses, 'I have no appetite for
a hero's death, if you must know. I am after all not a soldier.' But
Nettelbeck is contemptuous of such views: people like that, he says,
'would just decay, and they don't deserve to do anything else'. When
the French envoy comes for the Kolbergers' reply Nettelbeck informs
him:

Tell the Governor of the Emperor of France that the kings, princes
and counts have abandoned their oath to the German Emperor, and
the German Emperor has not kept his oath to the German Empire in
its hour of need. But the free citizens of the old Hanseatic city of
Kolberg would rather let themselves be buried under the rubble from
their walls than break their oath to King and Lord.

Napoleon is furious and declares what is in effect total war on the
inhabitants of the city: 'I order you to march on Kolberg with your
army. Attack the city without delay, without pity for its inhabitants
or its garrison.' He promises to make his victorious General Teulié
Duke of Kolberg when the battle has been won, dismissing Nettelbeck
contemptuously as nothing more than a mere brewer.

From Napoleon's tent we move back to the Werner household where
the New Year 1807 is being celebrated. Beethoven's Moonlight Sonata
plays on the sound track while Nettelbeck and Schill take stock of the
situation. Nettelbeck decides on the need for a new commandant.
There follows an interlude in which Maria's 'good' brother, Friedrich,
who is one of Schill's soldiers, asks his officer never to hurt her. To this
Schill makes the prophetic response: 'I shall never marry a woman. I am
married to war.' The next fleeting image shows Maria and Schill
together, drinking a toast. Then we return to matters of war and state.
It seems that Schill has reinforced the garrison's armaments without
consulting Lucadou, who is beside himself with rage. Nettelbeck
accuses him of having neglected the city's defences. Lucadou screams:
'Capitulation is better than suicide' and arrests him. Meanwhile the
French have occupied the Werner farmhouse and Maria goes to ask
Schill for help. In the farmhouse Claus, the violin-playing renegade,
drinks with the French troops and toasts Napoleon: 'Vive l'Empéreur!'
He is a collaborator. Werner himself is disgusted and cannot understand how such a thing could happen 'from my own flesh and blood
under my own roof'. His house has been disgraced. For this reason he
willingly agrees to Schill's suggestion that the house must be burnt
down as it would provide a refuge for French artillery in an attack on
Kolberg. This is the first sacrifice by Maria's family for Kolberg, but
not the last.

The citizens of Kolberg call on Lucadou to release Nettelbeck and
abandon the death sentence that has been passed. Schill also pleads
on the mayor's behalf. We return to the Werners. Claus is wandering
around muttering, 'Madness, idiotic', while the house burns. Werner
himself is missing: he has perished in the flames. Maria visits Nettelbeck

in his cell. He promises to be a father to her and entrusts a letter to the King of Prussia to her, for her to deliver to him in person. With Werner's death Maria's family has made its second sacrifice. But these sacrifices will be redeemed by the content of Bettelbeck's letter, for in it he asks the King to appoint a new commandant for the city of Kolberg.

Schill is surprised at Nettelbeck's action: he confesses to Maria that he is concerned about her and asks if his concern makes her happy. Her reply, in the circumstances, is a very correct one: 'I'd prefer it if you were proud of me.' It is their declaration of mutual love. The strength of their love will demonstrate the strength of their cause: Nettelbeck is freed. The scene changes once more: Maria is in Königsberg, arguing with an officer who will not grant her an audience with the King. When she is insistent, he suggests an audience with the Queen instead, and the magic words 'I come from Kolberg' make this possible. The Queen, played by Irene von Meyendorff, is an angelic and fairy-like apparition. In her presence Maria is speechless. She hands over Nettelbeck's letter and the Queen reveals that she is following the story of the city with close attention: 'I receive daily reports of Kolberg. You can be very proud of your native city.' She takes the letter with the words: 'In this way I press Prussia and Kolberg to my heart. There are only a few jewels left in our crown and Kolberg is one of them.' Thus Kolberg's pivotal role in Prussia's struggle for survival is underlined: it acts as an example for the rest of Germany, both in 1807 and in 1945.

The scene changes back to Kolberg. Nettelbeck discovers that Lucadou has ordered that the cobblestones should be lifted and the streets barricaded. Nettelbeck considers that this will endanger the safety of the city, particularly in case of fire, and countermands the military order. He goes to see Lucadou who, he now learns, has at his request been replaced by a younger man. That man is Gneisenau. They argue and the key to their argument lies in the following exchange:

Nettelbeck: I am the leader of the citizens of Kolberg.
Gneisenau: You want to to lead and you cannot obey?
Nettelbeck: Herr Kommandant, please explain. If we pull up the cobblestones now, we shall block the . . .
Gneisenau: I have nothing to say to you until you come and report to me that you have carried out the order.

Nettelbeck obeys Gneisenau's order and explains to his confused fellow citizens that 'orders are orders'. Immediately he reports back Gneisenau takes him into his confidence and consults him, but the hierarchy of leadership has been firmly and irrevocably established. As Gneisenau points out: 'What do you think would happen if everyone only carried out those orders that they considered right and just? Accepting that in this case you were right, is that the most important thing? We'd be well on the road to anarchy.' Nettelbeck protests but Gneisenau mollifies him with the words: 'We must work together — not at cross-purposes but hand in hand.' The message of the film, and its relevance to the Germany of 1945, is nowhere made clearer than in this scene.

Gneisenau's philosophy for the defence of Kolberg is spelled out in his speech to the citizens in the next scene. Echoing the order of priorities that is to be seen in Hitler's last orders of the day[12] he begins: 'Kolbergers, Prussians, Germans!' and continues:

No love is more sacred than love for one's fatherland. No joy is sweeter than the joy of freedom . . . Citizens and soldiers, from farm labourer to citizen general, you want to be as good as your fathers were. Dare to live up to them: you have their example, so set an example. The best way to defend a fortress is to attack.

Once more we find a speech in the film that could just as well be addressed to the Berliners of 1945 as to the Kolbergers of 1807. His words have their effect. The French attack, but the Prussians hold fire until it will have maximum effect. Then, in Schill's words, they 'fire to the last bullet'. This encounter over, Gneisenau decides that the low-lying land to the south of the city must be flooded to block a French attack. He is conscious of the fact that many families will be made homeless, but this is seen as a necessary sacrifice for the common good, and Nettelbeck is placed in charge. The work is rapidly accomplished and in the following scene we see the results. Claus, Maria's wayward brother, wades through the rising waters as if in a trance searching for his violin. He is swept away, and the Werner family has made its third sacrifice: the farmstead, Werner and now Claus. Claus's death is of course the only one that is not heroic. In a sense it is the film's only pointless sacrifice, although in another sense it does have a point in that it underlines the futility of his unworldly pretensions, and marks a fitting end to a traitor's life. Maria then learns that a further blow is about to fall: Schill is off to Sweden to summon assistance and is leaving without saying his farewells. She goes to meet him at the beach and reproaches him for not saying goodbye. But Schill is a true soldier, putting his patriotic duty before the interests of his personal life, and

he replies: 'A soldier does not always have time for such things.' He
gives her a medallion that belonged to his father and asks her to wear it
on her heart: 'It is a fine feeling for a soldier if a girl is crying for him.
Thank you for your love, Maria.' It is their final farewell and both of
them are conscious of the fact.

A French parliamentarian arrives to negotiate the city's surrender.
Gneisenau addresses the Kolbergers and delivers their answer: 'We'd
rather die than hand our city over to the enemy.' The French renew
their attack and amongst the soldiers we see a black man, to emphasise
to German audiences that the enemy is racially inferior, and indeed
racially mixed as well. The scenes of the bombardment of Kolberg look
like newsreel shots of German cities in 1945: there are fires everywhere,
alarm bells sound, buildings crumble. Even the churches, which provide
sanctuary for the homeless, are destroyed. Women and cripples fight
the fires: it is a true 'people's storm'. Nettelbeck's house is burnt down
but, as befits the mayor and civic leader, he is philosophical about it,
remarking only 'Life goes on', before resuming the struggle. At
different points in this sequence of battle and destruction he states:
'They can burn our houses but not our hearts' and 'Better to be buried
in the ruins than to capitulate'. Such are the sentiments that Goebbels
wanted to transmit to the beleaguered population of the war-shattered
Reich as the edifice of the Nazi state crumbled around them. The
general sacrifice is symbolised by the particular sacrifice of Maria,
whose sole surviving relative, her brother Friedrich, is killed in the
bombardment. She has lost her home, her father and her two brothers,
and her beloved Schill has left, never to return.

In making *Kolberg* Harlan managed to contrast the life and death
struggle of the Kolbergers with the relative coldness of the French.
They are distant in their manner, they sit around at tables in rather
effete fashion, and they wear wigs. There is an artificiality about their
general demeanour, while the Prussians are genuinely and totally involved in the heat of their struggle for their own city. The Kolbergers
are now united, whereas the French are divided over whether, in the
light of the peace negotiations at Tilsit, they should observe a cease-
fire. The Kolbergers' unity is their strength: in the ruins of the city we
hear the sounds of a hymn.[13] Nettelbeck kneels before Gneisenau,
pleading with him not to surrender. Gneisenau's reponse is unequivocal:
'That is what I wanted to hear from you, Nettelbeck. Now we can die
together.' In this complete unity of purpose Kolberg will find its
resurrection and serve as an example both for Prussia in 1813 and for
Germany in 1945. Because of the intensity of the resistance, and the

enormous losses inflicted on their troops, the French cease fire. Life begins again. Maria stands on the beach waiting for Schill who will never return. Nettelbeck goes to comfort her: 'You sacrificed all that you had here, Maria. But it was not in vain . . . The greatest things are always born out of pain . . . You stayed at your post, you did your duty, you too have won. You are a great woman, Maria!' The message for the film's audience in the ruins of the Reich could hardly be more explicit.

The final scene of the film takes us back to the framework story and Breslau in 1813. Gneisenau finishes telling Frederick William II the story of Kolberg and its heroic resistance. Outside, the crowd is restive. The King, who had at first hesitated to pursue the war against Napoleon, is convinced by the example of Kolberg: the hour of Germany's freedom, of the War of National Liberation, has arrived. The closing image of the film shows us Gneisenau's profile against a sea of fluttering banners as he proclaims: 'The people are rising up for the coming battle of the nations. The storm is breaking . . . Wherever there is danger, there is a way out, there is salvation too . . . From the ashes and the rubble there will rise, like a phoenix, a new people, a new Reich!' It was that same spirit of optimism against all odds that was to encourage Germans in 1945 to believe that their country would be saved from defeat at the last minute by the use of a new miracle weapon. But wars are not won by optimism alone, and certainly not by false optimism. Propaganda plays its part, but it must always have some basis in reality. By the beginning of 1945 it was clear that Germany had lost the war.

Kolberg received its world première in the Atlantic fortress of La Rochelle in occupied France on 30 January 1945. The fortress was surrounded by Allied forces and the film had to be parachuted in. It was the twelfth anniversary of Hitler's assumption of the Chancellorship. The Party newspaper urged: 'What the citizens under Nettelbeck and the Prussian soldiers under Gneisenau did then, we too can do now.'[14] On the same day the film was shown in Berlin. The Ufa-Palast am Zoo, where most of the major Nazi propaganda films had been shown first, already lay in ruins, and so the première was held in two other central cinemas, one on the Alexanderplatz and another on the Tauentzienstrasse. The finishing touches were still being put to the second negative when the Red Army marched into the Ufa studios in Neubabelsberg. On 6 March 1945 Goebbels dictated in his diary that the commandant of Kolberg, deeming further resistance futile, had wanted to surrender the city to the Russians, wishing to 'emulate a Lucadou rather than a

Gneisenau'. He had been replaced.[15] As Marx observed: 'Hegel remarks somewhere that all facts and personages of great importance in world history occur, as it were, twice. He forgot to add: the first time as tragedy, the second as farce.'[16] But Goebbels saw things otherwise: 'Have these depraved generals really no historical sensitivity or feeling of responsibility, and does the commandant of Kolberg at a time like this prefer to imitate a Lucadou rather than a Gneisenau?'[17] But less than a fortnight later even Goebbels had to admit that 'Our soldiers there are no longer in a position to offer organised resistance to the enemy.'[18] But even in defeat, the distinction between reality as it was and reality as it ought to be had to be maintained. On 19 March Goebbels recorded in his diary:

> Now we have had to evacuate Kolberg. The city, which had defended itself with such extraordinary heroism, could be held no longer. I shall see to it that the evacuation of Kolberg is not mentioned in the Wehrmacht report. We cannot use it at the moment because of the enormous psychological consequences it would have for the Kolberg film.[19]

Two days later Kolberg had fallen to the Russians.[20] None the less, on 17 April 1945 he told his staff at the Propaganda Ministry:

> Gentlemen, in a hundred years' time they will be showing a fine colour film of the terrible days we are living through. Wouldn't you like to play a part in that film? Hold out now, so that a hundred years hence the audience will not hoot and whistle when you appear on the screen.[21]

On 1 May Goebbels and his family committed suicide. On 8 May the Third Reich was surrendered unconditionally to the Allies. After the war Veit Harlan was twice tried for war crimes, above all in connection with *Jew Süss*,[22] and eventually acquitted. Gneisenau's prediction of ashes and rubble was amply confirmed but the phoenix that has risen from them has been at least a double-headed one, and certainly not recognisable as a new Reich. Kolberg itself is now Kołobrzeg, a town on the Baltic coast of Poland. As the Party newspaper remarked: 'We are no longer merely looking at what happened in 1806, we are living through it in 1945 as if it were part of us.'[23]

Notes

1. 'Uber die Aktualität des historischen Films – Wolfgang Liebeneiner und Veit Harlan sprachen zu dem neuen Ufa-Farbfilm *Kolberg*', *Film-Kurier*, 21 December 1943, quoted in J. Wulf, *Theater und Film im Dritten Reich. Eine Dokumentation* (Reinbek bei Hamburg, 1966), p. 397.

2. Dated 1 June 1943: quoted in E. Leiser, *Deutschland, erwache!* (Reinbek bei Hamburg, 1968), pp. 104-5. Cf. the English translation in *Nazi Cinema* (London, 1974), p. 122.

3. V. Harlan, *Im Schatten meiner Filme. Selbstbiographie* (Gütersloh, 1966), p. 181, note 1.

4. Quoted in Leiser, *Deutschland, erwache!* (Reinbek), p. 105, (London), p. 123.

5. Harlan, *Im Schatten meiner Filme*, p. 184.

6. Ibid., pp. 187-8. The section in brackets does not appear in the published German version but is included in the French translation, *Le Cinéma Allemand selon Goebbels* (Paris, 1974), pp. 263-4.

7. L.P. Lochner (ed.), *The Goebbels Diaries* (London, 1948), p. 207. The entry is dated 5 March 1943.

8. Wulf, *Theater und Film im Dritten Reich*, p. 397. See note 1.

9. Loc. cit.

10. 'Nun, Volk, steh auf, und Sturm brich los! Rede im Berliner Sportpalast', in J. Goebbels, *Der steile Aufstieg* (Munich, 1944), pp. 167-204.

11. This is my own translation from the screenplay held in the Deutsches Institut für Filmkunde, Wiesbaden. It has been checked against the copies of the film held in the Staatliches Filmarchiv der DDR, Berlin, GDR, and the British Film Institute, London, from whom it is available for hire. An English translation of the screenplay, by David and Ann Welch, is also held by the BFI.

12. Cf. the appeal of Hitler's last order of the day to his troops on the Eastern front, dated 15 April 1945, and quoted in: H.R. Trevor-Roper (ed.), *Hitler's War Directives, 1939-1945* (London, 1966), pp. 300-1: 'Form yourselves into a sworn brotherhood to defend, not the empty conception of a Fatherland, but your homes, your wives, your children, and, with them, our future.'

13. According to Harlan (p. 194) the film was originally intended to end with the people of Kolberg streaming from the ruins of their city to the music of the Lutheran hymn 'A safe stronghold our God is still', which had been used in *The Great King* in 1942. Goebbels, however, maintained that the words of this hymn had been written by Pastor Niemöller, who was currently held in a concentration camp. Instead, he insisted that a late nineteenth-century hymn of thanksgiving should be used, despite Harlan's protestations that it would be an anachronism. The rest of the music in the film, including the theme tune, was written by Norbert Schulte, best known outside Germany as the composer of 'Lili Marlen'.

14. '*Kolberg* – ein Film? Ein Beispiel!', *Völkischer Beobachter*, 1 February 1945.

15. J. Goebbels, *Tagebücher 1945. Die letzten Aufzeichnungen* (Hamburg, 1977), p. 126, translated as *The Goebbels Diaries. The Last Days*, ed. H.R. Trevor-Roper (London, 1978), p. 52.

16. K. Marx, 'The Eighteenth Brumaire of Louis Bonaparte', *Marx/Engels Selected Works*, vol. 2 (Moscow, 1962), p. 247.

17. Goebbels, loc. cit.

18. Entry dictated 17 March 1945; Goebbels (Hamburg), p. 286, cf. (London), p. 154.

19. Ibid. (Hamburg), p. 304, cf. (London) p. 166.

20. Entry dictated 21 March 1945; ibid. (Hamburg), p. 320, (London), p. 179.

21. Quoted in: Leiser, *Deutschland, erwache!* (Reinbek), p. 114, and (London), p. 132.

22. See, for instance: H. Pardo and S. Schiffner (eds), *'Jud Süss'. Historisches und juristisches Material zum Fall Veit Harlan* (Hamburg, 1949).

23. *Völkischer Beobachter*, loc. cit.

17 CONCLUSIONS

> Propaganda becomes ineffective the moment we are aware of it.
>
> Goebbels, 1937[1]

In this book I have taken Soviet Russia and Nazi Germany as two case studies in the use of film propaganda for political ends. They provide us with two clear and well documented examples of the deliberate, consistent and controlled use of the cinema in this way, and they also illustrate for us the archetypal themes of left- and right-wing propaganda. But Soviet Russia and Nazi Germany are of course by no means the only countries in which the cinema has been utilised to influence public opinion in a comprehensive fashion: Mussolini's Italy, Franco's Spain, and Eastern Europe in the 1950s furnish us with further instances of such use in peace-time, while yet other countries have mobilised the cinema's propaganda potential when they thought it expedient or necessary, above all in war-time. Its use has not therefore been confined to the examples that I have chosen.

The cinema then is, or has been, an important propaganda weapon. In Soviet Russia and Nazi Germany it was organised and utilised deliberately and directly as such, so that no film could be made without the consent, and indeed the encouragement, of the authorities. In other countries, such as Britain, France or the United States, the use of the cinema has been less well developed, less well systematised, and certainly less well centralised. In these other countries there has remained, even in war-time, a greater degree of spontaneity, perhaps a more authentic enthusiasm for the cause espoused, but above all a greater continuing obsession with commercial rather than political considerations. While this last factor may act as a brake on the use of the cinema for political propaganda, it has in its turn led to the hegemony of the somewhat spurious notion of 'giving the audience what they want'. In many ways this is as insidious as overt political propaganda in acting as an 'opium for the masses', and in some ways it is worse.[2] Both Lenin and Goebbels were well aware of the limitations of direct propaganda and both recognised the value of entertainment in the process of influencing public opinion. An audience that knows that it is being bombarded with propaganda will be on its guard, but an audience that imagines it is being entertained will more easily be lulled into submission. There is however a distinction between the escapist entertainment that

Hollywood tends to offer and that offered by the Soviet or Nazi cinemas, and that distinction lies in the *purpose* of the entertainment. If that conscious purpose is to lull the audience in order to manipulate its opinions for political ends, then we are concerned with film propaganda: if not, then we are concerned with entertainment pure and simple. It is, admittedly, a distinction that in practice may well be difficult to maintain, but that is not in itself a reason for abandoning it. In Soviet Russia and Nazi Germany the cinema, like the other arts, was concerned not to *reflect* reality in all its infinite variety but to *change* reality, to shape it in accordance with a predetermined mould, to convey what I have described as 'not reality as it is, but reality as it ought to be'.

It is fashionable nowadays to denounce objectivity and to decry the search for balance in what are now our principal media of mass communication, radio and television. How Goebbels would have agreed! In March 1933 he said:

> Where then can one find absolute objectivity? It is precisely that absence of tendentiousness that is dangerous, and we must look more closely at those who espouse it. In reality they want to hinder the thoroughgoing reform of the German nation. This reform is however the common denominator of our whole public life.[3]

To attack the quest for objectivity and balance is to attack the fundamental values, the critical doubts and uncertainties, that underpin the liberal political order, and this was of course Goebbels' purpose. In the same speech he prophesied that 'Liberalism of the spirit, which in fact means anarchy of the spirit, has been buried forever.' Fortunately his prophesy has so far proved unfounded: it is the tenets of National Socialism, rather than those of liberalism, that have been laid to rest. But this raises the question of how effective propaganda really is. It is a question to which we can provide no definitive answer. Propaganda of the word would appear to depend on propaganda of the deed: the victory of the Red Army at Stalingrad marks the turning point between the propaganda of *Triumph of the Will* and that of *Kolberg*. Propaganda reflects the moods and values of its time, it 'canalizes an already existing stream', but its task is to direct and change those moods and values for political ends. In the final analysis the effectiveness of propaganda depends on its audience. As George Bernard Shaw wrote to Werner Krauss, one of the leading actors in the Nazi cinema: 'All civilisations are kept in existence by the masses who collaborate with whatever governments are for the moment established in their country, native or foreign.'[4] That is the rationale for propaganda: but it must also be our protection against it. As Goebbels himself knew, the best defence against propaganda is awareness: awareness of ourselves and of our strengths and weaknesses, and awareness of the methods and aims of others who might wish to manipulate our opinions for their own ends. That awareness is perhaps even more crucial in a liberal society than in an authoritarian political system, for in the former propaganda is likely to be not only less prominent in its role but also less obvious in its techniques and therefore, at least potentially, more effective. Nowadays that awareness is probably better directed away from the cinema and towards those newer drug-pushers, radio and television. If this book has contributed to the development of such an awareness, it will have achieved its aim; if not, it will have failed. In his open letter to Goebbels, written in 1934, Eisenstein said:

> After pledging your high patronage to 'honest, artistic endeavour' in the film, you graciously add:
> 'But I do not insist that a film should begin and end with a National Socialist procession. Leave the National Socialist processions to us — we can do them better than you . . .' Well said! Very well said!!
> *Back to your drums, Herr Drummer-in-Chief!*
> Stop playing about with the magic flute of National Socialist realism in the cinema.
> Stop imitating your idol, Frederick the Great, on the flute as well.
> Stick to the instrument you're used to — the axe.
> And don't waste time.
> You don't have long to wield the executioner's axe.
> Make the most of it!
> *Burn your books.*
> *Burn your Reichstags.*
> *But don't imagine that a bureaucratic art fed on all this filth will be able to 'set the hearts of men on fire with its voice'.*[5]

Let us hope that Eisenstein was right. For if he was wrong, or if we fail to emancipate ourselves from the spell of propaganda, then we shall be condemned to live out our lives in the shadows of a dream — and of a dream that belongs to someone else.

Notes

1. From a speech to the Reich Film Chamber on 5 March 1937, quoted in: W. von Bredow and R. Zurek (eds), *Film und Gesellschaft in Deutschland. Dokumente und Materialien* (Hamburg, 1975), p. 33, note 41.

2. Lunacharsky pointed this out as early as 1926 in his article 'Kino – velichaishee iz iskusstv', *Komsomol'skaya pravda*, 15 December 1926, reprinted in A.M. Gak and N.A. Glagoleva (eds), *Lunacharskii o kino* (Moscow, 1965), p. 71.

3. Speech of 28 March 1933, quoted in: G. Albrecht, *Nationalsozialistische Filmpolitik* (Stuttgart, 1969), p. 440.

4. W. Krauss, *Das Schauspiel meines Lebens, einem Freund erzählt* (Stuttgart, 1958), p. 228.

5. S. Eizenshtein, 'O fashizme, germanskoi kinoiskusstve i podlinnoi zhizni', *Literaturnaya gazeta*, 22 March 1934, reprinted in *Izbrannye proizvedeniya*, vol. 5 (Moscow, 1968), p. 228. An English translation was published in *Film Art*, no. 5, Winter 1934, 7-11.

ALEXANDER NEVSKY
(Aleksandr Nevskii)

Direction: Sergei Eisenstein, assisted by Dmitri Vasiliev
Assistant directors: Boris Ivanov, Nikolai Maslov
Script: Sergei Eisenstein, Pyotr Pavlenko
Photography: Eduard Tisse
Design: Isaak Shpinel, Nikolai Solovyov, Konstantin Eliseyev, from
   drawings by Eisenstein
Music: Sergei Prokofiev

Cast: Nikolai Cherkasov (Alexander Nevsky); Nikolai Okhlopkov
   (Vasili Buslai); Alexander Abrikosov (Gavrilo Olexich); Dmitri
   Orlov (Ignat); Vasili Novikov (Pavsha, governor of Pskov); Vera
   Ivasheva (Olga); Nikolain Arsky (Domash, a boyar of Novgorod);
   Varvara Massalitinova (Amelfa, Buslai's mother); Anna Danilova
   (Vasilisa); Vladimir Ershov (Grand Master of the Teutonic Order);
   Sergei Blinnikov (Tverdilo, the traitor); Lev Fenin (Bishop);
   I. Lagutin (Ananias); Naum Rogozhin (Black monk)

Production: Mosfilm

Première: 23 November 1938, Moscow

Awards: Order of Lenin for Eisenstein and Cherkasov, 1939; State
   Prize, First Class, for Eisenstein, 1941

KOLBERG

Direction: Veit Harlan
Script: Veit Harlan, Alfred Braun
Photography: Bruno Mondi (Agfacolor)
Music: Norbert Schultze

Cast: Kristina Söderbaum (Maria); Heinrich George (Joachim Nettelbeck);
   Horst Caspar (Gneisenau); Paul Wegener (Lucadou); Gustav Diessl
   (Schill); Otto Wernicke (Werner); Kurt Meisel (Claus); Charles Schauten
   (Napoléon); Claus Clausen (Friedrich Wilhelm II); Irene von Meyendorff
   (Queen Luise of Prussia); Heinz Lausch (Friedrich); Paul Bildt (Rektor);

Jacob Tiedtke (Reeder); Hans Hermann Schaufuss (Zaufke); Franz Schafheitlin (Fanselow); Theo Shall (General Loison)

Production: Ufa

Première: 30 January 1945, La Rochelle and Berlin

Predicate: Especially valuable from the state political and artistic viewpoint; culturally and ethnologically valuable; commended; educational; suitable for juvenile audiences

Award: Film of the Nation, 1945

MOTHER
(Mat')

Direction: Vsevolod Pudovkin, assisted by Mikhail Doller and V.I. Strauss
Script: Natan Zarkhi, from the novel by Maxim Gorky
Photography: Anatoli Golovnya
Design: Sergei Kozlovsky

Cast: Vera Baranovskaya (Nilovna, the mother); Nikolai Batalov (Pavel, her son); Alexander Chistyakov (Vlasov, her husband); Anna Zemtsova (Anna, a student); Ivan Koval-Samborsky (Vesovshchikov); N. Vidonov (Misha); Vsevolod Pudovkin (Police officer)

Production: Mezhrabpom-Rus

Première: 11 October 1926, Moscow

Award: Voted one of the dozen 'Best Films of All Time' by an international jury, Brussels World Fair, 1958

OCTOBER
(Oktyabr')
Alternative title: *Ten Days That Shook the World*

Direction and script: Sergei Eisenstein, assisted by Grigori Alexandrov
Assistant directors: Maxim Strauch, Mikhail Gomorov, Ilya Trauberg
Photography: Eduard Tisse, assisted by Vladimir Popov and
    Vladimir Nilsen
Design: V. Kovrigin

Cast: The worker Nikandrov (Lenin); N. Popov (Kerensky); Boris Livanov (Minister Tereshchenko); Eduard Tisse (The German)

Production: Sovkino

Première: 7 November 1927, Moscow

THREE SONGS OF LENIN
(Tri pesni o Lenine)

Direction and script: Dziga Vertov, assisted by Elizaveta Svilova
Photography: D. Surensky, M. Magidson, B. Monastyrsky
Music: Yuri Shaporin

Production: Mezhrabpomfilm

Première: 1 November 1934, Moscow

Award: Prizewinner at Venice Film Festival, 1935

TRIUMPH OF THE WILL
(Triumph des Willens)

Direction, editing and artistic production: Leni Riefenstahl
Photography: Sepp Allgeier
Architect: Albert Speer
Music: Herbert Windt

Production: NSDAP

Première: 28 March 1935, Berlin

Predicate: Especially valuable from the state political and artistic viewpoint

Awards: National Film Prize, 1935; Grand Prix, Exposition Internationale des Arts et des Techniques, Paris, 1937

UNCLE KRUGER
(Ohm Krüger)

Direction: Hans Steinhoff, with the collaboration of Herbert Maisch and Karl Anton

Script: Harald Bratt, Kurt Heuser, based on the novel *Mann ohne Volk*
   by Arnold Krieger
Photography: Fritz Arno Wagner, Friedl Behn-Grund
Design: Franz Schroedter
Music: Theo Mackeben

Cast: Emil Jannings (Paul Kruger); Lucie Höflich (Mrs Kruger);
   Werner Hinz (Jan Kruger); Ernst Schröder (Adrian Kruger);
   Gisela Uhlen (Petra Kruger); Hedwig Wangel (Queen Victoria);
   Alfred Bernau (Prince of Wales); Gustaf Gründgens (Chamberlain);
   Ferdinand Marian (Rhodes); Franz Schafheitlin (Kitchener);
   Otto Wernicke (Camp commandant)

Production: Tobis

Première: 4 April 1941, Berlin

Predicate: Especially valuable from the state political and artistic
   viewpoint; culturally and ethnologically valuable; educational;
   suitable for juvenile audiences

Awards: Film of the Nation, 1941; Ring of Honour of the German
   Cinema for Emil Jannings, 1941; Mussolini Prize, Venice, 1941

THE WANDERING JEW
(Der ewige Jude)

Direction: Fritz Hippler
Script: Eberhard Taubert
Photography: A. Endrejat, A. Haffner, E. Strohl, R. Hartmann,
   F.C. Heere, H. Kluth, H. Winterfeld
Music: Franz. R. Fiedl

Production: D.F.G.

Première: 28 November 1940, Berlin

Predicate: Valuable from the state political and artistic viewpoint;
   suitable for juvenile audiences in its shortened version

APPENDIX B: BIBLIOGRAPHY

This bibliography is not intended to be comprehensive, but it should lead the reader towards the sources that I consider important either to the subject itself, to the development of my arguments, or both. A more complete bibliography on the Soviet cinema is included in my *The Politics of the Soviet Cinema, 1917-1929* (Cambridge, 1979). In the case of both the Russian and German sources I have tried, where possible, to indicate translations that are available in languages more accessible to the English-speaking reader, and more particularly in French. The names of Russian authors are spelt as in the text of the book and alternative spellings are given in brackets.

1. General

Albig, W., *Public Opinion* (New York, 1939)
Balázs, B., *Der Film. Werden und Wesen einer neuen Kunst* (Vienna, 1961)
—— *Der Geist des Films* (Halle, 1930)
—— *Der sichtbare Mensch oder die Kultur des Films* (Vienna, 1924)
—— *Theory of the Film* (New York, 1970)
Banham, R., *Theory and Design in the First Machine Age* (London, 1960)
Barnouw, E., *Documentary. A History of the Non-fiction Film* (London, 1974)
Barsam, R.M., *Nonfiction Film. A Critical History* (London, 1974)
Bartlett, F.C., *Political Propaganda* (Cambridge, 1940)
Benjamin, W., 'L'Oeuvre d'art à l'époque de sa reproduction mécanisée', *Zeitschrift für Sozialforschung* (Paris), 1 (1936), pp. 40-63, translated as 'The work of art in the age of mechanical reproduction' in *idem, Illuminations* (London, 1973), pp. 219-53
Bradby, D., and McCormick, J., *People's Theatre* (London, 1978)
Brown, J.A.C., *Techniques of Persuasion: from Propaganda to Brainwashing* (Harmondsworth, 1963)
Clark, M.J. (ed.), *Film and Politics in Camera* (Oxford, 1979)
Crossman, R.H.S. 'Psychological warfare', *Journal of the Royal United Services Institute*, vol. 97, no. 587, 1952, pp. 321-2

Doob, L.W., *Propaganda. Its Psychology and Technique* (New York, 1935)

Driencourt, J., *La propagande. Nouvelle force politique* (Paris, 1950)

Ellul, J., *Propaganda. The Formation of Men's Attitudes* (New York, 1973)

Ferro, M., *Cinéma et histoire. Le cinéma, agent et source de l'histoire* (Paris, 1977)

Fraser, L., *Propaganda* (London, 1957)

Furhammar, L., and Isaksson, F., *Politics and Film* (London, 1971)

Huaco, G.A., *The Sociology of Film Art* (New York, 1965)

Huxley, A., 'Notes on propaganda', *Harper's Monthly Magazine*, December 1936, pp. 34, 39

Konlechner, P., and Kubelka, P. (eds), *Propaganda und Gegenpropaganda im Film 1933-1945* (Vienna, 1972)

Lasswell, H.D., 'The person: subject and object of propaganda', *Annals of the American Academy of Political and Social Science*, vol. 179, p. 189

—— 'Propaganda' entry in *Encyclopedia of the Social Sciences*

—— 'The theory of political propaganda', *American Political Science Review*, vol. 21 (1927), pp. 627-31

Lewis, J., 'Before hindsight', *Sight and Sound*, Spring 1977, pp. 68-73

Lukács, G., *Schriften zur Literatursoziologie* (Neuwied, 1961)

Lumley, F.E., *The Propaganda Menace* (London, 1933)

MacCann, R.D., *Film: A Montage of Theories* (New York, 1966)

Mackenzie, A.J., *Propaganda Boom* (London, 1938)

Martin, K., *Propaganda's Harvest* (London, 1941)

Ophuls, M., *The Sorrow and the Pity* (London, 1975)

Phillips, B., *Swastika. Cinema of Oppression* (London, 1976)

Qualter, T.H., *Propaganda and Psychological Warfare* (New York, 1962)

Rhode, E., *A History of the Cinema from its Origins to 1970* (Harmondsworth, 1978)

Richards, J., *Visions of Yesterday* (London, 1973)

Roetter, C., *Psychological Warfare* (London, 1974)

Rotha, P., *The Film till Now* (London, 1967)

Russell, B., 'Free thought and official propaganda' (1922 Conway Memorial Lecture) in *Let the People Think. A Selection of Essays* (London, 1941)

Sadoul, G., *Histoire du cinéma mondial des origines à nos jours* (Paris, 1949)

Sarris, A. (ed.), *Hollywood Voices. Interviews with Film Directors* (London, 1971)

Smith, B.L., 'Propaganda' entry in *International Encyclopedia of the Social Sciences*
Smith, P. (ed.), *The Historian and Film* (Cambridge, 1976)
Stern-Rubarth, E., 'The methods of political propaganda' in Wright, ι
    Q. (ed.), *Public Opinion and World Politics* (Chicago, 1933)
Tudor, A., *Theories of Film* (London, 1974)
Wenden, D.J., *The Birth of the Movies* (London, 1975)

2. Soviet Russia

a. Works of Reference

Kinoletopis'. Annotirovannyi katalog kinozhurnalov i dokumental' nykh fil'mov ukrainskikh studii (1923-1941) (Kiev, 1969)
Kinoslovar' (2 vols., Moscow, 1966, 1970)
Sovetskie khudozhestvennye fil'my. Annotirovannyi katalog. I. Nemye fil'my (1918-1935) (Moscow, 1961)
Stsenaristy sovetskogo khudozhestvennogo kino, 1917-1967. Spravochnik (Moscow, 1972)
Vishnevskii, V., *25 let sovetskogo kino v khronologicheskikh datakh* (Moscow, 1945)

b. Other Works

Abramov, N.P., *Dziga Vertov* (Moscow, 1962), translated into French under the same title (Paris, 1965)
Abul-Kasymova, Kh. *et al.* (eds), *Istoriya sovetskogo kino 1917-1967* (4 vols., Moscow, 1969-74)
Aksel'rod, L., 'Dokumenty po istorii natsionalizatsii russkoi kinematografii', *Iz istorii kino*, 1 (1958), pp. 25-37
Amengual, B., *V.I. Poudovkine* (Paris, 1968)
Arossev, A. (ed.), *Soviet Cinema* (Moscow, 1935)
Art in Revolution. Catalogue (London, 1971)
Aumont, J., 'Un rêve soviétique', *Cahiers du Cinéma*, November 1976, pp. 26-44
Babitsky, P. and Lutich, M., *The Soviet Movie Industry – Two Studies* (New York, 1953)
Babitsky, P. and Rimberg, J., *The Soviet Film Industry* (New York, 1955)
Barale, F., 'Groupes et classes sociales en Russie soviétique de 1917 à 1925 à travers les films de l'époque', *Cahiers du Monde Russe et Soviétique*, vol. 17, no. 2/3 (April/September 1976), pp. 249-85
Barna, Y., *Eisenstein* (London, 1973)

Barthes, R., 'Le troisième sens. Notes de recherche sur quelques photogrammes de S.M. Eisenstein', *Cahiers du Cinéma*, July 1970, pp. 12-19

Batalov, N.P., *Stat'i, vospominaniya, pis'ma* (Moscow, 1971)

Beardow, F., 'Grigory Kozintsev and the Soviet cinema', *Essays in Poetics*, vol. 2, no. 1 (April 1977), pp. 8-29

Blyakhin, P., 'K partsoveshchaniyu', *Novyi zritel'*, 13 December 1927, p. 14

Boltyanskii, G.M., 'Iskusstvo budushchego', *Kino*, 1922, no. 1/2, pp.6-7

—— 'Kino i sovetskaya obshchestvennost', *Zhizn' iskusstva*, 7/10 November 1925, p.15

Bonitzer, P., 'Les machines e(x)tatiques', *Cahiers du Cinéma*, November 1976, pp. 22-5

Borland, H., *Soviet Literary Theory and Practice during the First Five-Year Plan 1928-32* (New York, 1950)

Bratolyubov, S., *Na zare sovetskoi kinematografii* (Leningrad, 1976)

Brown, E.J., *The proletarian episode in Russian literature 1928-32* (New York, 1953)

Bryher, W., *Film Problems of Soviet Russia* (Territet, Switzerland, 1929)

Bullitt, M.M., 'Toward a Marxist theory of aesthetics: the development of socialist realism in the Soviet Union', *Russian Review*, vol. 35, no. 1 (January 1976), pp. 53-77

Cahiers du Cinéma special issues:

—— 'Russie années vingt', May/June 1970

—— 'S.M. Eisenstein', January/February 1971

Carter, H., *The New Spirit in the Cinema* (London, 1930)

——, *The New Theatre and Cinema of Soviet Russia* (London, 1924)

——, 'The Soviet cinema and the people: their social unity', in Griffith, H. (ed.), *Playtime in Russia* (London, 1935)

Cherkasov, N., *Zapiski sovetskogo aktëra* (Moscow, 1953), translated as *Notes of a Film Actor* (Moscow, n.d.)

Christie, I., and Gillett, J. (eds), *Futurism/Formalism/FEKS: Eccentrism and Soviet Cinema, 1918-36* (London, 1978)

Cohen, L.H., 'The cultural-political traditions and developments of the Soviet cinema from 1917-1962' (unpublished PhD thesis, University of Southern California, 1973)

Constantine, M., and Fern, A., *Revolutionary Soviet Film Posters* (London, 1974)

Crofts, S., 'Ideology and form: Soviet socialist realism and *Chapayev*', *Essays in Poetics*, vol. 2, no. 1 (April 1977), pp. 43-59

De La Roche, C., 'The Moscow script studio and Soviet screenwriting', *Penguin Film Review*, 2 (1947), pp. 64-9

Dement'ev, V.M., *Kinematograf kak pravitel'stvennaya regaliya* (Petrograd, 1915)

Dickinson, T., and De La Roche, C., *Soviet Cinema* (London, 1948)

Dovzhenko, A.P., *Alexander Dovzhenko. The Poet as Filmmaker*, M. Carynnyk (ed.) (Cambridge, Mass., 1973)

—— *Sobranie sochinenii* (4 vols., Moscow, 1966-9)

Durham, F.G., 'Content and its control in the Russian and Soviet film' (unpublished Master's dissertation, Cambridge, Mass., 1963)

Dzidziguri, A., and Papava, A., *Cinematographic Art in Soviet Georgia* (Tbilisi, 1976)

Eastman, M., *Artists in Uniform* (London, 1934)

Eisenstein, S.M. (also: Eizenshtein, S.M.), 'Aleksandr Nevskii', in *Izbrannye proizvedeniya*, vol. 1 (Moscow, 1964), pp. 165-75

—— *The Battleship Potemkin* (London, 1968)

—— *Bronenosets Potëmkin*, N.I. Kleiman and K.B. Levina (eds) (Moscow, 1968)

—— *Eisenstein. Three Films*, J. Leyda (ed.) (London, 1974)

—— *Film Form* (New York, 1949)

—— *The Film Sense* (London, 1968)

—— 'Istinnye puti izobreteniya: *Aleksandr Nevskii*', in *Izbrannye proizvedeniya*, vol. 1 (Moscow, 1964), pp. 176-84

—— *Izbrannye proizvedeniya v shesti tomakh* (6 vols., Moscow, 1964-71)

—— *Notes of a film director* (New York, 1970)

—— 'O fashizme, germanskoi kinoiskusstve i podlinnoi zhizni', *Literaturnaya gazeta*, 22 March 1934, translated as 'Open letter to Dr Goebbels', *Film Art*, no. 5 (Winter 1934), pp. 7-11

—— 'Patriotizm – moya tema', in *Izbrannye proizvedeniya*, vol. 1 (Moscow, 1964), pp. 161-4, translated as 'My subject is patriotism', *International Literature*, 1939, no. 2, pp. 90-3

—— 'Perspektivy', *Iskusstvo*, 1928, no. 1/2

Eisenstein, S.M., and Aleksandrov, G.V., 'Eksperiment, ponyatnyi millionam', *Sovetskii ekran*, 5 February 1929, pp. 6-7

Eisenstein, S.M., and Pavlenko, P., 'Rus'', *Znamya*, December 1937

Eisenstein, S.M., Pudovkin, V.I., and Aleksandrov, G.V., 'Zayavka', *Zhizn' iskusstva*, 5 August 1928, pp. 4-5

Ekstsentrizm. Sbornik statei (Petrograd, 1922)

Enzensberger, M., 'Dziga Vertov', *Screen*, vol. 13, no. 4, pp. 90-107, reprinted in *Screen Reader 1* (London, 1977), pp. 394-411

—— 'Osip Brik: Selected writings. Introduction', *Screen*, vol. 15, no. 3, pp. 35-58

Ermolaev, H., *Soviet Literary Theories, 1917-1934. The Genesis of Socialist Realism* (Berkeley, Cal., 1963)

Fernandez, D., *Eisenstein* (Paris, 1975)

Ferro, M., 'The fiction film and historical analysis', in Smith, P. (ed.), *The Historian and Film* (Cambridge, 1976)

—— 'Le film, une contre-analyse de la société?', *Annales* no. 1 (January/February 1973), pp. 109-24

—— '1917: history and cinema', *Journal of Contemporary History*, vol. 3, no. 4 (October 1968), pp. 45-61

Filippov, B., 'Mat"', *Kino*, 26 October 1926

Le film muët soviétique (Brussels, 1965)

Fitzpatrick, S., *The Commissariat of Enlightenment. Soviet Organization of Education and the Arts under Lunacharsky, October 1917-1921* (Cambridge, 1970)

—— 'Cultural revolution in Russia, 1928-32', *Journal of Contemporary History*, vol. 9, no. 1 (January 1974), pp. 33-52

—— (ed.), *Cultural Revolution in Russia, 1928-31* (Bloomington, Indiana, 1978)

—— 'Culture and politics under Stalin: a reappraisal', *Slavic Review*, vol. 35 (1976), pp. 211-31

—— 'The emergence of *Glaviskusstvo*. Class war on the cultural front, Moscow, 1928-29', *Soviet Studies*, vol. 23 (1971-2), pp. 236-53

—— 'The "soft" line on culture and its enemies: Soviet cultural policy, 1922-27', *Slavic Review*, vol. 33 (1974), pp. 267-87

Freeman, J., Kunitz, J., and Lozowick, L. (eds), *Voices of October: Art and Literature in Soviet Russia* (New York, 1930)

Fridman, Yu., 'Dvizhenie pomoshchi mezhdunarodnogo proletariata Sovetskoi Rossii v 1921-1922 godakh', *Voprosy istorii*, January 1958, pp. 85-101

Fülöp-Miller, R., *Geist und Gesicht des Bolschewismus* (Vienna, 1926), translated as *The Mind and Face of Bolshevism* (London, 1927)

Gak, A.M., 'K istorii sozdaniya Sovkino', *Iz istorii kino* 5 (1962), pp. 131-44

Gibian, G., and Tjalsma, H.W. (eds), *Russian Modernism, Culture and the Avant-garde, 1900-1930* (Ithaca, NY, 1976)

Giercke, C., 'Dziga Vertov', *Afterimage* (London), April 1970, no page nos.

Ginzburg, S.S., *Kinematografiya dorevolyutsionnoi Rossii* (Moscow, 1963)

Glagoleva, N.A., *Vsevolod Pudovkin* (Moscow, 1968)

Goldobin, A., *Kino na territorii SSSR* (Moscow, 1924)
Herlinghaus, H. (ed.), *Der sowjetische Revolutionsfilm: Zwanziger und dreissiger Jahre. Eine Dokumentation* (Berlin, GDR, 1967)
Iezuitov, N., 'Cinema', in Holme, C.G. (ed.), 'Art in the USSR', *The Studio* special issue, Autumn 1935, pp. 95-122
—— 'Kinoiskusstvo dorevolyutsionnoi Rossii', *Voprosy kinoiskusstva*, 2 (1957), pp. 252-307
—— *Pudovkin. Puti tvorchestva* (Moscow, 1937)
Jacchia, P., *Cinema sovietico* (Florence, 1950)
James, C.V., *Soviet Socialist Realism. Origins and Theory* (London, 1973)
Kalashnikov, Yu.S. *et al.* (eds), *Ocherki istorii sovetskogo kino* (3 vols., Moscow, 1956-8)
Kamigulov, A. *et al.*, 'Posle *Potëmkina* – *Oktyabr'* plokh', *Zhizn' iskusstva*, 27 March 1928, p. 12
Karaganov, A.V., *Vsevolod Pudovkin* (Moscow, 1973)
—— *Sovetskoe kino: problemy i poiski* (Moscow, 1977)
Katsigras, A. (ed.), *Kino-rabota v derevne* (Moscow, 1925)
Kaufman, N., 'Kinoki', *Sovetskii ekran*, 18 January 1929, pp. 8-9
Kerr, A., *Russische Filmkunst* (Berlin, 1927)
Khrenov, N., 'K probleme sotsiologii i psikhologii kino 20-kh godov', *Voprosy kinoiskusstva*, 17 (1976), pp. 163-84
Kinematograf. Sbornik statei (Moscow, 1919)
Klaue, W., and Lichtenstein, M. (eds), *Sowjetischer Dokumentarfilm* (Berlin, GDR, 1967)
Konlechner, P. and Kubelka, P. (eds), *Sergej Michaelowitsch Eisenstein. Eine Übersicht* (Vienna, 1964)
Kozlov, L., 'Metodologicheskie problemy istorii sovetskogo kino', *Iskusstvo kino*, June 1972, pp. 122-4
Krasovskii, Yu., 'Kak sozdavalsya fil'm *Oktyabr'*, *Iz istorii kino*, 6 (1965), pp. 40-62
Krupskaya, N.K., 'O fil'me *Oktyabr'*', *Pravda*, 9 February 1928
—— 'Po gradam i vesyam sovetskoi respubliki', *Novyi mir*, November 1960, pp. 113-30
Kuleshov, L.V., *Iskusstvo kino* (Moscow, 1929)
—— *Kuleshov on Film*, R. Levaco (ed.), (Berkeley, Cal., 1974)
—— 'Souvenirs (1918-1920)', *Cahiers du Cinéma*, July 1970, pp. 20-5
Leaming, B.D., 'Engineers of human souls: the transition to socialist realism in the Soviet cinema of the 1930s' (unpublished PhD thesis, New York University, 1976)
Lebedev, A.A. (ed.), *Kinokamera pishet istoriyu* (Moscow, 1971)
Lebedev, N.A., 'Kino', *Pravda*, 3 January 1923

—— *Ocherk istorii kino SSSR: Nemoe kino (1918-1934)*, 2nd edn (Moscow, 1965), translated into Italian as *Il cinema muto sovietico* (Milan, 1962) from the 1947 edition

—— (ed.) *Partiya o kino* (Moscow, 1939)

—— *Vnimanie: kinematograf!* (Moscow, 1974)

Lemberg, E.G., *Kinopromyshlennost' SSSR: Ekonomika sovetskoi kinematografii* (Moscow, 1930)

Lenin, V.I., *Lenin and Stalin on Propaganda*, Little Lenin Library, vol. 24 (London, 1942)

—— *Lenin i kino*, G.M. Boltyanskii (ed.), (Moscow, 1925)

—— *Lenin o kul'ture i iskusstve*, N.I. Krutilova (ed.), (Moscow, 1956)

—— *Lenin on Culture and Cultural Revolution* (Moscow, 1970)

—— *Lenin. Sobranie fotografii i kinokadrov*, A.M. Gak *et al.* (eds), (2 vols., Moscow, 1970-2)

—— *Samoe vazhnoe iz vsekh iskusstv. Lenin o kino*, A.M. Gak (ed.), 2nd edn (Moscow, 1973)

Levaco, R., 'Kuleshov', *Sight and Sound*, Spring 1971, pp. 86-91, 109

Leyda, J., *Films Beget Films* (London, 1964)

—— *Kino: A History of the Russian and Soviet Film* (London, 1960)

Likhachëv, B.S., *Kino v Rossii (1896-1926). Materialy k istorii russkogo kino I. 1896-1913* (Leningrad, 1927)

Listov, V., *Istoriya smotrit v ob"ektiv* (Moscow, 1973)

—— 'Propaganda on wheels', *Soviet Film*, September 1969

London, K., *The Seven Soviet Arts* (London, 1937)

Lorenz, R. (ed.), *Proletarische Kulturrevolution in Sowjetrussland 1917-1921* (Munich, 1969)

Lunacharsky, A.V. (also: Lunacharskii, A.V., and Lunatscharsky, A.W.), *Anatoly Lunacharsky on Literature and Art*, A. Lebedev (ed.), 2nd edn (Moscow, 1973)

—— *Kino na Zapade i u nas* (Moscow, 1928)

——*Lunacharskii o kino*, A.M. Gak and N.A. Glagoleva (eds), (Moscow, 1965)

—— *Der russische Revolutionsfilm* (Zurich, 1929)

L'vov, A., *Kinematograficheskaya yazva izlechima* (Moscow, 1924)

Macdonald, D., 'The Soviet cinema 1930-38', *Partisan Review*, July 1938, pp. 37-50

Mal'tsev, K., *Na pomoshch' sovetskomu kino* (Moscow, 1927)

—— *Sovetskoe kino pered litsom obshchestvennosti. Sbornik diskussionnykh statei* (Moscow, 1928)

Mamatova, L., 'A.V. Lunacharskii i razvitie sovetskogo kinoiskusstva', *Iskusstvo kino*, November 1975, pp. 72-88

Marchand, R., and Weinstein, P., *L'art dans la Russie nouvelle: le cinéma* (Paris, 1927)

Markov, V., *Russian Futurism* (London, 1969)

Marshall, H., 'Eisenstein and others', *The Listener*, 22 March, 29 March and 5 April 1973

—— *Soviet Cinema* (London, 1945)

Mayakovsky, V.V. (also: Mayakovskii, V.V.), *Kino* (Moscow, 1940)

—— *Teatr i kino* (2 vols., Moscow, 1954)

Meyerhold, V.E.(also: Meierkhol'd, V.E.), *Stat'i, pis'ma, rechi, besedy* (2 vols., Moscow, 1968)

——*Meyerhold on theatre*, E. Braun (transl. and ed.), (London, 1969)

Meilakh, M., *Izobrazitel'naya stilistika pozdnikh fil'mov Eizenshteina* (Leningrad, 1971)

Michelson, A., 'The Man with the Movie Camera: from magician to epistemologist', *Artforum*, March 1972, pp. 63-72

Mitry, J., *S.M. Eisenstein* (Paris, 1961)

Montagu, I., 'Sergei Eisenstein', *Penguin Film Review*, 7 (1948), pp. 10-16

—— *With Eisenstein in Hollywood* (Berlin, GDR, 1968)

Moussinac, L., *Le cinéma soviétique* (Paris, 1928)

—— *Sergei Eisenstein* (New York, 1970)

Narboni, J., 'Le hors-cadre décide de tout', *Cahiers du Cinéma*, November 1976, pp. 14-21

Nikol'skaya, V., 'Kompozitsiya fil'ma S.M. Eizenshteina *Aleksandr Nevskii*', *Voprosy kinoiskusstva*, 2 (1957), pp. 205-45

'Novye vekhi', *Sovetskii ekran*, 21 June 1927

'Novyi kurs Sovkino', *Sovetskii ekran*, 8 January 1929, p.6

'O fil'me *Oktyabr*"', *Pravda*, 9 February 1928

'Octobre', *L'Avant-scène du Cinéma*, no. 74, October 1967, pp. 1-54

'Oktyabr'. Itogi diskussii', *Zhizn' iskusstva*, 27 May 1928, p. 8

Ol'khovyi, B.S. (ed.), *Puti kino. Pervoe Vsesoyuznoe partiinoe soveshchanie po kinematografii* (Moscow, 1929)

Oms, M., *Grigori Kozintsev* (Paris, 1976)

Oten, O., 'Kinokam', *Kino-Fot*, 19-25 September 1922, p. 9

'Otkrytoe pis'mo kinorezhissërov', *Zhizn' iskusstva*, 27 May 1928

'Partiya i kino', *Kommunisticheskaya revolyutsiya*, April 1928, pp. 3-9

Petrov-Bytov, P., 'U nas net sovetskoi kinematografii', *Zhizn' iskusstva*, 21 April 1929, p. 8

Piotrovsky, A. (also: Piotrovskii, A.), *Adrian Piotrovskii. Teatr, kino, zhizn'*, A.A. Akimova (ed.), (Leningrad, 1969)

—— 'Budem maksimalistami!', *Zhizn' iskusstva*, 13 December 1927, p. 4
—— 'Kino 1928 goda', *Zhizn' iskusstva*, 4 November 1928, p. 9
—— 'Oktyabr' dolzhen byt' peremontirovan!', *Zhizn' iskusstva*, 27 March 1928, p. 12
Plekhanov, G.V., *O zadachakh sotsialistov v bor'be s golodom v Rossii* (Geneva, 1892), partially translated by R. Taylor in N. Harding (ed.), *Marxism in Russia: Key Documents* (London, 1980)
Poluyanov, P., *Gibel' teatra i torzhestvo kino* (Nizhny Novgorod, 1925)
Polyanovskii, M., *My vidim Il'icha* (Moscow, 1969)
Preobrazhenskii, N.F., 'Vospominaniya o rabote V.F.K.O.', *Iz istorii kino* 1 (1958), pp. 85-91
Pudovkin, V.I., 'Alexander Nevsky', *International Literature*, 1939, no. 2, pp. 94-6
—— *Film Technique and Film Acting* (London, 1929)
—— 'K voprosu zvukovogo nachala v fil'me', *Kino i kul'tura*, May/June 1929, pp. 3-5
—— *Mat'*, N.A. Glagoleva (ed.), (Moscow, 1975)
—— *'Mat''*, *Kino*, 24 August 1926
—— *'Mat''*, *Sovetskii ekran*, 31 August 1926
—— 'Novaya fil'ma', *Novyi zritel'*, 7 September 1926
—— *On Film Technique* (London, 1929)
—— 'Pervaya fil'ma', *Kinogazeta*, 24 September 1932
—— 'S.M. Eizenshtein (Ot *Potëmkina* k *Oktyabryu*)', *Zhizn' iskusstva*, 14 February 1928, pp. 2-3
—— *Sobranie sochinenii v trëkh tomakh*, T. Zapasnik and A. Petrovich (eds), (3 vols., Moscow, 1974-6)
—— *Der sowjetische Film. Eine Vortragsreihe* (Berlin, GDR, 1953)
—— 'Vremya krupnym planom', *Proletarskoe kino*, April 1932, pp. 30-2
Rokotov, T., 'Pochemu malodostupen *Oktyabr'*?', *Zhizn' iskusstva*, 10 April 1928, p. 17
Room, A., 'Bytovaya i problemnaya fil'ma', *Zhizn' iskusstva*, 7 February 1928, p. 7
Rosolovskaya, V., *Russkaya kinematografiya v 1917 godu. Materialy k istorii* (Moscow, 1937)
Rostotsky, B., 'Mayakovsky and the cinema', in *Vladimir Mayakovsky: Innovator* (Moscow, 1976)
Rotha, P. *et al.*, *Eisenstein 1898-1948* (London, 1948)
Rühle, J., *Literature and Revolution* (London, 1969)
Sadoul, G., 'Actualité de Dziga Vertov', *Cahiers du Cinéma*, June 1963, pp. 23-31
Schnitzer, L. and J., *Vsevolod Poudovkine* (Paris, 1966)

—— and Martin, M., *Le cinéma soviétique par ceux qui l'ont fait* (Paris, 1966), translated as *Cinema in Revolution* (London, 1973)

Selezneva, T.F., 'Teoreticheskoe nasledie S.M. Eizenshteina', *Iskusstvo kino*, October 1975, pp. 110-23

—— *Kinomysl' 1920-kh godov* (Leningrad, 1972)

Seton, M., *Sergei M. Eisenstein*, 2nd edn (London, 1978)

Shklovsky, V.B. (also: Shklovskii, V.B.), 'Aleksandr Nevskii', *Kino*, 2 November 1938

—— *Eizenshtein* (Moscow, 1973)

—— 'Kuda shagaet Dziga Vertov?', *Sovetskii ekran*, 10 August 1926, p. 4

—— *Mayakovsky and His Circle* (London, 1974)

—— *Za sorok let* (Moscow, 1965)

—— *Zhili – byli* (Moscow, 1966)

Shtraukh, M. (also: Strauch, M.), *Glavnaya rol'* (Moscow, 1977)

Shub, E., *Zhizn' moya – kinematograf* (Moscow, 1972)

Shumyatsky, B., 'Fifteen years of Soviet cinema', in Arossev, q.v. *Socialist Realism in Literature and Art* (Moscow, 1971)

Sokolov, I.V. (ed.), *Istoriya sovetskogo kinoiskusstva zvukovogo perioda* (2 vols., Moscow, 1946)

Solski, W., 'The end of Sergei Eisenstein: case history of an artist under dictatorship', *Commentary*, March 1949, pp. 252-60

Sorlin, P., and Ropars, M.-C., *Octobre. Ecriture et idéologie* (Paris, 1976)

Soviet Writers' Congress. The Debate on Socialist Realism and Modernism (London, 1977)

Sudendorf, W., *Sergej M. Eisenstein. Materialien zu Leben und Werk* (Munich, 1975)

Swallow, N., *Eisenstein. A Documentary Portrait* (London, 1976)

Tait, A.L., 'The literary works of A.V. Lunačarskij (1875-1933)' (unpublished PhD thesis, Cambridge University, 1971)

Talmadge, I.D.W., 'The confession of Sergei Eisenstein. A study of artistic servitude', *New Leader*, 7 December 1946, pp. 11, 14

Taylor, R., 'Agitation, propaganda and the cinema: the search for new solutions, 1917-21', in N.A. Nilsson (ed.), *Literature, Language and Society in Russia, 1917-21* (Stockholm, 1979)

—— 'From October to *October*: the Soviet political system in the 1920s and its films', in Clark, M.J. (ed.), *Politics in Camera* (Oxford, 1979)

—— 'A medium for the masses: agitation in the Soviet Civil War', *Soviet Studies*, vol. 22 (1971), pp. 562-74

—— *The Politics of the Soviet Cinema, 1917-1929* (Cambridge, 1979)

—— 'The spark that became a flame: the Bolsheviks, propaganda and the cinema', in Rigby, T.H. *et al.* (eds), *Authority, Power and Policy in the USSR* (London, 1979)

Tertz, A., *On Socialist Realism* (New York, 1960)

Thomson, B., *Lot's Wife and the Venus of Milo* (Cambridge, 1978)

—— *The Premature Revolution. Russian Literature and Society 1917-1946* (London, 1972)

Trainin, L., *Kino-promyshlennost' i Sovkino* (Moscow, 1925)

Trotsky, L., *Literature and Revolution* (New York, 1957)

—— *Problems of Life* (London, 1924)

Two Russian classics: 'Mother' and 'Earth' (London, 1973)

Vainshtok, V., and Yakobzon, D., *Kino i molodëzh'* (Leningrad, 1926)

Vertov, D., *Dziga Vertov. Stat'i. Dnevniki. Zamysli*, S.V. Drobashenko (ed.), (Moscow, 1966)

—— 'Eshchë o Mayakovskom', *Iskusstvo kino*, April 1957, pp. 118-20

—— 'Fabrika faktov. (V poryadke predlozheniya)', *Pravda*, 24 July 1926

—— 'Fil'my o zhenshchine', *Iskusstvo kino*, April 1957, pp. 123-4

—— 'Kino-glaz', in *Na putyakh iskusstva* (Moscow, 1925)

—— 'Kino-glaz', *Pravda*, 19 July 1924

—— 'Kinoki. Perevorot', *Lef*, June/July 1923, pp. 135-43

—— 'Kino-Pravda', *Kino-Fot*, 8 January 1923, p. 13.

—— 'Kinopravda', *Sovetskoe kino*, November/December 1934

—— 'My. Variant manifesta', *Kino-Fot*, 25-31 August 1922, pp. 11-12

—— 'Novoe techenie v kinematografii', *Pravda*, 15 July 1923

—— 'On i ya', *Kino-Fot*, 8-15 September 1922, pp. 9-10

—— 'Otvet na pyat' voprosov', *Kino-gazeta*, 21 October 1924

—— 'Poslednyi opyt', *Literaturnaya gazeta*, 18 January 1935

—— *Tri pesni o Lenine*, Vertova-Svilova, E.I., and Furtichev, V. (eds), (Moscow, 1972)

Vertova-Svilova, E.I., and Vinogradova, A.L. (eds), *Dziga Vertov v vospominaniyakh sovremennikov* (Moscow, 1976)

Woroszylski, W., *The Life of Mayakovsky* (London, 1971)

Yurenev, R.N. (ed.), *Eizenshtein v vospominaniyakh sovremennikov* (Moscow, 1974)

Yutkevich, S.I., 'V.E. Meierkhol'd i teoriya kinorezhissury', *Iskusstvo kino*, August 1975, pp. 74-82

Zetkin, C. (also: Tsetkin, K.), *Vospominaniya o Lenine* (Moscow, 1966)

Zhdan, V.N. (ed.), *Kratkaya istoriya sovetskogo kino* (Moscow, 1969)

Zorkaya, N.M., *Sovetskii istoriko-revolyutsionnyi fil'm* (Moscow, 1962)

3. Nazi Germany

a. Works of Reference

Bauer, A. (ed.), *Deutscher Spielfilmalmanach 1929-1950* (Berlin, 1950)
Bucher, F. (ed.), *Germany (Screen Series)* (London, 1970)
Deutscher Film-Katalog 1930-1945 (Ufa. Tobis. Bavaria) (Frankfurt-am-Main, no date)

b. Other Works

Albrecht, G., 'Korrektur zum Nazifilm', *Film* (Hanover), October 1963, p. 46f
—— *Nationalsozialistische Filmpolitik. Eine soziologische Untersuchung über die Spielfilme des Dritten Reichs* (Stuttgart, 1969)
Allgeier, S., *Die Jagd nach dem Bild* (Stuttgart, 1936)
Altenloh, E., *Zur Soziologie des Kino* (Jena, 1914)
Amengual, B., 'Vichy entre le réel et l'irréel', *L'Ecran* (Paris), August 1972, pp. 5-8
Aubry, Y., *Slatan Dudow* (Paris, 1970)
Bächlin, P., *Der Film als Ware* (Basle, 1945)
Baird, J.W., *The Mythical World of Nazi War Propaganda 1939-1945* (Minneapolis, 1974)
Barsam, R.M., *Filmguide to 'Triumph of the Will'* (Bloomington, Indiana, 1975)
Bateson, G., 'An analysis of the Nazi film *Hitlerjunge Quex*', in Mead, M., and Métraux, R. (eds), *The Study of Culture at a Distance* (Chicago, 1953)
Baudot, M., 'L'opinion publique devant la propagande allemande et l'invasion de l'U.R.S.S.', *Revue d'Histoire de la Deuxième Guerre Mondiale* vol. 64 (1966), pp. 63-80
Belling, C., *Der Film im Dienste der Partei* (Berlin, 1937)
—— *Der Film in Staat und Partei* (Berlin, 1936)
Belling, C., and Schütze, A., *Der Film in der Hitler-Jugend* (Berlin, 1937)
Bénac, G., 'La première femme du Reich: Leni Riefenstahl: animatrice des Jeux Olympiques', *Paris-Soir*, 22 August 1936
The Blue Angel (London, 1968)
Boberach, H. (ed.), *Meldungen aus dem Reich. Auswahl aus den geheimen Lageberichten des Sicherheitsdienstes der SS 1939-1944* (Neuwied, 1965)
Boelcke, W.A. (ed.), *Kriegspropaganda 1939-1941. Geheime Ministerkonferenzen im Reichspropagandaministerium* (Stuttgart, 1966)

Bramsted, E.K., *Goebbels and National Socialist Propaganda 1925-1945* (London, 1965)

Brandenburg, H., 'Was ist eigentlich das Kino?', *Deutsche Rundschau*, 1926, no. 10, July, pp. 54-7

Brauneck, M. (ed.), *Die rote Fahne: Kritik, Theorie, Feuilleton, 1918-1933* (Munich, 1973)

Brecht, B., 'Der Dreigroschenprozess. Ein soziologisches Experiment', in *Versuche*, vol. 3 (Frankfurt-am-Main, 1959)

Bredow, W. von, and Zurek, R. (eds), *Film und Gesellschaft in Deutschland. Dokumente und Materialien* (Hamburg, 1975)

Brenner, H., *Die Kunstpolitik des Nationalsozialismus* (Reinbek, 1963)

Brentano, B. von, 'Der verbotene Film *Kuhle Wampe*', *Die literarische Welt*, 22 April 1932

The Cabinet of Dr Caligari (London, 1972)

Cloet, R., 'Les directives de Goebbels', *Revue d'Histoire de la Deuxième Guerre Mondiale*, vol. 64 (1966), pp. 1-6

Courtade, F., and Cadars, P., *Histoire du cinéma nazi* (Paris, 1972)

Delahaye, M., 'Leni et le loup. Entretien avec Leni Riefenstahl', *Cahiers du Cinéma*, September 1965, pp. 42-51, 62-3

Demeter, K., 'Die Entwicklung des deutschen Films zu einem Faktor der Weltpolitik und Weltwirtschaft', *Archiv für Politik und Geschichte*, 1925, no. 2, pp. 606-38

—— 'Die Filmpropaganda der Entente im Weltkriege', *Archiv für Politik und Geschichte*, 1925, no. 8, pp. 214-31

—— 'Die soziologischen Grundlagen des Kinowesens', *Deutsche Rundschau*, July 1926, pp. 57-62

Deutschland und der deutsche Film (Berlin, 1935)

Donner, W., 'Politik hat sie nie interessiert. Leni Riefenstahls Comeback', *Die Zeit*, 18 August 1972

Doob, L.W., 'Goebbels' principles of propaganda', *Public Opinion Quarterly*, Fall 1950, pp. 419-42

Dreyer, E.A. (ed.), *Deutsche Kultur im neuen Reich. Wesen. Aufgabe und Ziel der Reichskulturkammer* (Berlin, 1934)

Duenschmann, H., 'Kinematograph und Psychologie der Volksmenge. Eine sozialpolitische Studie', *Konservative Monatsschrift für Politik, Literatur und Kunst*, September 1912, pp. 920-30

Eisner, L., *Fritz Lang* (London, 1976)

—— 'The German films of Fritz Lang', *Penguin Film Review* 6 (1948), pp. 53-61

—— *The Haunted Screen* (London, 1969)

Esslin, M., *Brecht: A Choice of Evils* (London, 1959)

Ewen, F., *Bertolt Brecht. His Life, His Art and His Times* (London, 1970)

Fischer, R., *Stalin and German Communism* (Cambridge, Mass., 1948)

Foertsch, 'Propaganda. Eine Kriegswaffe!', *Militär-Wochenblatt*, 11 April 1935

Ford, C., *Emil Jannings* (Paris, 1969)

Freiwald, H., 'Filmdokumente über die Jugend unter Hitler und ihre Bedeutung für die politische Bildung', *Beiträge zur Erziehungswissenschaft (Oldenburger Hochschulbrief)*, no. 16/17, November 1966, pp. 116-35

Fünfundzwanzig Jahre Kinematograph (Berlin, no date)

Funk, A., *Film und Jugend. Eine Untersuchung über die psychischen Wirkungen des Films im Leben der Jugendlichen* (Munich, 1934)

Gersch, W., *Film bei Brecht. Bertolt Brechts praktische und theoretische Auseinandersetzung mit dem Film* (Berlin, GDR, 1975)

Gersch, W., and Hecht, W. (eds), *Bertolt Brecht. 'Kuhle Wampe'. Protokoll des Films und Materialien* (Frankfurt-am-Main, 1969)

Giese, H.-J., *Die Film-Wochenschau im Dienste der Politik* (Dresden, 1940)

Goebbels, J., *Der Angriff, Aufsätze aus der Kampfzeit*, 3rd edn (Munich, 1936)

—— *Das eherne Herz. Reden und Aufsätze aus den Jahren 1941-42* (Munich, 1943)

—— *Der Faschismus und seine praktischen Ergebnisse* (Berlin, 1934)

—— *The Goebbels Diaries*, L.P. Lochner (ed.), (London, 1948)

—— *Der Kampf um Berlin. Der Anfang*, 4th edn (Munich, 1932)

—— *Reden* (2 vols., Düsseldorf, 1971-2)

—— *Revolution der Deutschen. 14 Jahre Nationalsozialismus* (Oldenburg, 1933)

—— *Signale der neuen Zeit* (Munich, 1934)

—— *Der steile Aufstieg. Reden und Aufsätze aus den Jahren 1942-43* (Munich, 1944)

—— *Tagebücher 1945. Die letzten Aufzeichnungen* (Hamburg, 1977), translated as *'The Goebbels Diaries. The Last Days*, ed. H.R. Trevor-Roper (London, 1978)

—— *Vom Kaiserhof zur Reichskanzlei* (Munich, 1935)

—— *Wesen und Gestalt des Nationalsozialismus* (Berlin, 1934)

—— *Die Zeit ohne Beispiel. Reden und Aufsätze aus den Jahren 1939-41* (Munich, 1941)

Gombrich, E.H., *Myth and Reality in German War-time Broadcasts* (The Creighton Lecture in History, 1969), (London, 1970)

Gregor, J., *Meister deutscher Schauspielkunst. Krauss − Klöpfer − Jannings − George* (Bremen, 1939)

Günther, W., *Der Film als politisches Führungsmittel. Die anderen gegen Deutschland* (Leipzig, 1934)

Hadamovsky, E., *Propaganda und nationale Macht. Die Organisation der öffentlichen Meinung für die nationale Politik* (Oldenburg, 1933)

Hale, O.H., *The Captive Press in the Third Reich* (Princeton, 1964)

Harlan, V., *Im Schatten meiner Filme. Selbstbiographie* (Gütersloh, 1966), translated into French as *Souvenirs; ou le cinéma allemand selon Goebbels* (Paris, 1974)

Hauptmann, C., 'Der Film in totalitären Staaten', *Politische Studien*, 1960, pp. 532-42

Hempel, R., *Carl Mayer. Ein Autor schreibt mit der Kamera* (Berlin, GDR, 1968)

Herma, H., 'Goebbels' conception of propaganda', *Social Research*, vol. 10, no. 2, May 1943, pp. 200-18

Heyde, L., *Presse, Rundfunk und Film im Dienste der Volksführung* (Dresden, 1943)

Hippler, F., *Betrachtungen zum Filmschaffen* (Berlin, 1942)

Hitler, A., *Die deutsche Kunst als stolzeste Verteidigung des deutschen Volkes* (Munich, 1934)

——— *Hitler's War Directives 1939-45*, H.R. Trevor-Roper (ed.), (London, 1966)

——— *Mein Kampf*, R. Manheim (transl.), (London, 1969)

Hollstein, D., *Antisemitische Filmpropaganda. Die Darstellung des Juden im nationalsozialistischen Spielfilm* (Munich, 1971)

Hombourger, R., *Goebbels. 'Chef de publicité du IIIe Reich* (Paris, 1939)

Hoppe, W., *Die Führerpersönlichkeit in der deutschen Geschichte* (Berlin, 1934)

Hull, D.S., *Film in the Third Reich* (Berkeley, Cal., 1969)

Hunger, F., 'Der ideelle und psychologische Gehalt des historischen Films' (unpublished doctoral thesis, Hamburg University, 1939)

Jannings, E., *Theater – Film – Das Leben und ich* (Berchtesgaden, 1951)

——— 'Über den Film. Aus einer Runfunk-Rede zu seinem Film *Ohm Krüger*', *Nationalsozialistische Monatshefte*, June 1942, pp. 342-3

Jensen, P., *The Cinema of Fritz Lang* (London, 1969)

Kalbus, O., *Vom Werden deutscher Filmkunst* (2 vols., Altona-Bahrenfeld, 1935)

Kallmann, A., 'Die Konzernierung in der Filmindustrie, erläutert an den Filminudstrien Deutschlands und Amerikas' (unpublished doctoral thesis, Jena, 1932)

Kauer, E.T., *Der Film: vom Werden einer neuen Kunstgattung* (Berlin, 1943)

Kelman, K., 'Propaganda as vision – *Triumph of the Will'*, *Film Culture*, Spring 1973, pp.162-7

Klaren, G.C., *Der deutsche Film und der Autor* (Berlin, 1937)

Kliesch, H.J., 'Die Film- und Theaterkritik im NS-Staat' (unpublished doctoral thesis, Freie Universität, Berlin, 1957)

Klimsch, G.W., *Die Entwicklung des national-sozialistischen Film-Monopols von 1933-1940* (Munich, 195 ;)

Koch, H., *Heinrich George. Ein Mann voi echtem Schrot und Korn* (Berlin, 1940)

Koch, H., and Braune, H., *Von deutscher Filmkunst. Gehalt und Gestalt* (Berlin, 1943)

Kochenrath, H.-P. (ed.), *Der Film im Dritten Reich* (Cologne, 1963)

Kolb, R., and Siekmeier, H., *Rundfunk und Film im Dienste nationaler Kultur* (Düsseldorf, 1933)

'*Kolberg* – ein Film? Ein Beispiel!', *Völkischer Beobachter*, 1 February 1945

Kracauer, S., *From Caligari to Hitler. A Psychological History of the German Film* (Princeton, 1947)

—— 'The conquest of Europe on the screen. The Nazi newsreel 1939-40', *Social Research*, vol. 10, no. 3, September 1943, pp. 337-57

Krauss, W., *Das Schauspiel meines Lebens, einem Freund erzählt* (Stuttgart, 1958)

Kriegk, O., *Der deutsche Film im Spiegel der Ufa. 25 Jahre Kampf und Vollendung* (Berlin, 1943)

Kris, E., and Speier, H., *German Radio Propaganda. Report on Home Broadcasts during the War* (London, 1944)

Kühn, G., Tümmler, K, and Wimmer, W. (eds), *Film und revolutionäre Arbeiterbewegung in Deutschland 1918-1932* (2 vols, Berlin, GDR, 1975)

Lang, F., 'La nuit viennoise', *Cahiers du Cinéma*, August 1965, pp. 42-60

Leiser, E., '*Deutschland, erwache!';Propaganda im Film des Dritten Reiches* (Reinbek, 1968), translated as *Nazi Cinema* (London, 1974)

Lévy, C., 'L'Organisation de la propagande allemande en France', *Revue d'Histoire de la Deuxième Guerre Mondiale*, vol. 64 (1966), pp. 7-28

Lévy-Klein, S., 'France 1940-1944: le cinéma de Vichy', *Positif*, January 1973, pp. 51-5

Liss, U., *Westfront 1939/40. Erinnerungen des Feindbearbeiters im OKH* (Neckargemünd, 1959)

Lüdecke, W., *Der Film in Agitation und Propaganda der revolutionären deutschen Arbeiterbewegung (1919-1933)* (Berlin, 1973)

Luft, H.G., *E.A. Dupont* (Paris, 1970)

M (London, 1968)

Manvell, R., and Fraenkel, H., *The German Cinema* (London, 1971)

Manz, H.P., *Ufa und der frühe deutsche Film* (Zurich, 1963)

Maraun, F., 'Der Held: die Gemeinschaft', *Der deutsche Film*, August 1939, pp. 49-52

Mermet, P., and Danan, Y.M., 'Les thèmes de la propagande allemande après le 22 juin 1941', *Revue d'Histoire de la Deuxième Guerre Mondiale*, vol. 64 (1966), pp. 39-62

Messter, O., *Mein Weg mit dem Film* (Berlin, 1936)

Metropolis (London, 1973)

Mohóly-Nagy, L., *Painting, Photograph, Film* (London, 1969)

Monaco, P., *Cinema and Society: France and Germany during the Twenties* (New York, 1976)

Mosse, G.L., *The Nationalization of the Masses. Political Symbolism and Mass Movements in Germany from the Napoleonic Wars through the Third Reich* (New York, 1975)

Müller, G.W., *Das Reichsministerium für Volksaufklärung und Propaganda* (Berlin, 1940)

Münzenberg, W., *Die dritte Front* (Berlin, 1930)

—— *Fünf Jahre Internationale Arbeiterhilfe* (Berlin, 1926)

—— *Propaganda als Waffe* (Paris, 1937)

NSDAP, *Der Kongress zu Nürnberg vom 5. bis 10. September 1934. Offizieller Bericht über den Verlauf des Reichsparteitages mit sämtlichen Reden* (Munich, 1934)

Neumann, C., Belling, C. and Betz, H.-W., *Film- 'Kunst', Film-Kohn, Film-Korruption. Ein Streifzug durch vier Jahrzehnte* (Berlin, 1938)

Nollau, G., *International Communism and World Revolution* (London, 1961)

Novik, W., 'Four years in a bottle. A critical study of French film production under the Occupation', *Penguin Film Review*, 2 (1947), pp. 45-53

Ohm Krüger. Zur festlichen Aufführung des Emil Jannings Films der Tobis (Berlin, 1941)

Ohm Krueger. Un film d'Emil Jannings de la Tobis (Paris, 1941)

Oley, H., and Hellwig, J., . . . *wie einst Lili Marleen* (Berlin, 1963)

Oms. M., *Josef von Sternberg* (Paris, 1970)

Pandora's Box (London, 1971)

Pardo, H., and Schiffner, S., *Jud Süss. Historisches und juristisches*

Material zum Fall Veit Harlan (Hamburg, 1949)

Petersen, J., *Schiller. Der Triumph eines Genies* (Berlin, 1940)

Pevsner, M., 'Les actualités cinématographiques de 1940 à 1944', *Revue d'Histoire de la Deuxième Guerre Mondiale*, vol. 64 (1966), pp. 88-96

—— 'Les thèmes de propagande avant le 22 juin 1941', *Revue d'Histoire de la Deuxième Guerre Mondiale*, vol. 64 (1966), pp. 29-38

Phillips, M.S., 'The German film industry and the New Order', in Stachura, P.D. (ed.), *The Shaping of the Nazi State* (London, 1978), pp. 257-81

—— 'The Nazi control of the German film industry', *Journal of European Studies*, vol. 1, no. 1, pp. 37-68

'Propaganda im Dienste grosser Ideale und zukunftskräftiger Prinzipien. Dr Goebbels erstattet Bericht', *Völkischer Beobachter*, 11 September 1938

Rabenalt, A.M., *Film im Zwielicht. Über den unpolitischen Film des Dritten Reiches und die Begrenzung des totalitären Anspruches* (Munich, 1958)

Reimers, K.F., 'Der Führer als völkische Erlösergestalt. Die Berliner NS-Weihnachtskundgebung 1933 im offiziellen Filmbericht', *Geschichte in Wissenschaft und Unterricht*, vol. 3, (1968), pp. 164-75

Rhades, J., 'Von der nationalsozialistischen 'Filmkunstbetrachtung' zur Filmkritik der Gegenwart. Dargestellt an Beispielen aus der Bayerischen Presse' (unpublished doctoral thesis, Ludwig-Maximilians Universität, Munich, 1955)

Richards, J., 'Two Titanics', *Focus on Film*, October 1977, pp. 43-6

Riefenstahl, L., *Hinter den Kulissen des Reichsparteitag-Films* (Munich, 1935)

Riess, C., *Das gab's nur einmal* (Hamburg, 1956)

Sander, A.U., *Jugend und Film* (Berlin, 1944)

Scheffler, K.N., 'Die Verstaatlichung der deutschen Filmwirtschaft 1937 bis 1942 und die Bildung der 'Ufa-Film GmbH' ('Ufi')', *Deutsche Filmkunst*, vol. 9, no. 1, 1961, pp. 20-3

Schenzinger, K.A., *Der Hitlerjunge Quex* (Berlin, 1932)

Schulberg, B., 'Nazi pin-up girl', *Saturday Evening Post*, 30 March 1946

Semmler, R., *Goebbels. The Man next to Hitler* (London, 1947)

Sington, D., and Weidenfeld, A., *The Goebbels Experiment. A Study of the Nazi Propaganda Machine* (London, 1942)

Siska, H.W. (ed.), *Wunderwelt Film. Künstler und Werkleute einer Weltmacht* (Heidelberg, 1943)

Speer, A., *Inside the Third Reich* (London, 1970)

Speier, H., 'Nazi propaganda and its decline', *Social Research*, vol. 10, no. 3, September 1943, pp. 358-77

Stephan, W., *Bismarck. Dem Drehbuch nacherzählt* (Berlin, 1940)

Stern-Rubarth, E., *Die Propaganda als politisches Instrument* (Berlin, 1921)

Terveen, F., *Die Entwicklung der Wochenschau in Deutschland: Ufa-Tonwoche Nr 451/1939. Hitlers 50. Geburtstag* (Göttingen, 1960)

—— 'Das Filmdokument der Nazis und sein Wahrheitsgehalt. Wochen-schauen aus der Hitlerzeit erfordern kritische Beobachter', *Das Parlament*, 25 May 1955

—— 'Historischer Film und historisches Filmdokument', *Geschichte in Wissenschaft und Unterricht*, vol. 7 (1956), pp. 750-2

Traub, H., *Der Film als politisches Machtmittel* (Munich, 1933)

—— *Die Ufa. Ein Beitrag zur Entwicklung des deutschen Filmschaffens* (Berlin, 1943)

Turovskaya, M., 'Brekht i kino', *Iskusstvo kino*, April 1976, pp. 82-97

Wagner, F., 'I believe in the sound film', *Film Art*, 1936, no. 8, p. 11

Walsh, M., 'The complex seer: Brecht and the film', *Sight and Sound*, Autumn 1974, pp. 222-7

Wedel, H. von, *Die Propagandatruppen der deutschen Wehrmacht* (Neckargemünd, 1962)

'Wie der Olympia-Film entstand', *Hakenkreuzbanner*, 19 April 1938

Wiers, H., 'Die politische Bedeutung der Wochenschau', *Politische Studien*, 1954, pp. 33-8

Wippermann, K.W., *Die Entwicklung der Wochenschau in Deutschland: Ufa-Tonwoche Nr 410/1938* (Göttingen, 1970)

—— *Die Entwicklung der Wochenschau in Deutschland: 'Die Deutsche Wochenschau' Nr 10/651. Februar 1943* (Göttingen, 1970)

Witte, K. (ed.), *Theorie des Kinos. Ideologiekritik der Traumfabrik* (Frankfurt-am-Main, 1972)

Wolf, K., *Entwicklung und Neugestaltung der deutschen Filmwirtschaft seit 1933* (Heidelberg, 1938)

Wulf, J. (ed.), *Theater und Film im Dritten Reich. Eine Dokumentation* (Reinbek, 1966)

Zglinicki, F. von, *Der Weg des Films. Die Geschichte der Kinemato-graphie und ihrer Vorläufer* (Berlin, 1956)

Ziegler, M., *'Blut und Boden. Ein Film von den Grundlagen deutscher Zukunft'*, *Völkischer Beobachter*, 25 November 1933

Zimmereimer, K., *Die Filmzensur* (Breslau-Neukirch, 1934)

INDEX